This is a pioneering research study on a vitally important subsector of the industry in the Indian economy. The authors, Dr Meenakshi Parida and Professor S. Madheswaran, employ appropriate methodology and data to analyse total factor productivity (TFP) and technical efficiency (TE) of coal mining in India and explore the social and environmental compliance aspect rigorously and systematically. Public policy analysts and research students will benefit from reading the book.

Professor K. L. Krishna, former Director, Delhi School of Economics; founding Managing Editor, Journal of Quantitative Economics; former President, the Indian Econometric Society

This comprehensive study delves into India's mining sector, analysing its economic impact, productivity trends, and the challenges faced by both public and private enterprises. The mining industry in India faces significant challenges, which include environmental regulations, complex compliance requirements, and slow technological adoption. The need to balance economic growth with environmental sustainability remains a pressing concern. The book offers insights and analysis for a deeper understanding of this critical sector. It is an essential read for policymakers, industry stakeholders, and researchers interested in understanding the mining sector in India.

Professor T. C. A. Anant, former Chief Statistician of India; Secretary, Ministry of Statistics and Programme Implementation, Government of India; former Professor, Delhi School of Economics; Member, Union Public Service Commission (retired); Visiting Professor, Institute for the Study of International Development, Delhi; Adjunct Professor, Tata Institute of Social Sciences, Hyderabad

This book, *The Indian Mining Industry: An Economic, Social, and Environmental Analysis*, by Meenakshi Parida and S. Madheswaran is a scholarly work. It examines the Indian mining industry and its complex realities through three interconnected lenses. The book delves into the sector's productivity and efficiency, focusing on total factor productivity, energy efficiency, and economic impacts at subsectoral levels. Beyond the economic metrics, it sheds light on the social dimensions of mining and the often overlooked social dimensions, investigating the social compliance measures. This book is invaluable for policymakers, researchers, industry professionals, and anyone concerned about the future of India's natural resources and the communities dependent upon them.

Professor Ram Singh, Director and Professor, Delhi School of Economics; Director, Delhi School of Public Policy and Governance, University of Delhi

This book by Meenakshi Parida and S. Madheswaran provides an economic, social, and environmental analysis of the mining industry in India. The study shows that the mining industry had a significant impact on the Indian economy because of its great interconnectedness with other sectors. The economic impact is high, as shown by the higher multipliers for output, income, and employment. Total factor productivity for the whole industry shows a declining trend. Productivity for the private sector is much higher than the public sector, and the need for more participation of the private sector is obvious. Energy efficiency must be improved. There are significant concerns on the adverse impact on the social and environmental aspects of the mining industry. As India aspires to become a developed country by 2047, the policy implications of this book are very useful for improving efficiency, including energy and taking care of social and environmental concerns. This volume on the mining industry is very useful for all stakeholders, including students, researchers, and policymakers.

Professor S. Mahendra Dev, Chairman, Economic Advisory Council to the Prime Minister (EAC-PM); former Director Indira Gandhi Institute of Development Research; former Chairman of the Commission for Agricultural Costs and Prices, Government of India; Editor-in-Chief, Economic and Political Weekly

This book provides an innovative analysis of India's mining industry, employing a rigorous methodology that integrates secondary data from various sources with primary research. As the study highlights, while the industry makes a substantial contribution to gross domestic product and employment—both directly and indirectly—its technical and energy efficiencies remain below optimal levels. Moreover, with increasing concerns over climate change and growing public awareness and scrutiny, the industry must adopt and enforce robust social and environmental compliance measures. This book is a valuable resource for experts, scholars, policymakers, and other stakeholders engaged in the sector.

Alakh N. Sharma, Professor and Director, Institute for Human Development; President, Indian Society of Labour Economics

The Indian Mining Industry

An Economic, Social, and Environmental Analysis

MEENAKSHI PARIDA
S. MADHESWARAN

OXFORD
UNIVERSITY PRESS

OXFORD
UNIVERSITY PRESS

Great Clarendon Street, Oxford, OX2 6DP,
United Kingdom

Oxford University Press is a department of the University of Oxford.
It furthers the University's objective of excellence in research, scholarship,
and education by publishing worldwide. Oxford is a registered trade mark of
Oxford University Press in the UK and in certain other countries.

Published in the United States of America by Oxford University Press
198 Madison Avenue, New York, NY 10016, United States of America.

British Library Cataloguing in Publication Data
Data available

Library of Congress Control Number is on file at the Library of Congress

ISBN 9780198954361

DOI: 10.1093/9780198954392.001.0001

Printed and bound in India by
Replika Press Pvt. Ltd.

The manufacturer's authorised representative in the EU for product safety is
Oxford University Press España S.A., Parque Empresarial San Fernando de Henares,
Avenida de Castilla, 2 – 28830 Madrid (www.oup.es/en or product.safety@oup.com).
OUP España S.A. also acts as importer into Spain of products made by the manufacturer.

Foreword

The mining industry has been a focal point of economic development, providing essential raw materials for various sectors and contributing significantly to the national economy. Given India's rich mineral resources and the critical role mining plays in promoting industrial growth, this industry enjoys a unique position in India. Nevertheless, the industry is facing numerous challenges, including environmental degradation, social displacement, and regulatory issues. This book, *The Indian Mining Industry: An Economic, social, and Environmental Analysis*, provides an excellent comprehensive analysis of the industry incorporating the nation's mindset on economic, social, and environmental concerns.

The book is a timely and valuable contribution in the arena of 'sustainable renewable energy' to the ongoing discussion about the sustainable development of the mining industry in India. It explores the economic impact of mining with special reference to its contributions to output, income, and employment. The authors have demonstrated (particularly in Chapters 5 and 6) their expertise on measuring productivity and productive efficiency. The authors' meticulous examination of the productivity and efficiency of the industry, comparing public- and private-sector performance, and identification of areas for improvement deserves our appreciation. The analysis of energy efficiency within the mining sector is particularly pertinent, given the global emphasis on reducing carbon footprints and enhancing sustainability.

One of the book's most significant strengths is its focus on social and environmental compliance. The authors provide a nuanced understanding of the challenges faced by mining-affected communities and the industry's efforts—or lack thereof—in addressing these issues. By incorporating the perspectives of project-affected households, the book offers a ground-level view of the social and environmental impacts of mining, making it a crucial resource for policymakers, industry stakeholders, and researchers.

The policy recommendations presented in this book are both feasible and forward-thinking. The authors emphasize the need for improved data generation, transparent resource allocation, streamlined regulatory processes, and enhanced infrastructure. The authors also advocate for skill development, the adoption of advanced mining technologies, and a stronger focus on sustainability practices.

The implementation of these recommendations has the potential to transform the Indian mining industry, making it more efficient, equitable, and environmentally responsible. As we navigate the complexities of modern industrial development, it is imperative to strike a balance between economic growth and environmental stewardship. This book provides a road map for achieving this balance, offering insights and strategies that can guide the mining industry towards a more sustainable future. It is a must-read for anyone involved in, or concerned with, the mining sector, from industry professionals and policymakers to academics and environmental advocates not only in India but also in developing countries with similar characteristics to India.

In conclusion, *The Indian Mining Industry* is a comprehensive and insightful exploration of the diverse challenges and opportunities within the Indian mining industry. It is a testament to the authors' dedication to advancing our understanding of this critical industry and their commitment to promoting sustainable development. I commend them for their thorough research and thoughtful analysis, and I am confident that this book will serve as an invaluable resource for years to come.

Kaliappa Kalirajan
21 February 2025
Emeritus Professor, Arndt-Corden Department of Economics,
Crawford School of Public Policy Australian National
University, Canberra

Preface and Acknowledgements

This book develops an empirical, analytical, and methodological insight to examine the Indian mining industry by exploring its complex realities through three interconnected lenses. This book offers an empirical examination into the sector's productivity and efficiency by measuring total productivity growth, technical efficiency, and energy efficiency, at various subsectoral levels. In addition to the estimation of economic metrics, the book analyses the industry's economic impact on the national income, output, and employment while also identifying challenges and ways forward for improvement. It explores the operational challenges; opportunities present and the potential for a more responsible and sustainable mining future. Further, the book sheds light on the often neglected social dimensions through its inquisitive investigation into the social compliance measures. Furthermore, the book critically examines environmental compliance, examining the ecological footprint of mining activities, compliance with regulatory frameworks, and the pursuit of sustainable practices. Summing up, the book analyses the performance of the mining industry in India from three perspectives—economic (productivity and efficiency), environmental, and social. In the process, it attempts to examine the veracity of four broad questions related to the industry: (i) its economic impact and challenges, (ii) productivity growth and efficiency, (iii) energy-use efficiency, and (iv) environmental and social compliance. The findings reveal a noticeable impact on the macroeconomic variables, though not significant. The findings further highlight the productivity gap between private and public mining firms, raising questions about the stability of state ownership over time. Additionally, this book finds the presence of a considerable proportion of medium-efficient firms in the coal-mining industry and the existence of energy-saving potential among the mining firms. In the end, it offers empirical evidence on the non-compliance of mining firms to social and environmental commitments, indicating tangible failures of government regulatory and monitoring systems. Considering these results, the book suggests the policymakers allow for the expansion of the mining projects in the possible locations by envisaging a trade-off between how much to produce and social and environmental concerns. It recommends the policymakers take appropriate and requisite steps to strengthen the public-sector firms by identifying the causes of their slow productivity. It proposes to focus more on energy-efficient mining equipment to cash in on the energy saving potential. It further proposes for more stringent environmental monitoring and swift actions to compel mining firms to adhere to environmentally sustainable practices.

We offer our sincere gratitude to several people without whom it would have been truly difficult for us to complete this piece of work. This study was conducted with the help of financial support received from the Indian Council of Social Science Research (ICSSR). It would not have been possible without the financial support of the ICSSR. We gratefully acknowledge Ms B. P. Vani, Professor, Institute for Social and Economic Change, for her unconditional emotional support and invaluable comments and suggestions provided to us at every stage of our work. We express our gratitude to the former director of the Delhi School of Economics, Padmashri Professor K. L. Krishna, who offered invaluable mentorship and guidance to us from the very beginning and as and when required.

We also thank several officials at the Indian Bureau of Mines, Nagpur; Bhubaneswar; Odisha State Pollution Control Board; Directorate of Mines, Bhubaneswar; Department of Steel and Mines, Bhubaneswar; Collectorate of Jajpur; deputy directors of mines and mines officers at Odisha Mines Corporation; and director and welfare officers of the Industrial Development Corporation (IDC), Odisha. We thank all the respondents from our surveyed villages of the Jajpur district where the primary survey was conducted. Without their generous help, this book would not have been possible. We also thank the Institute of Social and Economic Change, Bengaluru, where the research study was conducted.

We wish to thank our respective family members for their immense and unconditional moral support and encouragement during this journey.

We thank Professor Kaliappa Kalirajan, professor at the Australian National University, for writing the foreword to the book and providing valuable suggestions to the work at different stages.

Finally, we thank Oxford University Press for publishing the book with care and on time.

Contents

Figures

Tables

1
Introduction

1.1 Motivation

Minerals are considered vital natural resource endowments that have enormous value for any nation. The finite nature and non-renewability of minerals makes them more valuable in the commodity basket. Almost every aspect of modern life depends on minerals and mineral products, such as base metals, precious metals, coal, iron, sand, limestone, and industrial minerals. Everything that people use—household appliances, computers, farm equipment, mobile phones, fertilizers, medicines, transport vehicles, beauty products—relies heavily on minerals and mineral products for their production and distribution. As such, minerals constitute key raw materials for many basic industries and are therefore considered as a major source of development (GoI, 2010). India is a nation blessed with many key mineral resources, and their availability makes India a resource-rich nation among the global key players and has led to the development of the mining industry.

Since Independence, India's development strategy has placed more emphasis on the creation of industrial development to materialize the goal of achieving industry-led economic development. This is evident from all the five-year plans, where much attention has been paid to the performance of industrial sectors. As the performance of industrial sectors and economic growth move in tandem with each other, it is envisaged that the growth of industrial sectors is key to a nation's prosperity. Again, the growth of industrial sectors brings to the fore the issues of enhancing productivity and efficiency as they are considered to be the prime components of any sector's economic performance. However, improving these indicators can be seen as a step towards other goals (i.e. social welfare), not as an end in itself.

The Indian Mining Industry. Meenakshi Parida and S. Madheswaran, Oxford University Press.
 DOI: 10.1093/9780198954392.003.0001

In realizing industry-led development, almost all the industrial units have played their role and contributed to their capacities. The history of India's economic development stands witness to this fact. In this context, the Indian mining industry is slightly behind. Surprisingly, even though India is rich in mineral endowments, its contribution to the development process is abysmally low. The contribution of India's mining industry to economic growth is estimated to be around 2%, and the contribution of the mining sector to India's gross domestic product (GDP) has continuously declined (RBI, 2018).

The mining sector contributed 3.4% of India's GDP in 1992–1993. This declined to 3.0% in 1999–2000 and further to 2.3% in 2009–2010. With the sector contracting in absolute terms, the contribution of the mining sector to India's GDP came down to 2% in 2012–2013. Although in 2013–2014, this sector's growth performance showed a slight improvement to 2.8% in terms of its contribution to gross value added (GVA), the figure once again come down to 2.4% for the year 2014–2015 and made a slight improvement in 2018 to 2.7% (RBI, 2018). This shows that the performance of this sector has remained almost stagnant at around 2–3% over the years, which is a matter of concern for the policymakers.

The mining sector has suffered under a lethal mix of high borrowing costs, on the one hand, and policy paralysis on the part of the government, on the other. Mining projects across the country remain stalled owing to environmental, regulatory, and land acquisition issues (FICCI Mines and Metals Division, 2013).

Though India is considered to be substantially endowed with mineral resources, many mineral-rich states have experienced a 'resource curse'. The 'resource curse' is a paradoxical situation where states rich in natural resources often experience economic backwardness, poorer development outcomes, and increased inequality compared with resource-poor states. In India, it has been observed that mineral-rich states such as Odisha, Chhattisgarh, and Jharkhand have low economic growth, higher levels of poverty, and higher levels of infant mortality, malnutrition, and morbidity in comparison to states that are poorly endowed with mineral resources (Das, 2013). This 'resource curse' points out the fact that the benefits of the richness of the mineral resources have not been effectively tapped in India.

Moreover, despite India's significant geological potential, the country does not rank very high in terms of its mineral resource base amongst similarly geologically endowed nations. It is also a matter of concern that though (as per the National Mineral Policy 2008) the private sector should have been at the forefront of mineral production, the public sector continues to play a dominant role, accounting for 62% of mineral production during 2019–2020 (GoI, 2020). This shows that a conducive environment in the form of liberal policies and incentives has not been framed to invite more active private-sector participation.

There is significant mineral potential that remains untapped in India for the growth of mining (Table 1.3), but history stands witness to the fact that the Indian mining industry has struggled to exploit the mining potential for several reasons. The most important factors responsible for this fall under three categories, that is, regulatory and administrative procedures, inadequate infrastructure facilities, and sustainability (FICCI Mines and Metals Division, 2013). Because of these challenges, the overall investment in mining and exploration activities in India has become low, as is evident from a very low inflow of foreign direct investment (FDI) in the mining sector (GoI, 2019). India's spending on mineral exploration was less than 0.5% of the global spending on exploration in 2010, much below its fair share, given the size of mineral resource potential (MOM, 2011).

Given the availability of mineral wealth in India, the Ministry of Mines, Government of India, has targeted a significantly higher share of GDP from mining. It aims to increase the share of mining and quarrying in GDP from the current 2% to 5% over the next twenty years. This requires mining to grow at 10–12% per annum (FICCI Mines and Metals Division, 2013). On the other hand, within two decades of opening up the economy, mining as a sector has come to be associated with many problems, such as low productivity, high costs, scams, conflicts, violence, and environmental degradation. The conflict it causes is huge and all-pervasive.

Hence, looking at the problems and challenges that engulf the mining industry and the potential it has to contribute to the nation's growth, this book aims to focus on the economic analysis of the mining industry from three perspectives: productivity and efficiency, social, and environmental. Productivity and efficiency improvement is considered to be of paramount importance to maximize the growth of this core industrial sector, which in turn is expected to contribute to the overall growth of the economy. As the nature of this industry is such that it causes significant social and environmental damages, it is also imperative to analyse the industry from these two dimensions so that loopholes can be plugged to derive maximum benefits from this sector.

1.2 The Indian Mining Industry: Key Facts

1.2.1 Product Structure

India is a nation blessed with several huge mineral resources. India is endowed with vast amounts of iron ore, manganese, coal, bauxite, chromite, limestone, gold, diamonds, asbestos, and other diverse kinds of minerals. Like many other developing nations, in India, mining has become an important component of the economy and has a long history. Gold, copper, iron ore, manganese, bauxite, and coal have been mined since the Harappa age (Rábago et al., 2001), and in recent years, extraction has been further intensified owing to the global increase in demand for mineral commodities.

India produces about ninety varieties of minerals, out of which four are fuel minerals, ten are metallic, seventy-one are non-metallic, and five are atomic minerals. The Indian mineral sector is comprised of four broad categories: fuel, metallic, non-metallic, and minor minerals. Among these, fuel minerals contribute around 68%, followed by metallic minerals (19%), minor minerals (11%) and non-metallic minerals (2%) (GoI, 2019).

India also occupies a remarkable position in the world mineral market in respect of some commodities (Table 1.1). It is the second-largest producer of coal and holds the fourth rank in chromite and iron ore production for the year 2018–2019 (GoI, 2020). In India, a major deficiency in production is observed in the case of industrial minerals (such as petroleum, lead, copper, zinc, kyanite, rock phosphate, and fluorspar), while some of the other minerals (such as bauxite, chromite, gypsum, limestone, magnesite, rutile, silicon minerals, barites, manganese, and talc) are in surplus supply, creating a favourable situation for exports.

In the past, coal and iron ore received significant focus among all the minerals, as these were used as the basic raw materials in many industries.

Table 1.1 India's production rank across key minerals, 2018

Minerals	Unit of commodity	Total production	Contribution (percentage)	India's rank in global production
Coal	Million tonnes	753.9	12	2nd
Iron ore	Million tonnes	206	7.05	4th
Bauxite	Thousand tonnes	23,688	7.27	5th
Chromite	Thousand tonnes	3,971	9.73	4th
Zinc metal	Thousand tonnes	696	5.23	3rd
Manganese ore	Thousand tonnes	2,820	5.32	7th
Lead metal	Thousand tonnes	620	5.17	4th
Copper	Thousand tonnes	454	1.90	11th
Aluminium	Thousand tonnes	3,696	5.89	4th

Source: GoI (2018a).

However, in recent years, the trend has shifted from iron ore and coal to other important minerals: petroleum, natural gas, lignite, lead, zinc, copper, silver, diamond, rock phosphate, etc. At the current consumption rank, India has proven coal reserves for 175–200 years and iron ore and limestone for 40–50 years (Table 1.2).

In addition to the proven and probable 'reserves', India has a significant quantity of mineral 'resources', which are still under various stages of exploration. The amount of mineral potential that is still untapped in India can be seen from the data in Table 1.3. With appropriate investments in infrastructure and technology used in exploration, there is significant potential for further increase in the realizable mineral wealth of India.

In India, there are currently as many as 3,834 mining leases spreading over 24 states, out of which, 92% of mining leases are in the private sector and the remaining 8% are in the public sector (GoI, 2018). Madhya Pradesh tops the list in obtaining the maximum number of leases (19%), followed by Tamil Nadu (14%), Andhra Pradesh (13%), Gujarat (12%), Karnataka (10%), Odisha (7%), Rajasthan (5%), Chhattisgarh (5%), Maharashtra (5%), and Jharkhand (4%), and the clear dominance of the private sector over the public sector in the distribution status (according to the industry experts) is due to the high competence and efficiency of the private sector.

Table 1.2 India's rank in reserves and reserve life across key minerals

Minerals	Current reserves (million tonnes)	India's rank in reserves	Reserve life (years)
Coal	11,300	4th	187
Limestone	12,715	–	55
Iron ore	7,000	7th	47
Bauxite	900	6th	66
Barite	34	2nd	30
Chromite	66	3rd	24
Zinc metal	11	7th	8
Manganese ore	138	5th	47
Lead metal	3	7th	26
Copper	4	–	9
Aluminium	2.3	5th	–

Source: Goldman Sachs & Morgan Stanley Metals Playbook (2013); Ministry of Mines, GoI; US Geological Survey.

Table 1.3 Untapped mineral potential in India

Minerals	Reserves (% of total resources)	Remaining resources (% of total resources)	Total resource (tonnes)
Silver	59	41	10.2 thousand
Zinc	46	54	24 million
Coal	40	60	280 billion
Copper	39	61	11.4 million
Manganese	37	63	378 million
Chromite	31	69	213 million
Iron ore	28	62	25 billion
Bauxite	27	73	3.3 billion
Gold	17	83	490
Nickel	NA	100	188 million

Source: GoI (2013a).

Currently, the industry is largely fragmented, and dominated by small-scale mining operations. The total number of reporting mines[1] (excluding minor minerals, petroleum (crude), natural gas, and atomic minerals) for the year 2017–2018 was 1,430 as against 1,616 in 2017–2018, showing a decline of 0.13% from that of the previous year (GoI, 2016a). Out of this, 42.78% belonged to non-metallic minerals, followed by metallic minerals (31.88%) and fuel minerals (25.34%). Many mines were reported from the private sector amounting to 69%, and the public sector accounted for only 31% of reporting mines. Of the total number of about ninety minerals, the three key minerals are coal, limestone, and iron ore. There are 560 coal mines (19% of the total number), 553 limestone mines (19% of the total number) and 316 iron ore mines (11% of the total number). They comprise about half of the total number of reporting mines. The number of mines engaged in extraction was also significant in cases of bauxite (189), manganese (141), dolomite (116), and Steatite (113).

1.2.2 Production

The total value of mineral production (excluding atomic minerals and also excluding the value for February and March in respect of thirty-one minerals notified as minor minerals for the year 2017–2018 stands at rupees 1,12,632 crore, reflecting an increase of 10.65% as compared with that of the previous year due to an increase in the production of some of the important minerals—lignite, natural gas (ut), petroleum (crude), gold, manganese ore, phosphorite, garnet (abrasive), magnesite, wollastonite, etc.—and also the reduction in the average unit prices of important minerals—coal, iron ore, graphite, vermiculite, etc. The public sector, which accounted for 62% of the total value of mineral production, continues to dominate the industry. Regarding shares of value of mineral production by mineral groups, fuel minerals continue to dominate the total production with a share of about 67%, followed distantly by

[1] Reporting mine refers to a mine reporting production or reporting 'Nil' production during a year but engaged in developmental work such as overburden removal; underground driving; winzing; sinking work; or exploration by pitting, trenching, or drilling as evident.

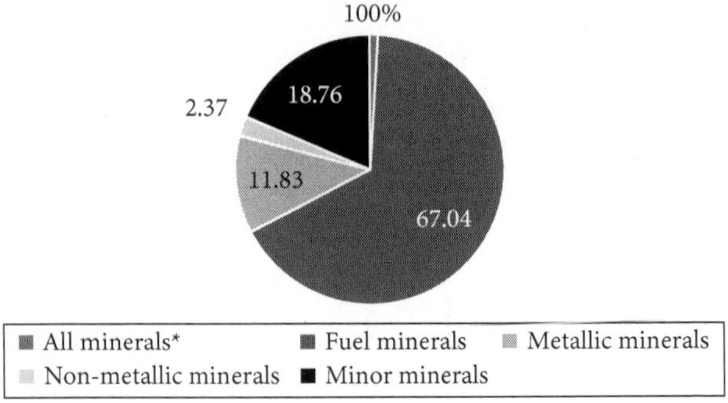

Fig. 1.1 Shares of mineral groups in value of mineral production (%)
Source: Author's estimation.

non-metallic, minor, and metallic minerals, in the range of 19, 12, and 2%, respectively (Fig. 1.1).

Among the fuel minerals, coal contributes about half of the fuel production and is a major resource for power generation. Despite the emerging clamour for shifting the focus towards gas-based power generation in the field of energy production, coal is likely to remain the main energy resource because of its abundant domestic availability and lower cost. The value of production of minerals by groups other than atomic minerals from 2005–2006 to 2014–2015 at 2004–2005 constant prices is provided in Fig. 1.2 below. From the year 2014–2015 onwards, data is available only for metallic and non-metallic groups.

The production trend of some key minerals over the years shows that the domestic mining industry has registered negative year-on-year growth in minerals such as iron, coal, gold, and manganese over the previous year 2015, whereas positive growth has been registered in minerals such as chromite, bauxite, and lead concentrate (Table 1.4).

In terms of geographical distribution of mineral resources, during 2017–2018, about 63% of mineral production came from the five states of Rajasthan (19%), Odisha (18%), Andhra Pradesh (9%), Chhattisgarh (9%), Karnataka (8%), and another 18% from Telangana, Gujarat, and Uttar Pradesh. Most of the metallic and non-metallic minerals are produced by states such as Rajasthan, Odisha, Madhya Pradesh, Andhra Pradesh, Karnataka, Goa, and Gujarat, while a majority of coal resources were confined to states such as Odisha, Jharkhand, Chhattisgarh, West

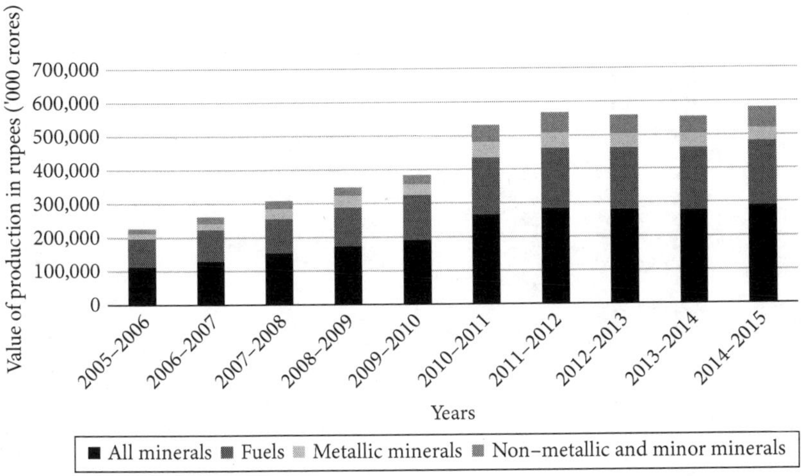

Fig. 1.2 Value of mineral production by mineral groups, in Rs '000 crores
Source: GoI (2015a; 2016a).

Table 1.4 Production trend of key minerals in India, 2016–2017

Minerals	Production, 2016	Year-on-year growth (%)
Iron ore (million tonnes)	1,559	–20.1
Coal (million tonnes)	639	–1.0
Bauxite (million tonnes)	281	18.2
Gold (kg)	1,323	–10.8
Lead concentrate (kt)	262	39.8
Manganese	215	–35.1
Chromite	289	22.6
Diamonds	36,070	1.3

Source: Ministry of Mines, *Indian mineral year book, 2016–17*; author's calculation.

Bengal, Madhya Pradesh, Andhra Pradesh, and Maharashtra. At present, nearly half of India's total mineral production (including oil and gas offshore production, which is about 19%) comes from the five key mining states. The share of key mining states in India's mineral production is presented in Fig. 1.3 below. These mining states are relatively economically backward, which shows that growth in mining could play a catalytic role in the social and economic upliftment of the people of these states as

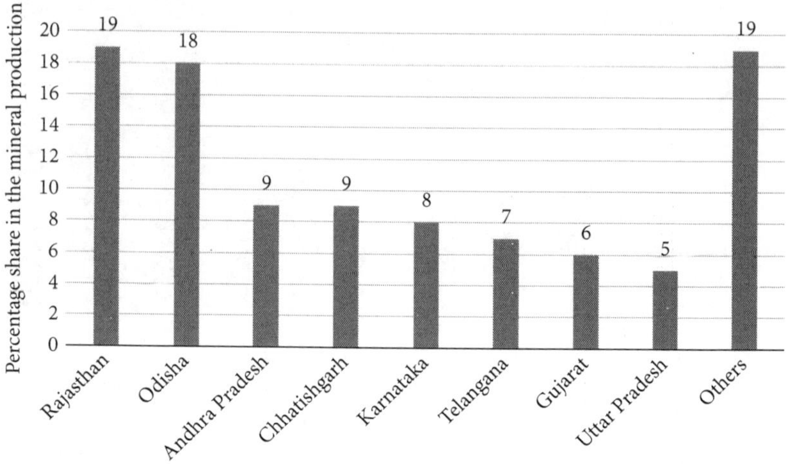

Fig. 1.3 Share of key mining states in India's mining production, by value, 2017–18

Source: Author's estimation using data from GoI (2017a; 2018a).

Table 1.5 Percentage share of key mining states in India's mineral reserves by volume, 2016–2017

States	Coal	Iron ore	Bauxite	Manganese	Lead and zinc	Chromite
Rajasthan	–	2	–	1	89	–
Odisha	25	23	4	44	–	96
Chhattisgarh	18	15	4	–	–	–
Jharkhand	26	16	6	2	–	0.21
Telangana	7	0.37	–	0.31	–	0.05
Madhya Pradesh	9	1	4	12	2	–
Andhra Pradesh	1	5	16	–	3	–
Karnataka	–	–	1	22	–	–

Source: GoI (2016a).

these five states also account for a majority of the key mineral reserves in India (Table 1.5).

The change in the share of each state regarding the value of total mineral production also points to the structural shift in the Indian mining industry. The mining industry has shifted its base from region to region due to the depletion of mineral resources and the resultant increased operational expenditure. The location of the mining industry has also depended, to a certain extent, on factors such as the availability of raw materials, skilled personnel, market access, availability of other services, feasibility conditions, and financial assistance. Thus, because of the depletion of mineral deposits in some areas and discoveries in other regions and the availability of factors determining industrial locations, the share of each state in the production of total mineral output has changed periodically, albeit at a slow pace.

1.2.3 Contributions

1.2.3.1 Contribution to GVA

The industry made a total value addition to the economy amounting to rupees 3,820 billion for the year 2017–2018 (Table 1.3). At the national level, the mining and quarrying sector (M&Q) had a very small share in GVA, around 3% for the year 2017–2018. The share remained almost stagnant for most of the years since 2012–2013, hovering around 3%. It can be seen from Table 1.6 that the annual growth rate of the mining industry shows a high rate of fluctuation.

The mining industry's contribution to India's growth in GVA declined from 5.73% in 2016–17 to 1.5% for the year 2017–2018. This was because of the closure of some of the mines in the country, which were adding value to the country's output growth rate. The comparison of

Table 1.6 Growth of the M&Q sector in India

Years	Value of output (*)	Share of M&Q sector in GVA	Annual growth rate (%)	Sectoral contribution to growth in GVA
2012–2013	2,626	3.07	0.60	0.36
2013–2014	2,631	2.90	0.19	0.1
2014–2015	2,887	2.97	9.72	3.94
2015–2016	3,285	3.13	13.78	5.03
2016–2017	3,711	3.30	12.97	5.73
2017–2018	3,820	3.19	2.94	1.5

Note: * At factor cost in rupees (billion) at 2011–2012 base year prices.

Source: Author's estimation from RBI (2018).

this industry with other sectors (see Table 1.4) shows that the share of mining and quarrying was more than that of electricity, gas, water supply, etc. but way below that of manufacturing, agriculture, and allied services. Mining, although a basic raw material provider to the other industries, contributes very little in terms of its share to the GVA compared with other industries (Table 1.7). The industry's growth lags behind the overall growth of the economy primarily due to infrastructure bottlenecks, policy paralysis, and other challenges. This inherently implies that the economic performance of the sector is not up to the mark, and there is a lot of scope for improvement.

The growth of the mining sector has also been very low over the years (Table 1.8). The sector grew at a rate of 2.94% in the year 2017–2018 as

Table 1.7 Percentage share in GVA by economic activity

Year	Agriculture, forestry, and fishing	Mining and quarrying	Manufacturing	Electricity, gas, water supply, and other utility services
2011–2012	18.53	3.22	17.39	2.3
2012–2013	17.84	3.07	17.4	2.24
2013–2014	17.75	2.9	17.22	2.2
2014–2015	16.53	2.97	17.34	2.2
2015–2016	15.38	3.13	18.08	2.13
2016–2017	15.26	3.3	18.21	2.18
2017–2018	14.82	3.19	18.09	2.19

Source: RBI (2018).

Table 1.8 Sectoral growth at 2011–2012 prices

Year	Mining and quarrying	Agriculture and allied	Manufacturing	Electricity, gas, and water supply
2012–2013	0.6	1.49	5.45	2.66
2013–2014	0.19	5.57	4.97	4.16
2014–2015	9.72	−0.22	7.9	7.24
2015–2016	13.78	0.59	12.76	4.74
2016–2017	12.97	6.29	7.9	9.25
2017–2018	2.94	3.37	5.74	7.17

Source: RBI (2018).

against the growth rate of 12.97% for the year 2016–2017. The growth of this sector also presents a dismal picture when compared with other sectors. It can be seen from Table 1.8 that all other sectors (for instance, manufacturing and electricity, gas, and water supply) have grown at a much higher rate than the mining sector. The poor growth performance of this sector may be due to policy paralysis and lack of proper planning and implementation of industry development programmes.

Mining in India contributed around 2.7% to the GDP for the year 2018, showing a marginal increase from that of the previous year (Fig. 1.4). The contribution declined from 3.2 to 2.7% owing to the closure of some mines in recent years. However, the domestic mining industry's contribution to the industrial sector is around 10–11%, reflecting the positive role that this industry plays in the overall growth of industrial output.

1.2.3.2 Contribution to employment

The Indian mining sector employs only a meagre (0.3%) percentage of India's population, and employment in this sector has grown at the very slow pace of about 3% per annum over the years (MOM, 2011). During 2018–2019, the estimated average daily employment of labour engaged in the mining sector (excluding atomic and minor minerals) was 4,82,752, out of which 78% was in the public sector and 22% in the private sector. Fuel minerals accounted for 76%, metallic minerals for 18%, and

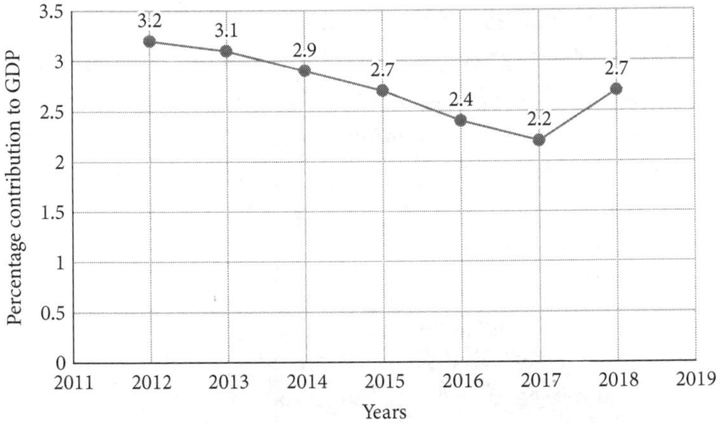

Fig. 1.4 Contribution to GDP (%) in India, 2012–2018
Source: Author's calculation using data from RBI (2017).

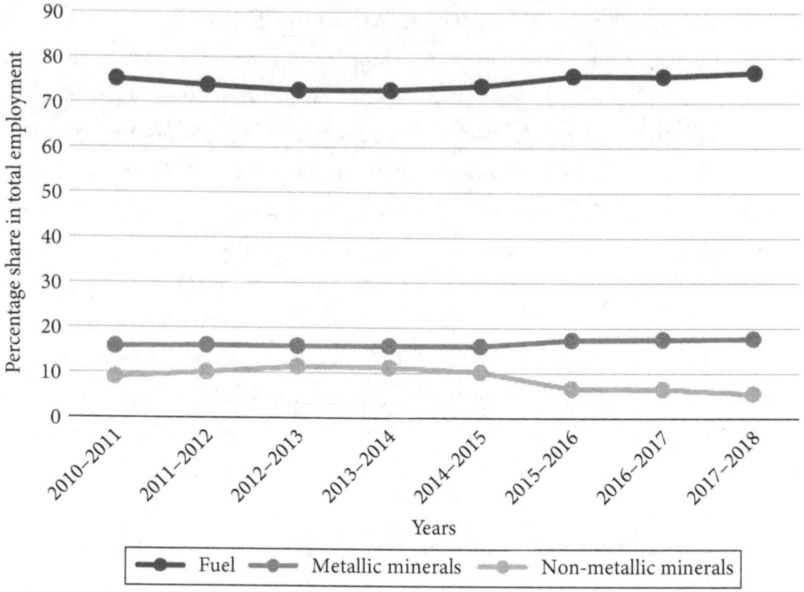

Fig. 1.5 Trends in employment by groups of minerals
Source: GoI (2017a; 2018a).

non-metallic minerals for 6% of the total labour force during 2019–2020. Over the years, the employment trend among the groups of minerals has declined (Fig. 1.5). The year-on-year growth rates of employment of various mineral groups also exhibit a negative trend (Table 1.9). For instance, while the total employment generated in mining has come down by 1.1% for 2017–2018, the same for mineral groups such as metallic and non-metallic minerals have reduced by 0.2 and 16.6%, respectively. For fuel minerals, the employment numbers have remained almost the same, indicating no growth rate changes. The huge reduction in non-metallic group employment may be due to the closure and non-operation of some important mines under this category.

1.2.3.3 Contributions to trade

With the contribution of 10% in merchandise exports and 29.67% in merchandise imports during 2019–2020, the mineral sector remained an important component of India's foreign trade. However, no visible diversification of trade was observed during this period. While the mineral

Table 1.9 Year-on-year employment growth rates for mineral groups .

Year	Total year-on-year growth (%)	Fuel year-on-year growth (%)	Metallic minerals year-on-year growth (%)	Non-metallic minerals year-on-year growth (%)
2010–2011	0.1	0.2	2.3	−4.3
2011–2012	0.3	−1.5	1.8	12.8
2012–2013	−1.7	−3.2	−2.6	10.3
2013–2014	−0.8	−0.7	−0.4	−2.2
2014–2015	−0.6	0.7	−0.5	−9.1
2015–2016	−6.1	−3.2	2.1	−39.7
2016–2017	0.1	0	1	−0.4
2017–2018	−1.1	0	−0.2	−16.6

Source: Indian Bureau of Mines; author's estimation.

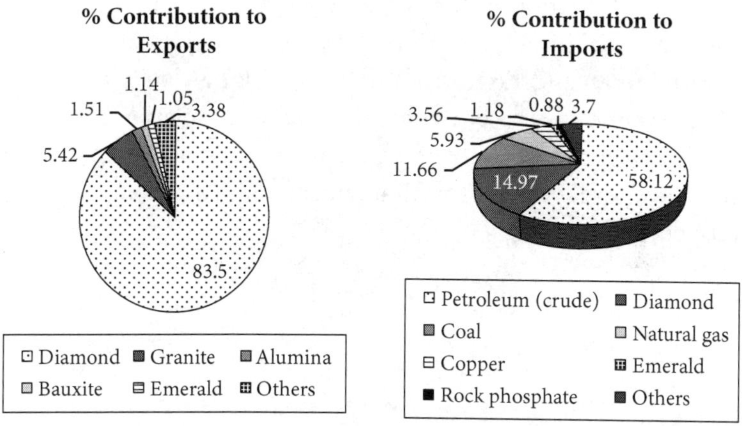

Fig. 1.6 Percentage contribution to exports and imports, 2019–2020
Source: GoI (2019a; 2020a).

exports have been dominated by diamonds (83.5% during 2019–2020), more than 84% of mineral imports during 2019–2020 were contributed by crude petroleum (58.12%), uncut diamond (14.97%), and coal (11.66%) (Fig. 1.6). Although India has huge coal reserves (as per the National Mineral Inventory, 2015), the fact that it has to import coal to the extent of 13% is quite disheartening and may be due to a lack of rigorous exploration activities and difficulty in extraction. Similarly, even though India has emerged as one of the world's best and largest cutting and polishing centres for rough diamonds, it is still deprived of the opportunity to do so, maybe because of the action of the international cartels that control the allocation of cutting centres in line with their own wishes.

The trends in mineral exports and imports (Fig. 1.7) over the years show that India experienced almost stagnant mineral exports until 2014–2015, whereas the import trend shows a constant increase, indicating a negative impact on the balance-of-payment situation of the country. However, of late, this increasing import trend has started to come down slowly and gradually due to the lower import of certain minerals such as diamond and coal. Yet, exports have not increased much, as a result of which the direction of trade is still negative, as imports are always greater than exports over the years. This trend presents a paradoxical situation in the Indian context. Even though it is considered a mineral resource-rich country, the nation is not self-sufficient in many minerals and has to depend on others for providing an impetus to the economic growth of the nation. Higher imports also points towards the lower productivity of the sector, which may be due to several reasons: low level of mechanisation, unskilled manpower, low level of investment, etc.

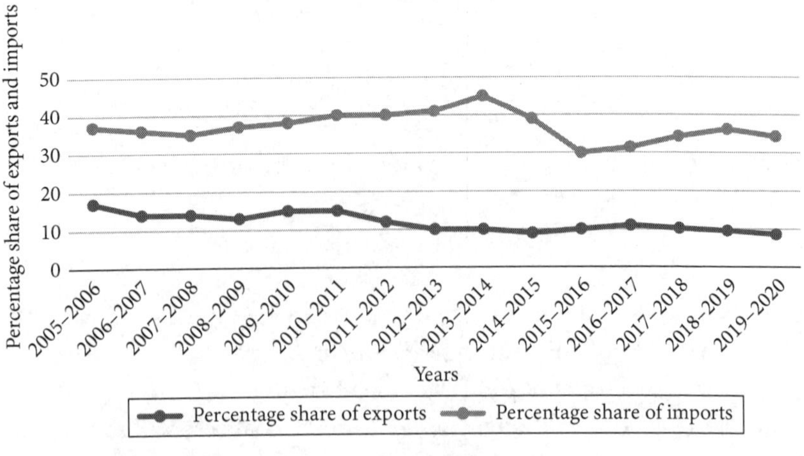

Fig. 1.7 Trends in mineral exports and imports

Source: GoI (2020a); author's own analysis.

1.3 Rationale for Choosing the Mining Industry

The Indian mining industry is an interesting case for examining the above issues for several reasons. The mining industry is of critical importance to the economy, as minerals are considered to be the backbone of any country's industrial development. The industry is a basic raw material supplier to many key industries such as manufacturing and thermal power generation. For instance, thermal power generation necessitates an uninterrupted supply of coal. The manufacturing industry largely depends on this industry for its basic inputs: almost all the products that we use for our survival are some kind of mineral. Starting from automobile production to medicinal products, all types of consumer products use minerals as the basic input. The growth of the manufacturing industry is thus heavily impacted by the mining industry. Similarly, the construction industry, which uses steel and aluminium as its primary inputs, is also largely affected by the mining industry. Hence, this industry is expected to have a wider effect on the economy as a whole and other industries in particular. Another reason for considering the mining industry for exploring the issues related to productivity and efficiency is that the low level of production and productivity may constrain the production of related manufacturing sectors and adversely affect the overall economic growth. The industry also makes an interesting case for examining energy-related issues, as the growth of this sector requires huge energy consumption.

1.4 Objectives of the Study

The present study seeks to examine the following research questions:

1. Does the mining industry have an impact on the Indian economy? What are the challenges encountered by the Indian mining industry?
2. What is the all-India trend in productivity in the mining sector? What is the scenario of factor productivity in the mining industry across the component subsectors such as metallic, non-metallic, coal, and petroleum? Has the productivity growth in the mining

industry changed over a period of time? Are private mining firms more productive than public firms?

3. Are mining firms energy efficient? Do they exhibit interfirm heterogeneity in energy-use efficiency?
4. How do mining firms perform socially and environmentally? Are the public firms more environment-compliant than private firms?

1.5 Methodology and Data

These four research questions have been examined independently in Chapters 2, 3, 4, 5, 6, and 7. First, for examining the economic impact of the mining industry on macroeconomic variables such as income, output, and employment, the input–output methodology is used, considering its advantage over other methods. Identifying the challenges that this industry faces has been conducted through desktop-based research. For evaluating the economic impact of the mining industry on the Indian economy, the input–output transaction table for 2013–2014 has been used, and for the purpose of identification of the mining industry's challenges, data has been collected from secondary sources such as publications from the Indian Bureau of Mines, the Reserve Bank of India *Handbook of statistics*, *National accounts statistics* and other relevant documents, Directorate General of Mines Safety reports, nongovernmental organization (NGO) publications, and podcasts of interviews of mining experts.

For the second objective, the total factor productivity (TFP) of the mining industry and its component subsectors has been estimated using the Levinsohn and Petrin (2003) method. It is noteworthy to mention here that the TFP can be measured by the ordinary least square (OLS) method, where the measure of TFP can be obtained as the residual in the production function relationship. Several methodological issues arise when the TFP at firm level is estimated by using traditional methods such as OLS. First, since productivity and input choices are likely correlated, OLS estimation of firm-level production functions may result in a simultaneity or endogeneity problem. The literature provides various estimators (parametric and semi-parametric) that can be used to resolve these methodological issues. However, traditional estimators (i.e. fixed effects, instrumental variables, and generalized method of moments or GMM) used to overcome endogeneity issues have not proved satisfactory for the case of production functions. The unsatisfactory performance of these estimators may be due to their underlying assumptions. Therefore, a number of semi-parametric alternatives have been proposed in the literature to address these issues. Both Levinsohn and Petrin (2003) and Olley and Pakes (1996) have developed a semi-parametric estimator that addresses the simultaneity bias (and the selection bias in the case of the Olley and Pakes estimator). Out of these, in recent times, the Levinsohn and Petrin method has become popular as it has advantages over the Olley and Pakes method. The Levinsohn and Petrin method directly estimates the TFP at levels for individual firms, thereby assuming importance from the analysis viewpoint. The present study, to estimate the TFP at firm levels, uses Levinsohn and Petrin method because of its merits over other methods. For comparing the private- and public-sector mining firms productivity difference, the TFP of the two groups has been estimated for four component subsectors of the mining industry—coal, metallic, non-metallic, petroleum—for the periods 2000–2001 and 2016–2017.

Further, the technical efficiency of a specific subsector—coal has been measured using the stochastic frontier approach. As against the non-frontier approach, in the frontier approach, benchmarking is done where a firm's actual performance is compared with its maximum potential performance, which makes it more suitable to describe the industry or firm's behaviour, whereas benchmarking has little room in the non-frontier approach. Since this book aims to address the questions on maximum productive or best practice output levels, given the inputs and technology, it uses the frontier approach. Corresponding to this objective, which focuses on productivity growth and efficiency measurement, the firm-level data has been used, extracted from the Centre for Monitoring Indian Economy (CMIE). Prowess is a database of large and medium Indian firms and comprises all companies traded on India's major trade exchanges. As regards the data from the Prowess database, it contains financial information for over 40,000 companies in general and 255 mining companies in particular. The data are available from 1989.

For measuring the energy-use efficiency at the firm level for the various subsectors of the mining industry (coal, metallic, non-metallic, and petroleum), the parametric frontier approach has been used due to its advantage in providing a benchmark where a firm's actual performance is compared with its maximum possible performance in terms of energy-use efficiency. Thereafter, a second stage panel data regression analysis is performed using these efficiency scores to derive the determinants of energy-use efficiency. The detailed methodology of estimating energy-use efficiency is discussed in Chapter 5 of this book. To accomplish this objective, the book refers to the same sources of data, that is, the Prowess database of the CMIE.

Finally, an examination of the social and environmental performance of mining firms in terms of their compliance with the social and environmental damages inflicted by their operations has been conducted with the help of a primary survey. For this purpose, the study considers the state of Odisha as the proposed study area and conducts a household survey in the Jajpur district of Odisha. To compare social compliance, using a pre-tested questionnaire, the survey collects information on variables such as mode of land transfer, nature of compensation, the satisfaction of households concerning compensation received, capacity-building exercise undertaken, and any other development activities performed. For comparing the environmental compliance between public and private mining firms, the study gathers information on various measures undertaken by the mining companies: improving the quality of air and water, reducing noise pollution, treatment of mine drainage water, tree plantation, etc. Based on this information, the study discusses whether or not the mining firms are complying in respect of their environmental performance from the mining-affected households' perspective. Thereafter, these results are discussed against the environmental compliance indicators that mining firms submit to the State Pollution Control Board to identify the existence of any possible performance difference.

1.6 Chapter Outline

The book has been organized into eight chapters. The first chapter introduces the purpose of the study, which spells out the need for a detailed economic analysis of the mining industry from three different dimensions: productivity, social, and environmental. The analysis of the mining industry in these three different dimensions necessitates a unique treatment for each. Therefore, the review of previous studies and the description of the methodology and data sources used for examining the four different research questions have been mentioned separately. Chapter 2 examines the first research question concerning what is the economic impact of the mining industry and its subsectors on the Indian economy. Chapter 3 examines the challenges faced by the mining industry in the context of India. Chapter 4 provides an empirical examination of the second research question, which attempts to investigate the trend, scenario, and ownership and efficiency link. The technical efficiency of coal-mining firms has been estimated in Chapter 5. Chapter 6 probes the third research question of whether or not mining firms are energy efficient and if there is any interfirm heterogeneity. Chapter 7 investigates the fourth research question of whether or not ownership affects the social and environmental performance of mining firms. A summary of the results is provided in Chapter 8, followed by policy implications, a description of the limitations of the study, and suggestions of direction for areas for future research.

1.7 Policy Reforms in the Indian Mining Industry

The regulation and development of mines in India were based on the first regulatory framework, constituted in 1948, and termed as the Mines and Minerals (Regulation and Development) Act. The Constitution of India entrusted power to both the central government and the state governments for mining regulation and minerals development (GoI, 2006). The ownership rights were accorded to the state governments. The central government kept possession of the regulatory authority over all major minerals defined in Schedule A of Industrial Policy Resolution, 1956, while the management of all minor minerals fell under the ambit of state governments. The Mines and Minerals (Regulation and Development) Act of 1957 framed two important rules, namely, the Mineral Concession Rule (MCR, 1960) and the Mineral Conservation and Development Rules (MCDR, 1958). The MCR dealt with all the major minerals, and the state governments were given the liberty to frame their own concession rules with minor minerals.

The MMDR Act (1957) was amended for the first time in 1972, and this extended the central government's control over mining. An array of new measures, such as the power to modify mining leases, premature termination of mining leases, the right of the central government to conduct prospecting and mining operations in specific areas, removal of the ceiling on the royalty charged on minerals, inclusion of provision for collection of dead rent, and increase of penalties were initiated. A further amendment to the MMDR Act (1957) was made in 1986, which brought in several rigorous measures. Subsequently, the Act has been amended several times to streamline the mining business in India. The latest amendment, made in 2023, focused on strengthening the exploration and extraction of critical minerals essential for India's economic development and national security.

The Indian mining industry has thus undergone significant policy reforms in recent years aimed at boosting investment, increasing domestic production, and ensuring sustainable practices. The key changes have been brought in the areas of liberalization and auctioning, ease of doing business, focus on exploration and value addition, sustainability, and the environment. As per the latest amendment, the Indian mining sector has been opened to private players through auctions so as to bring in competition to increase the efficiency of the business. In this respect, a transparent auction process for mineral blocks has been implemented, attracting investments and ensuring fair allocation. To introduce ease of doing business, simplified procedures and digitalization of the mining process have been introduced to facilitate the smooth operation of mining. As per the recent policy changes, a National Mineral Exploration Trust (NMET) has been established to fund exploration activities and reduce risks for private players. To create value addition for the business, policies encouraging the domestic processing of minerals have been initiated to generate employment opportunities and boost the economy. The policy reforms also focus on stricter environmental norms emphasizing sustainable mining practices, including rehabilitation and afforestation. To reduce the industry's carbon footprints, and thereby contribute to the mitigation of the climate crisis, the MMDR Act calls for the promotion of environment-friendly clean technologies. The Indian mining industry is undergoing a transformative phase with several policy reforms aimed at making it globally competitive while ensuring environmental sustainability.

1.7.1 Reforms in the Indian Coal-Mining Subsector

Since the establishment of the MMDR Act of 1957, the Indian coal-mining subsector has undergone tremendous transformation, the significant changes made in recent years. Key policy reforms include the introduction of commercial coal mining; a transparent auction process for coal blocks; a focus on sustainable mining practices, including environmental clearances, rehabilitation, and afforestation; and the adoption of improved mining technology. The reforms also lay stress on the simplification of procedures, reduction of clearances, and promotion of digitalization in the subsector. These reforms aim to make the coal-mining subsector more efficient, competitive, and environmentally responsible while ensuring India's energy security.

1.7.2 Key Policy Changes in the Metallic-Mining Subsector

In recent years, India has undergone significant policy reforms to boost its metallic-mining subsector to attract investment, increase domestic production, and reduce reliance on imports. In these respects, the noteworthy policy changes emphasize the establishment of the NMET, which aims to boost mineral exploration, reduce exploration risks for private players, and enhance mineral availability. In addition, to bringing in more competition and increasing revenue, the government has adopted a transparent auctioning process for allocating mineral blocks, replacing the earlier discretionary system. Further, to increase domestic production and curtail import dependency, the government has started to recognize the importance of critical minerals and has subsequently included twenty-four minerals in the 'Critical and Strategic minerals' category.

1.7.3 Key Policy Changes in the Non-Metallic-Mining Subsector

With respect to policy reforms in the non-metallic-mining subsector, the government has attempted procedure simplification and reduction in regulatory impediments to ease the process for businesses to operate in this subsector. Initiatives are also being undertaken to promote domestic manufacturing of non-metallic minerals-based products, thereby helping to reduce import dependency. In addition, the policy changes also place more emphasis on sustainable practices in non-metallic mining.

1.7.4 Key Policy Changes in the Petroleum-Mining Subector

The key policy reforms concerning the petroleum-mining subsector in recent years focus on the introduction of the Open Acreage Licensing Policy (OALP), the Hydrocarbon Exploration and Licensing Policy (HELP) and prioritizing gas. With the objective of promoting exploration activities, the OALP permits companies to explore and produce hydrocarbons in identified areas without prior bidding. The government has also introduced a hydrocarbon exploration and licensing policy to usher in a new era of exploration and production to attract investments and enhance domestic oil and gas production. The recent policy changes focus on gas as a cleaner fuel and have implemented policies to encourage gas production and utilization.

2

The Economic Impact of the Mining Industry in India

2.1 Introduction

Minerals are valuable natural resources, being finite and non-renewable. Besides catering to the energy requirements of the world, they are useful inputs for diverse industrial activities. Thus, the mining sector, being one of the core sectors of the economy, provides basic raw materials to many important industries: power generation (thermal), iron and steel, cement, petroleum and natural gas, petrochemicals, fertilizers, precious and semi-precious metals/stones, electrical and electronics equipment, glass and ceramics, etc. Natural endowment of minerals increases the potential wealth of a country, but their distribution across the world varies substantially.

Minerals play a vital role in the development process of any country, particularly developing nations (Hilson, 2002b). The large mineral resources can serve as a basis for a country's development, provided the required policies are in place. Mining can have a colossal impact on a nation's macroeconomic variables, and the economic impact can be felt at local, regional, and national levels (Dorian, 1994). Commercial mining activities will generate a series of economic impulses that reverberate across society (Dorian, 1994).

The economic impacts of mining can be observed across a nation's economy in terms of output expansion, employment generation, and revenue creation. Mining's economic impact can be segregated into three categories—direct, indirect, and induced effects (PwC, 2012). The total economic impact arising out of mining activities would be the total of these direct, indirect, and induced impacts. Direct effects primarily occur as a result of mining operations (for instance, from the expenses associated

The Indian Mining Industry. Meenakshi Parida and S. Madheswaran, Oxford University Press.
 DOI: 10.1093/9780198954392.003.0002

with constructing and operating a mine), whereas the indirect effects result from the linkage that the mining industry has with other sectors. In other words, the indirect effect emanates from the suppliers of the mine purchasing goods and services and hiring workers to meet the demands of the mining sector. These second-round effects (indirect effects) occur only due to mine expansion. The induced effect, on the other hand, results from the wages and salaries that the mine workers receive, which they use for purchasing goods and services at the household level. Thus, the mining industry is expected to generate a series of economic impacts through these direct, indirect, and induced impacts that have the potential to catalyse the long-term development of a nation. Another channel through which the mining industry can have an impact is through the spending of taxes and royalties paid to the government. However, it has been revealed that this channel, which involves government revenue and associated expenditure, is likely to be a small part (15–20%) of the total economic value generated by any mining project (ICMM, 2014).

The economic impact of the mining sector depends on the structure of a nation's economy and accordingly varies from country to country. For India, which has opened up its mineral sector to the world economy since 1990 and is becoming more and more decentralized (and even privatized, to some extent) in its mining operations, leaving few strategic minerals, the economic ramifications of this sector assume great importance. Thus, this chapter attempts to analyse the economic impacts of mining on the Indian economy in terms of direct and indirect effects concerning macroeconomic variables such as output, income, and employment.

2.2 Role of Mining in the Indian Economy

India is a nation blessed with a diversity of huge mineral resources according to the Geological Survey of India. India is endowed with a vast amount of iron ore, manganese, coal, bauxite, chromite, limestone, gold, diamonds, asbestos, and other diverse types of minerals. As in many other developing nations, in India, mining has become an important component of the economy and has a long history. Gold, copper, iron ore, manganese, bauxite, and coal have been mined since the Harappa age (MMSD, 2001), and in recent years extraction has been further

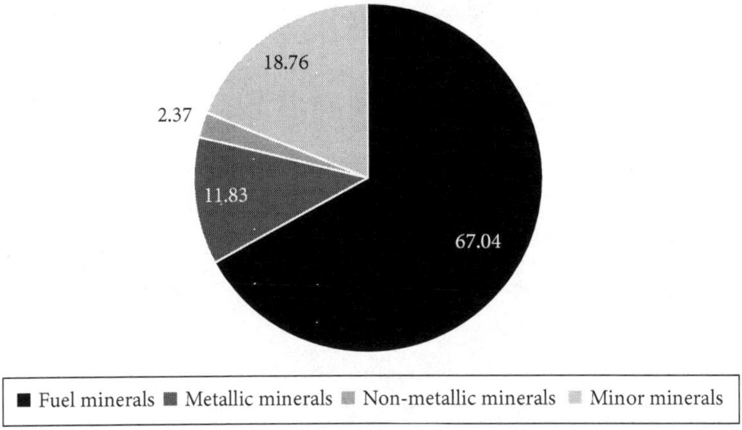

Fig. 2.1 Shares of mineral groups in value of mineral production
Source: GoI (2016a).

intensified owing to a global increase in demand for mineral commodities. India produces about 90 varieties of minerals (Rábago et al., 2016). The Indian mineral sector is comprised of four broad categories of minerals: fuel, metallic, non-metallic, and minor minerals. Among these, fuel minerals contribute around 68% of the sector, followed by metallic minerals (19%), minor minerals (11%), and non-metallic minerals (2%) (GoI, 2016a) (Fig. 2.1).

The mining and quarrying sector contributes around 2.4% of the gross domestic product (GDP) with a total value of rupees 3,18,672 crores in 2015–2016 (GoI, 2016a) (Fig. 2.2). The index of mineral production with base 2011–2012 prices touched 129.3 points in 2015–2016, showing an increasing trend of mineral production in India. In addition to this, India has also been able to occupy a remarkable position in the world mineral market in respect of some commodities. It produces one-third of all coal, lignite, barite, and steel (crude) and held the fourth rank in bauxite, chromite, and iron ore production for the year 2015–2016 (GoI, 2016a).

In terms of export earnings, India is considered to be a leading exporter of minerals and ores. In 2015–2016, minerals contributed significantly to India's export trade, which accounted for about rupees 1,70,946 crores, with a share of about 10% in the total value of merchandise trade. The major minerals in terms of export earnings are diamond, granite,

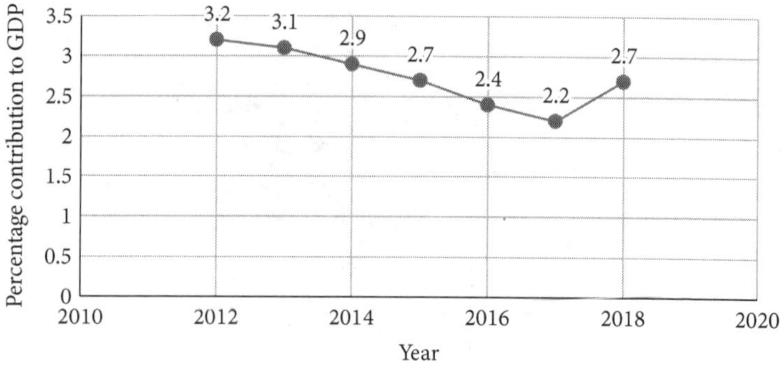

Fig. 2.2 Contribution to GDP (%) in India, 2012–2018
Source: Author's calculation using data from RBI (2017).

alumina, bauxite, and emerald. However, diamond alone holds 83.50% of the total value of mineral exports from India, followed by granite (5.42%), alumina (1.51%), bauxite (1.41%), and emerald (1.05%), and the rest of the minerals individually are less than 1%. Apart from mineral production and export earnings, the mineral sector is considered to be an important source of employment generation in India. On average, the mining sector employed 4,88,694 people in 2015–2016, out of which 68% were in the public sector and 32% in the private sector (GoI, 2016a).

The above estimates point out the increasing importance of mining in the Indian economy. Thus, the mining sector is gaining importance in the official circles of the Government of India due to the nature of its impact on the economic, environmental, and social fabric of the country. As these estimates suggest, the Indian mining industry can significantly contribute to the national economy (primarily as a raw material provider) in respect of output growth, employment creation, export earnings, and revenue generation. However, mineral development can also bring a series of negative effects, such as social tensions and the destruction of the ecological environment, especially for the mineral-rich regions. Moreover, more emphasis on mineral development may lead to the concentration of one kind of industry and employment structure in many mineral regions, creating problems such as mineral resource depletion and a decline in sustainable development.

However, despite these negative effects, the importance of the sector for the country's economy cannot be ignored. Again, as India moves through rapid urbanization and industrialization, the mineral sector is expected to grow at a rapid rate in the future. Hence, future demand in this sector is expected to reach a new high. This may lead to the development of other industries and simultaneous increases in the output, employment, and income of the economy. It is envisaged to have a big impact on investment, employment opportunities, and output growth, as well as income. Thus, it can be said, without a doubt, that mineral development will not only provide important raw materials for India's industrialization but will also engender a wide impact on the fixed assets investment, employment opportunities, economic growth, and industrial structure, as well as income. Therefore, it is necessary to comprehensively analyse the combined economic effects of the mineral sector in India.

To this end, this chapter seeks to analyse the impact of the mining industry on output, income, and employment at the national level. The structure of the chapter is as follows. Section 2.3 discusses the theoretical and empirical literature about the impact and challenges of the mining industry, and 2.4 discusses the choice of methodology for examining the impact of the mining industry. Section 2.5 describes the theoretical and methodological framework. The results of the economic impact of mining are discussed in section 2.6, while section 2.7 provides the discussion and conclusion.

2.3 Studies Based on Economic Impact and Challenges

There is extensive literature discussing the relationship between mining and economic growth. With the perspective of studying the effects of mineral development on the economy and society, many scholars have focused on the relationship between mining development and socio-economic development and thereby have drawn disparate conclusions about the effects of mineral development on society and economy. At one extreme, some studies have found that mining activity has a positive impact on incomes, housing affordability, communication access, education, and employment across regional and remote Australia (Hajkowicz et al. 2011), while some have found a positive impact on economic growth (Davis, 1995; Habakkuk,1962). At the other extreme, some empirical research has found a negative effect of mining activity on economic growth (Auty, 1993; Gelb, 1988).

Habakkuk (1962) analysed the economic effects of mineral resource development from the productivity perspective. By linking high productivity to mineral resource endowment, he claimed that the United States became the world leader in terms of industrial production due to mineral resource extraction. Davis (1995) believed that mineral-abundant countries can enhance their economic growth by exporting raw materials. On the contrary, Gelb (1988) considered mineral endowment as a curse and argued that nations with rich mineral resources have had lower growth rates than nations that import raw minerals. One of the front runners of resource curse literature, Auty (1993), believed that abundant natural resources not only failed to promote growth but also rather limited the country's potential for economic growth. Both Auty and Gelb also provided the reasons why countries with huge mineral endowments have not performed well on the economic growth front. They ascribed economic and political factors to be the key reasons for this dismal performance. Similarly, Sachs and Warner (1995, 1997, 1999, 2001) conducted a series of empirical tests associated with a prospective resource curse and found that very few (two of the eighteen) resource-abundant countries sustained a growth rate greater than 2% between 1970 and 1989. They argued that the primary reasons why these countries were experiencing low growth were due to their trade policies, investment rates, terms of trade volatility, income inequalities, and bureaucratic inefficiencies. Many scholars have offered political and economic explanations for the low economic growth of mineral-rich countries (Lane and Tornell, 1995; Sachs and Warner, 1995).

In an attempt to analyse the impact of the mining industry on the South African economy, Stilwell et al. (2000) suggested that South African mining activity would have a positive impact on income and employment only when exports increase and linkage is established between mining and the rest of the South African economy. Edwards (1985), in his study, advocated that South Africa should take advantage of its rich mineral resource base for creating domestic secondary industries and suggested that South Africa could be a rich nation using its mineral wealth as intermediate input to develop a strong manufacturing sector.

However, in the context of India, very few studies have been published from the perspective of measuring the economic impact of the mining industry. Moreover, the existing published work focuses on the relationship between mining production, exports, and economic growth (Sahoo et al., 2014). Few have attempted to investigate the relationship between energy resources (gas and coal development) and regional economic growth. There are relatively few studies on other minerals, such as metallic and non-metallic mineral resources. Some scholars have analysed the economic effects of the mining sector from the perspective of the regional economy (Panda, 2014). However, the economic effect of the mineral development industry is seldom analysed at the national level in India. There is hardly any study that attempts to examine the impact of the mining industry on output, income, and employment. In addition, previous research tends to focus on certain categories of minerals in individual states (Panda, 2014), with little work addressing the national effects of mineral development. Thus, it is difficult to comprehend the wholesome effects of the mining industry and compare them across other industries.

In this regard, this book attempts to take a small step by focusing on the impact of the mineral development industry on the Indian economy as a whole. The book, therefore, endeavours to carry out a systematic examination of the effect of the mining industry on output, income, and employment.

2.4 Choice of Methodology

Assessing the impact of mining expansion is complex as these impacts arise through different dynamic channels. For impact assessment, varied methodologies were reviewed in terms of their pros, cons, and pragmatism. In general, three approaches can be used for impact assessment: econometric modelling, which includes regression analysis and structural macroeconomic modelling; input–output multiplier analysis; and computable general equilibrium (CGE) models.

Traditional econometric tools that study the influence of mining output expansion on GDP levels do not provide estimates for specific mining projects. At the same time, GDP is not the only macroeconomic variable that is impacted by the mining industry expansion. These studies are also associated with serious issues, such as omitted variable bias, discussed in the review of the literature. The unavailability of time series data for all the macroeconomic variables related to this industry renders this technique redundant for the particular purpose of mining impact study.

However, the CGE approach might be preferable to the input–output multiplier analysis from the theoretical standpoint. However, larger data and programming requirements make practicality of use difficult. CGE models, however, can be more applicable in cases where larger data and resources are available, especially for detailed ex-post analysis of a specific project.

Thus, the input–output methodology is found to be the most appropriate method for the present task. As such, we use this method for our multiplier modelling as a practical tool that can be applied with minimum programming and data requirements. The approach is also associated with several assumptions and limitations, which are discussed in section 2.5.

2.5 Theoretical and Methodological Framework

This book uses the standard input–output analysis for the impact estimation, as is usually the case in literature. The input–output analysis was originally conceived by Leontief (1966), who first used it to analyse the structure of the US economy (Leontief 1936, 1941). The major application of this approach has been discussed in O'Connor and Henry (1975), Leontief and Inchausti (1984), and Miller and Blair (2009). Some of the most important theoretical assumptions on which the model is based are the following (Miller and Blair 2009; Rose and Miernyk 1989):

1. Each sector produces only one good and there cannot be any instances of firms producing the same output in different sectors.
2. Constant returns to scale prevail in the economy.
3. There is no substitution of intermediate inputs, or in other words, the input–output coefficients are fixed.
4. There is no technological change.
5. The model is demand-driven.

Along with these assumptions, one of the most important limitations of this model is that it is considered to be static. These models provide intersectoral transactions in an economy at a given point in time and do not reflect what happens to the economic transactions when there are endogenous changes in the variables, thereby they do not contain a mechanism that can best describe a dynamic model.

Despite all these limitations of the input–output analysis, this method is widely used in the literature as it offers a direct solution to the estimation of the total impact of a particular activity or sector. Moreover, the method is used in many similar kinds of studies that aim to assess economic activity at the national level. Similar studies undertaken include the Stillwell et al. (2000) analysis of the South African economy, and Li et al.'s (2017) analysis of China.[1]

2.5.1 Input–Output Methodology

The input–output (IO) analysis is a mechanism for estimating the impact of an expansion in any sector's activity. With the help of IO analysis, three types of impact can be estimated for a sector: direct impact (total expenditure arising out of the sector's productive activity), its indirect impact (arising out of the linkages between the aforementioned sector and the rest of the domestic economy's sectors), and its induced effect (arising out of the consumption expenditure of the sector's employees).[2]

The core of IO analysis is the IO model. The IO model is based on the intermediate transaction matrix that describes the relationships among the productive sectors of an economy. Every row of this matrix shows the distribution of output of a sector among the rest of the sectors in the economy, and each column of the matrix exhibits the inputs that the particular sector uses in its production process.

[1] The study of San Cristobal and Bizema (2006) should be added to this list as this is the only study in the literature that focuses on the impact of mining on the European Union. However, the study emphasizes linkage estimation, and no efforts have been made to quantify the economic impact.

[2] Besides the quantification of impacts, which is considered to be a main application of IO analysis, other applications of this method are also found in the literature. In this context, a noteworthy study is by Wagner and Dellar (1998), who (in the context of a regional economy) used this model to derive the economic diversity, taking into account inter-industry linkages.

The IO model is a demand-driven model; its intermediate use matrix embodies both the demand and cost aspects. The demand aspect relates to the intermediate demand of other sectors for the output of the sector in question for their use and the cost aspect is represented by the column of the IO table as this reflects the input requirement of the sector from the rest of the economy. The model explains two mathematical identities from both demand and cost perspectives. From a demand perspective, the total output must be equal to the sum of the total intermediate use and the final demand, whereas, from the cost perspective, it must equal the sum of the intermediate good's cost and gross value added net of taxes and subsidies.

A very general and simplified IO model is presented in Table 2.1 below.

The transactions among various sectors presented in Table 2.1 can be described by the following equation:

$$X_i = \Sigma X_{ij} + Y_i \tag{1}$$

where X_{ij} is the amount of inputs sector j purchases from the selling sector i, X_j is the output for sector j, and Y_i is the final demand of sector i.

Table 2.1 Simplified framework of India input–output table

Supply from ith industry	Intermediate uses (uses in jth industry)	Final uses					Total output
	Ind-1	Ind-2	In-n	PFCE	Other output final use	Net final demand	
Ind-1	X11	X12	X1n	C1	G1	Y1	X1
Ind-2	X21	X22	X2n	C2	G2	Y2	X2
Ind-n	Xn1	Xn2	Xnn	Cn	Gn	Yn	Xn
Value added	V1	V2	Vn	–	–	–	–
Value of output	X1	X2	Xn	–	–	–	–

Source: Author's presentation.

2.5.2 Data

2.5.2.1 India IO table

In India, the Central Statistical Office (CSO) compiles and publishes official statistics, including IO tables. The first IO table for India was published in 1968–1969 jointly by the CSO and the Planning Commission. Since 1973, the CSO has been constructing and publishing these tables at an approximate five-yearly interval. The latest IO table available for India is for 2007–2008. Before that, the official IO tables (brought out by the CSO) were prepared for the reference years 1968–1969, 1973–1974, 1978–1979, 1983–1984, 1989–1990, 1993–1994, 1998–1999, and 2003–2004. The published tables for 1989–1990, 1993–1994 and 1998–1999 are for 115 sectors of the economy while, for the earlier years, these relate to 60 sectors only. The tables for 2003–2004 and 2007–2008 have 130 sectors. However, after 2007–2008, no attempt has been made by the CSO to publish IO tables; rather, for the years 2011–2012 and 2012–2013, the CSO has come up with the supply use tables that can be employed to construct an IO table for India. To do this, using the supply use table for 2012–2013, K. Singh and M. R. Saluja (2017) have brought out the IO table for 2013–2014. For the present analysis, this chapter uses the IO table prepared by Singh and Saluja (2017).[3] The advantage of using this IO table is that they have used the same methodology and procedure as was used by the CSO in the construction of IO tables, and like 2007–2008, this IO table also contains 130 sectors, which makes comparison easy if desired. As the official IO table (CSO) dates back over a decade and a half, it would be inappropriate to use this IO table for impact analysis as the results would not reflect the proper scenario and impact analysis and would not serve any purpose. Hence, this book uses the IO table for 2013–2014 constructed by Singh and Saluja with the view that, although the table dates back ten years, as is assumed in many economic analyses, no major changes are expected to have occurred in the transactions among different sectors within this short period. Thus, this table would be more appropriate from the standpoint of our analysis.

[3] For a detailed structure and methodology, refer to Singh and Saluja (2017).

Table 2.2 Aggregated sectors

Sector No.	Sectors aggregated	Aggregated rows in the IO table
1	Agriculture	1–26
2	Mining and quarrying	27–37
3	Manufacturing	38–105
4	Construction	106
5	Other industries	107–108
6	Business services	118–120, 123, 125, 126, 127
7	Trade, hotel, transport, and communication	109–117
8	Community, social, and personal services	121, 122, 124, 128, 129, 130

Source: Author's estimation using input–output table 2013–2014.

Thus, the IO table (India) for 2013–2014 comprises the data for this analysis. Notwithstanding the limitations of the IO analysis, this table is the best reference to trace the impact of the mining sector as well as other sectors on the national economy.

The first step in our methodology involves organizing and consolidating information in the IO tables. We aggregate the 2013–2014 IO table into eight sectors to simplify the calculation and interpretation of results.[4] The aggregation has been done by the National Accounts Statistics of India (CSO, 2015), which gives the figures for all macroeconomic variables for these same eight segregated sectors. The sole purpose underlying the classification of 130 sectors into 8 is to make a comparison of the mining industry compared with other industries at the broader level. Further, this aggregation also helps in easy enumeration and interpretation of the IO table. For our analysis, the aggregated sectors are provided in Table 2.2. The detailed sectoral classification is provided in Appendix A2 at the end of the chapter.

[4] The 2013–2014 IO table for the Indian economy classifies 130 sectors. Table 2.2 gives the aggregated eight sectors.

2.5.2.2 IO technique to estimate the impact of mining activity

The IO table represents the starting point in estimating the output, income, and employment multipliers used in conducting the economic impact analysis. The next step employed after consolidating the IO table from 130 to 8 sectors was to build an IO model by converting the intersectoral transactions into an A matrix (technical coefficient matrix) showing the direct requirements of a sector to produce a unit of its product. The technical coefficients are estimated by dividing the values taken from the transaction matrix by the total output, respectively:

$$a_{ij} = \frac{x_{ij}}{x_j} \tag{2}$$

Each column of the direct requirement matrix represents the production function for the corresponding sector. The technical coefficients are non-negative $a_{ij} \geq 0$ and also $\sum_{j=1}^{n} a_{ij} \leq 1$, which implies that input requirements cannot exceed the total output produced.

From equation (2), it can be written as

$$x_{ij} = \alpha_{ij}\ X_j \tag{3}$$

Now, equation (1) can be rewritten as follows:

$$\sum_{i}^{n} X_{ij} = \sum_{i}^{n} a_{ij} {}^{*}X_j + \sum_{i}^{n} Y_i \tag{4}$$

Equation system (4) exhibits that the output level of each sector is dependent on the output of other sectors and the final demand. In other words, an industry's total output (X) equals the sum of the intermediate demand for its output and the total final demand. Thus, the model's basic equation can be written as

$$\mathrm{X} = \mathrm{AX} + \mathrm{Y} \tag{5}$$

Solving equation (5), we get

$$\mathrm{X} = (\mathrm{I} - \mathrm{A})^{-1}\, Y \tag{6}$$

where 'I' is the (nxn) identity matrix. The matrix $(I-A)^{-1}$ is called Leontief's inverse or the total requirement matrix and shows the extent to which output production changes to the variations of final demand (i.e. the extent to which final demand multiplicatively affects total output). Each sector's simple multipliers (the sum of direct and indirect effects divided by the direct effects) are simply the sums of the elements of the respective column of Leontief's inverse matrix.[5]

To estimate the induced effect, the IO matrix is required to have one additional row and column each, the additional row showing the household income (compensation to the employees) and the extra column exhibiting the household's private final consumption expenditure. Once the IO model is augmented by the extra information as described above, the total multiplier estimation can be done from this table directly in a similar way as the simple multiplier estimation. However, this analysis-induced effect could not be estimated due to data constraints (unavailability of wage and salary data). We restrict ourselves to simple multiplier estimation because of these data constraints.

2.5.3 Calculating the IO Multipliers

IO multipliers are summary measures used to estimate the impact of all industries in an economy of changes in the demand for the output of any one industry. The multipliers are derived from the constructed IO table. However, as the IO table often dates back several years, questions can be raised concerning the applicability of the table in a time of fast technological change. The tables date back a few years as the agency entrusted with the responsibility of producing them could not do so within the stipulated time period due to the enormous amount of data required and the complexities of the tasks involved in compilation. Technological change does not occur very fast in most industries, so it is possible to obtain reasonable results for the latest year even though the latest IO tables may be a few years old. So, the calculated multipliers remain fairly stable over time.

[5] Although IO analysis is the most widely used method for estimating output, income, and employment multipliers, there are several other techniques to do the same. For instance, using a simple econometric model, Fleming and Measham (2014) have been able to estimate the local employment multipliers. Similarly, Ahmmad and Clements (1999) and Clements et al. (1996) used CGE modelling to calculate the multipliers of the Western Australian economy.

Using the standard demand-side IO model, we generate different types of IO multipliers that represent the measures used for estimating the likely effects of mining output expansion.

2.5.3.1 Output multipliers

The output multiplier for the mining industry is defined as the total value of all outputs from each domestic industry of the economy required to produce an extra rupee worth of mining output. This initial requirement for an extra rupee worth of mining output is referred to as the 'initial output effect'. By definition, it is equal to one in total for all industries since an extra rupee worth of output from any industry will require the initial one rupee worth of output from that industry plus any induced extra output. The first-round effect is the amount of output needed from all industries of the economy to produce the initial output effect. For instance, if the mining industry's output increased by one rupee, then inputs from other industries, such as construction and manufacturing, will be required, as well as inputs from mining itself. These are referred to as 'backward linkages' as the demand for an extra rupee worth of mining output is considered to have induced the output production of these industries supplying inputs to it. The first-round effect can be measured from the technical coefficient matrix (i.e. A), which is otherwise referred to as the 'direct requirement matrix'. The column total of each of the industries provides the first-round effects, which also measures the strength of the backward linkages.

The simple output multipliers are the column sums $\sum_i L_{ij}$ of Leontief inverse matrix L_{ij}. This is given as follows:

$$O_{multj} = \sum_i L_{ij} \tag{7}$$

Once the simple multiplier is calculated, the industrial supports effect and the subsequent rounds of induced production can be estimated as follows:

Industrial support effects = simple multiplier − initial effects − first-round effects

Production-induced effects = first-round effects + industrial supports effects

Output multipliers estimate the direct and indirect effects of marginal increase in a sector's value added on output. The direct effects are the increased value added to the sector. The indirect effects are the value added by other sectors to satisfy the increased demand of the industry in question for intermediate inputs.

2.5.3.2 Income multipliers

The income multipliers for a particular industry are defined as the total value of income from wages, salaries, and supplements required to satisfy a rupee worth of final demand for the output of that industry. For this, we are required to calculate the household income coefficient, which can be done by dividing the value-added income (in the form of wages, salaries, and supplements) of each industry with the total output of that industry. For estimation purposes, let us refer to them as vector $\boldsymbol{h}$. These are the initial income effects. The remaining effects and multiplier are calculated as follows:

$$\text{First-round effect} = \boldsymbol{h}^{*}\boldsymbol{A}$$
$$\text{Simple income multiplier} = h^{*}\left(\mathbf{I}-\mathbf{A}\right)^{-1}.$$

The remaining production-induced income effects can be calculated in a similar way as the corresponding output multipliers.

2.5.3.3 Employment multipliers

The employment multipliers show the total increase in employment throughout the economy resulting from an increase in final demand that is enough to create one additional job in that industry. The employment multiplier can be calculated by using employment coefficients, **e**. The employment coefficients are estimated by dividing the number of employed persons in a given industry by the level of output generated by that industry. The employment coefficients are regarded as initial employment effects. These effects are then used to estimate the subsequent rounds of effects and multipliers:

$$\text{First-round effect} = \boldsymbol{e}^{*}\boldsymbol{A}$$
$$\text{Simple employment multiplier} = \boldsymbol{e}^{*}\left(\mathbf{I}-\mathbf{A}\right)^{-1}.$$

The remaining production-induced employment effects can be calculated in a similar way to the corresponding output multipliers. The employment multiplier gives the number of jobs created throughout the economy directly and indirectly per job created in the sector in which unit expansion in output has occurred.

Similarly, the employment multipliers estimated the number of jobs generated due to one unit expansion in a particular sector's output. Employment multipliers give the number of jobs created throughout the economy directly and indirectly per job created in the sector in which unit expansion in output has occurred.

2.6 Results and Analysis

As discussed above, multipliers are the mechanism through which total impact on the economy can be measured due to change in final demand; we estimated the output, income, and employment multipliers for our impact assessment purposes using the constructed IO table.

The results presented in this section throw light on the economic impact of the mining sector on the Indian economy as a whole. The results are presented in the form of output multipliers, income multipliers, and employment multipliers, each one of which includes direct and indirect effects. Each type of multiplier is discussed in detail individually in subsection 2.6.1, showing the importance of mining in the context of the Indian economy. Also, a comparative picture of the mining industry concerning other sectors of the economy is given in respect of all these multipliers to show how the mining industry can affect the economy in comparison to other sectors in the economy. Table 2.3 presents the output multiplier.

2.6.1 Output Multipliers

The output multiplier of the mining industry is the total value of the output produced by all the industries of the economy required to satisfy one extra rupee worth of final demand for that economy. As Table 2.3 shows, in the case of the mining industry, the simple multiplier (which

Table 2.3 Output multipliers, 2013–2014

	Sectors	Initial effects	First-round effects	Industrial support effects	Production-induced effects	Simple multipliers
1	Agriculture	1.00	0.26	0.26	0.52	1.52
2	Mining and quarrying	1.00	0.42	0.46	0.88	1.88
3	Manufacturing	1.00	0.74	0.86	1.59	2.59
4	Construction	1.00	0.63	0.80	1.43	2.43
5	Other industries	1.00	0.73	0.86	1.59	2.59
6	Business services	1.00	0.25	0.29	0.54	1.54
7	Trade, hotel, transport, and communication	1.00	0.42	0.54	0.96	1.96
8	Community, social, and personal services	1.00	0.33	0.38	0.71	1.71

Source: Author's estimation.

is the sum of both direct and indirect effects divided by direct effect) is 1.88. This implies that rupees 1.88 of additional output from the Indian economy is induced by an extra output of rupees 1 in the mining industry. In other words, to produce an additional output of 1 unit in 'mining', the economy's output must increase by an extra rupees 0.42 to provide inputs to 'mining' and, in turn, to increase by rupees 0.46 to provide inputs to the suppliers to 'mining', along with its own additional unit of output. Thus, the mining multiplier embodies the initial effects of (rupees 1.00), the first-round effects (rupees 0.42), and the industrial support effects (rupees 0.46). The indirect effect here is the sum of first-round effects and industrial-support effects (rupees 0.42 + rupees 0.46), which is quite impressive as it signifies that when mining grows by one unit, the rest of the economy expands by almost 0.88. After the first round and industrial-support effects, this leads to a cycle of second and subsequent rounds of effects, which can be termed 'induced effects'. Induced effects can result from both production and consumption perspectives. From the production side, it is quite obvious that as the mining industry expands by one unit, this leads to expansion in the production of other industries, which further induces production from each industry in the economy. From the consumption perspective, as the income of the mining employees increases due to more employment owing to mining expansion, they tend to spend more on goods and services, which in turn leads to expansion in the production of other industries. These consumption-induced effects are taken into consideration in the case of the total multipliers. Our study does not estimate the consumption-induced effect.

Comparison of this industry's economic impact with the rest of the industries in the economy shows that the total direct and indirect effect of this industry given by the simple multipliers amounts to rupees 1.88, which is above that of agriculture, business services, and community and personal services but behind manufacturing; construction; other industries; and trade, hotel, and transport industries. This low performance of the mining industry as against other sectors could be due to insufficient exploration, use of underdeveloped mining techniques, and lack of proper implementation of mining policies. However, even though it lags behind many of the industries in terms of its contribution to total output, it occupies a higher rank than that of important sectors such as agriculture and business services, indicating that this industry has the potential to surpass some of the key sectors in terms of its contribution to output if proper mining policies are put in place.

As the multiplicative impact of mining on output is reasonable and impressive, it can certainly be said that the industry has high interconnectedness with the rest of the sectors. This is also proven by the basic nature of the industry as a primary resource provider. Hence, once the mineral output expansion happens owing to increased demand (both domestic as well as export) for mineral products, it would create a ripple effect in the economy as a whole through its multiplier effect. Hence, the Government of India should come forward to take policy initiatives to boost export and domestic demand. Thus, if constructive policy decisions are taken towards mineral expansion and development in the area of resource allocation, it would lead to more income and employment.

2.6.2 Income Multiplier

The mining industry can affect the income of the economy through income multiplier. Table 2.4 shows the income multipliers for the economy.

Table 2.4 Income multipliers, 2013–2014

	Sectors	Initial effects	First-round effects	Industrial support effects	Production-induced effects	Simple multipliers
1	Agriculture	0.77	0.13	0.12	0.25	1.02
2	Mining and quarrying	0.57	0.21	0.20	0.42	0.98
3	Manufacturing	0.25	0.33	0.39	0.72	0.97
4	Construction	0.35	0.25	0.36	0.62	0.96
5	Other industries	0.25	0.33	0.39	0.71	0.96
6	Business services	0.75	0.12	0.13	0.25	0.99
7	Trade, hotel, transport and communication	0.57	0.17	0.24	0.41	0.98
8	Community, social, and personal services	0.67	0.15	0.17	0.32	0.99

Source: Author's estimation.

It can be seen from Table 2.4 that every one unit of mining output expansion would lead to 0.98 units of income generation for the national economy and even more of such units when the effect of employee expenses are taken into consideration. From this table, it can be enumerated that the income-generating impact of the mining industry is reasonably high as compared with other industries, such as manufacturing, construction, and a little lower than the agriculture industry. The probable reason for this is higher wage and salary payment in this sector due to the nature of risk involved in the mining activity, which is then translated into increased demand for goods and services of other industries which, in turn, employs more workers to satisfy the increased demand, thereby leading to more income generation.

2.6.3 Employment Multiplier

The employment coefficients and multipliers for India for 2013–2014 are presented in Tables 2.5 and 2.6. These coefficients were calculated by dividing the total number of employed persons of different sectors by their respective output for the year 2013–2014. For employment figures, we

Table 2.5 Employment coefficients, 2013–2014

	Sectors	Employment coefficient
1.	Agriculture	0.04
2.	Mining and quarrying	0.50
3.	Manufacturing	0.09
4.	Construction	1.15
5.	Other industries	0.04
6.	Business services	0.09
7.	Trade, hotel, transport and communication	0.67
8.	Community, social, and personal services	0.08

Source: Author's estimation.

Table 2.6 Employment multiplier, 2013–2014

	Sectors	Initial effects	First-round effects	Industrial support effects	Production-induced effects	Simple multipliers
1.	Agriculture	0.04	0.05	0.06	0.11	0.15
2.	Mining and quarrying	0.52	0.09	0.12	0.20	0.72
3.	Manufacturing	0.09	0.19	0.21	0.40	0.49
4.	Construction	1.13	0.13	0.20	0.33	1.46
5.	Other industries	0.04	0.19	0.22	0.41	0.45
6.	Business services	0.09	0.06	0.07	0.14	0.23
7.	Trade, hotel, transport and communication	0.66	0.11	0.13	0.24	0.90
8.	Community, social, and personal services	0.08	0.12	0.10	0.22	0.30

Source: Author's estimation.

referred to the sixty-eighth round unit-level data on employment and unemployment given by the National Sample Survey Office (NSSO).

It can be visualized from Table 2.6 that every ten units of mining output are translated into seven units of employment for the national economy, and the results would be even more such units when the effects of worker's expenditure are taken into account. In other words, the mining industry is capable of creating approximately seven units of total additional employment (direct and indirect) by the production of ten extra units of output. However, these employment multipliers should be viewed with caution. This is because, as the mining industry employs a large number of subcontractors who employ their own people, they do not appear in the company's payroll; therefore, it hugely underestimates the indirect employment effect of this industry as well as the induced effect. This is evident from the indirect impact figure, which is 0.20 for an extra unit of mining output production. One interesting fact that can be noticed here is that the mining sector employment multipliers are generally smaller than their income multipliers, which suggests that mining activities generated less employment but larger incomes. This larger income is an indication of the considerably high wage rate prevailing in the mining industry due to the nature of the risk associated with it, which is also confirmed by our high values of income multipliers. The testimony to our results is the wage rates provided by India KLEMS data. which shows that a regular employee of this industry gets approximately rupees 782 per day, which is larger than any other industry except the chemical industry. And when both casual and self-employed workers' wage rate is taken into account, this rate is even more about rupees 2,613 per day.[6]

In this study, we attempted to analyse the economic impact of the whole mining industry in terms of its impact on output, income, and employment multipliers. We also provided a comparison of this sector with that of seven other broad sectors to compare the performance of the mining industry across other industries. However, as the mining industry is composed of different subsectors, such as coal, metallic, non-metallic, and petroleum, it is imperative to analyse the economic impact of these individual subsectors to gain some additional insights into the mining industry's economic impact. To achieve this goal, we attempted a within-mining industry analysis by expanding the mining sector (disaggregation of the mining industry). The results for all three multipliers—output, income, and employment multipliers—for all the eleven subsectors of the mining industry are presented in Table 2.7.

[6] For more on wage and employment of the mining industry, refer to Das et al. (2015).

Table 2.7 Output, income, and employment multipliers for subsectors of the Indian mining industry, 2013–2014

Sectors	Output multiplier	Input multiplier	Employment multiplier
Iron ore	2.118	0.984	0.134
Manganese ore	2.569	0.953	0.278
Bauxite	2.014	0.981	0.129
Copper ore	2.424	0.959	0.282
Other metallic minerals	2.003	0.979	0.117
Limestone	2.334	0.963	0.366
Mica	2.687	0.961	0.378
Other non-metallic minerals	1.211	0.982	0.243
Natural gas	2.001	0.982	0.213
Crude petroleum	2.012	0.971	0.115
Coal and lignite	2.121	0.978	0.197

Source: Author's estimation.

In the IO table of 2013–2014, the whole mining industry is presented in eleven subsectors (Table 2.7). For meaningful analysis, we place all these subsectors under four broad groups: metallic, non-metallic, petroleum, and coal. Under the metallic group, five subsectors—iron ore, manganese, bauxite, copper, and other minerals—are placed. The non-metallic group consists of limestone, mica, and other non-metallic minerals. Further, petroleum includes natural gas and crude petroleum under its ambit, and finally, coal consists of both coal and lignite. For easy analysis, we present the pictorial representation of Table 2.7 in Fig. 2.3.

It can be observed from Fig. 2.3 that in the total mining industry, mica produces the highest output multiplier values, followed by manganese and copper. Income multiplier values remain more or less the same for all the subsectors of the mining industry. The reason may be due to the same prevailing wage rate across the industry. Further, the employment multiplier values are high for mica and limestone, followed by copper and manganese.

Sector-wise analysis reveals that in the metallic subsector, the output multiplier is highest for manganese, followed by copper and iron ore (Fig. 2.4). This may be due to the increased use of these minerals in most

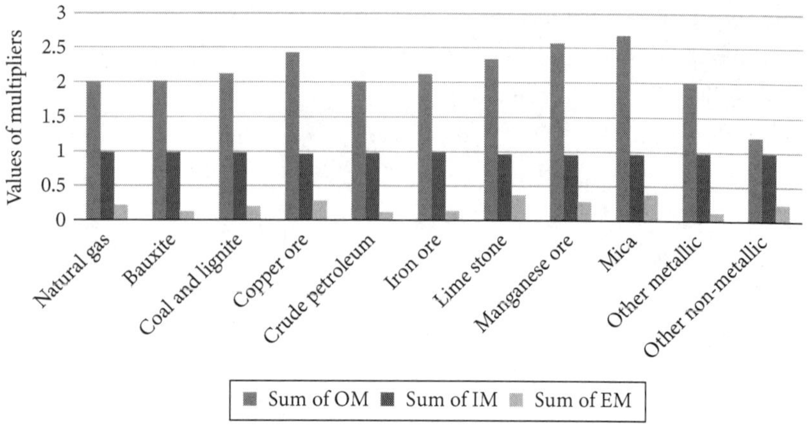

Fig. 2.3 Output, income, and employment multipliers for subsectors of the mining industry, 2013–2014
Source: Author's estimation.

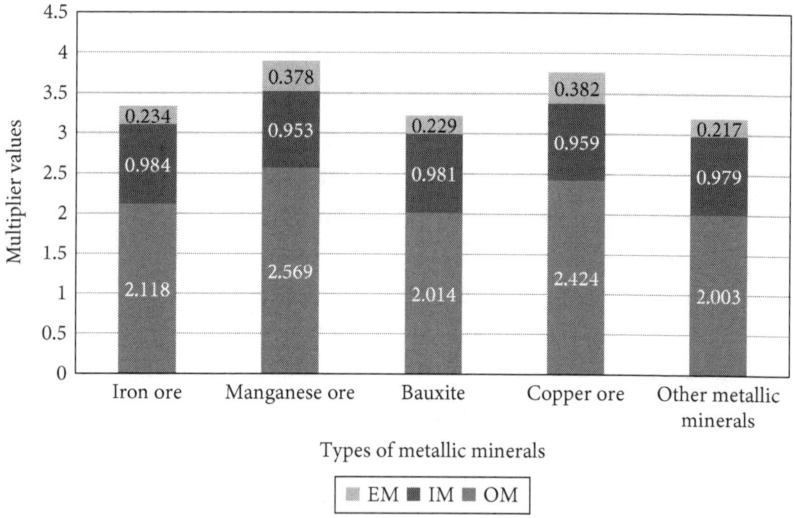

Fig. 2.4 Multiplier values for the metallic mineral subsector
Source: Author's estimation.

of the products by other subsectors. On the other hand, one unit of expansion in iron ore produces higher income compared with other metallic minerals. Regarding employment multiplier values, copper ore adds to the employment creation more, followed by manganese and iron ore. The reason for what drives one subsector to produce a high output multiplier and the other subsector to a high employment multiplier requires further in-depth investigation into the individual subsector.

Again, in the case of the non-metallic minerals group, mica occupies the highest position concerning output multiplier values, implying that one unit of expansion in this subsector's output can have a larger output expansion effect as compared with other non-metallic groups (Fig. 2.5). However, other non-metallic groups occupy the highest position in terms of income multiplier effects, followed by limestone and mica. Concerning employment multipliers, mica once again is the front runner, followed by limestone and other non-metallic minerals.

In the petroleum category, both crude petroleum and natural gas have almost the same impact in terms of output expansion. However, the natural gas subsector has a slightly higher income and employment multiplier (Fig. 2.6).

Finally, for the coal subsector, the multiplier values for output, income, and employment come out to be 2.121, 0.978, and 0.197, respectively (Fig. 2.7).

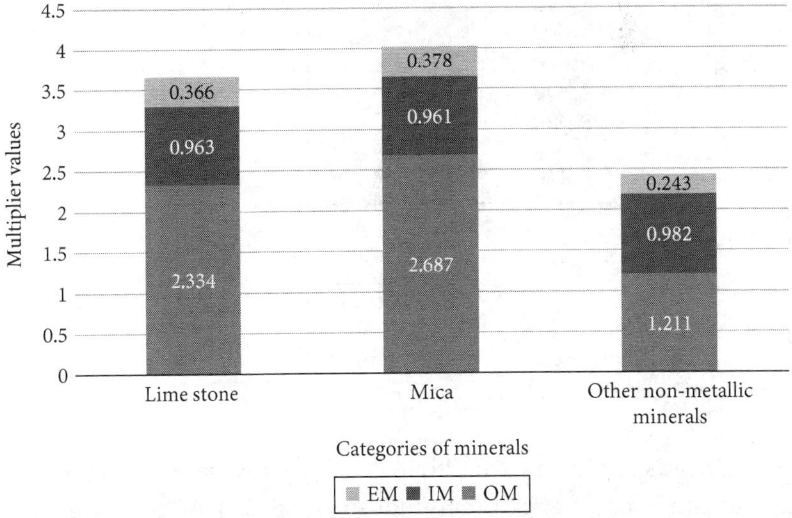

Fig. 2.5 Multiplier values for the non-metallic mineral subsector
Source: Author's estimation.

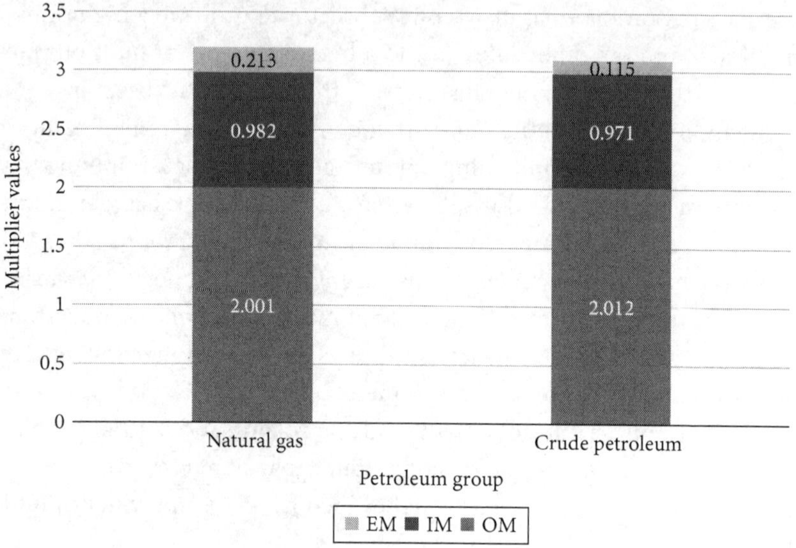

Fig. 2.6 Multiplier values for the petroleum subsector
Source: Author's estimation.

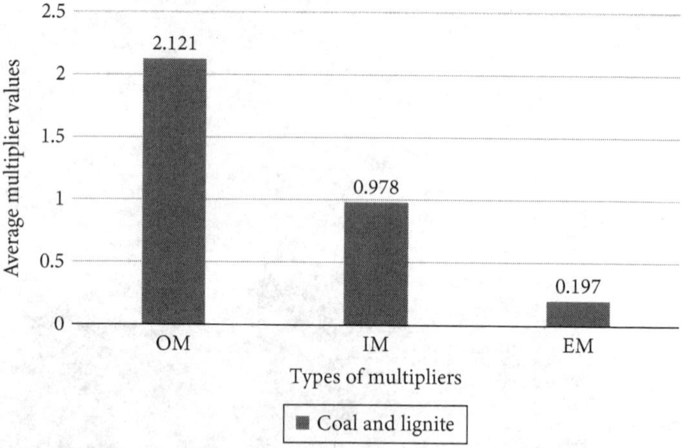

Fig. 2.7 Multiplier values for the coal subsector
Source: Author's estimation.

A comparison of average multiplier values across subsectors brings to light an interesting feature of this industry (Fig. 2.8). Across the groups, the output-expanding effect is higher for the metallic subsector, followed by coal, non-metallic, and petroleum. While almost all the subsectors

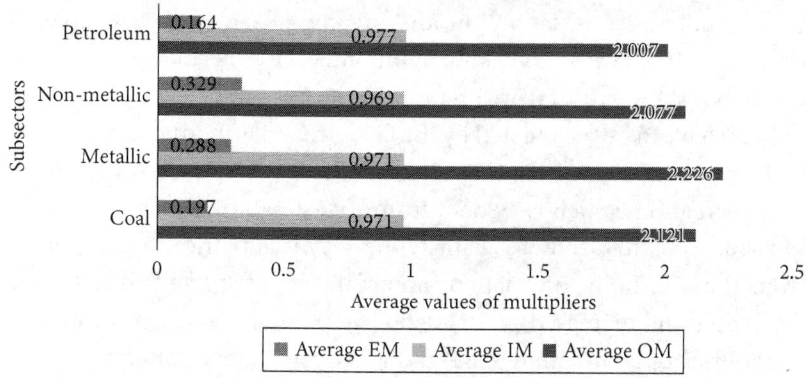

Fig. 2.8 Comparison of multipliers across subsectors of the mining industry
Source: Author's calculation.

exhibit more or less the same income expansion effect, the employment-expanding effect is highest for the non-metallic subsector, followed by metallic, coal, and petroleum.

2.7 Discussion

The preceding analysis has examined empirically the economic impact of the mining industry on output, income, and employment creation, using the IO transaction table for 2013–2014. The examination of the effect of mining on output reveals that with one extra unit's production of mining output, the total output of the economy can increase by 1.88 (approximately 2 units), out of which the total indirect effect of this mining output expansion is 0.88 (industrial support effects + production-induced effects), which signifies the interconnectedness that this industry has with others. The mining industry's high interconnectedness with the suppliers of the inputs industry and the industries that use its product as their intermediate product is expected to bring positive results in both directions, such as productivity generation throughout the economy and supporting the productive activity of others. The results also show a high-income multiplier for this industry (0.98) which is an indication of higher wage rates prevailing in this sector. Our results also suggest that this industry would contribute to the output and income of the country if demand (both export as well as domestic) requirements for this industry increase, and to boost the export demand for the mineral products, proper mining policies have to be formulated by the Government of India.

These results show that the mining industry has a noticeable impact on job creation, which is evident from a reasonable employment multiplier (0.72) of this sector as against others. This is all the more important from the viewpoint of a labour-abundant country like India. A large workforce and increased capital–labour ratio in the organized sector for a labour-abundant country like India is truly a grave concern that has been well highlighted by the Government of India (GoI, 2013a). If India has to meet the demographic dividend challenge anyway, it has no choice but to target industries where the employment multiplier is higher. In this context, the mining industry assumes importance due to its high employment-generating potential. A study by Chakravarty (2013) points out that roughly 10 million people would need a job every year for the next 15 years. Finding productive jobs for such a huge number is a big challenge, and clearly, the answer lies in stepping up the employment intensity of growth. Also, these additional jobs would have to be created bearing in mind the overall structural changes that the Indian labour market has been going through, particularly in terms of movement of people away from agriculture. Thus, the non-farming sector has to gear up to shoulder the burden of agriculture. Amongst the non-farming sector, while the services sector has already led India's growth and employment story for some time, it is now high time for the mining industry to play an important role in creating jobs in the coming years as employment in manufacturing has also reached a stagnant position. This piece of work also reveals that within the mining industry, the output expansionary impact is high for the metallic subsector, which is followed by coal, non-metallic, and petroleum. Again, within the metallic subsector, manganese ore has the highest output expansionary impact. For non-metallic and petroleum, the output multipliers are highest for mica and crude petroleum, respectively. The income expansionary impact is more or less the same for all the subsectors, implying that across the subsectors the wage rate is the same. However, the average employment multiplier values are highest for the non-metallic subsector, followed by metallic, coal, and petroleum.

The results of this analysis have important policy implications for specializing in the production of abundant resources. As India is endowed with significant mineral resources, it is quite natural to use those mineral resources wisely, keeping in mind the sustainability issues. As our results suggest, this industry has a noticeable impact in terms of its output, income, and employment effect when compared with other broad sectors, therefore it can be considered as an important sector. Thus, looking at the output, income, and employment impact of this sector, the Government of India should prioritize this sector in its budget allocation by allowing for an increased share in its allocation of resources. Our findings also reveal a few key areas, such as non-metallic, metallic, and coal, where both employment and output expansionary effects are high. Keeping this in mind, the Government of India should focus on mining development by identifying key areas for investment within these groups. Finally, it is worth mentioning here that though mining has a noticeable impact on the Indian economy, it does not necessarily call for uncontrollable expansion of this industry. It is a well-known fact that the industry has its negative side too in terms of having negative social and environmental effects. Thus, we suggest here that the policies supporting industrial development (mining) should not ignore the mining ecosystem and the businesses across the associated value chain. Hence, the Indian Government should promote the development of mineral resources giving priority to its social, economic and environmental sustainability issues, as the nation still has a long way to go in terms of industrialization and urbanization, and a substantial quantity of minerals is required.

Appendix A2

Table A2 Sectoral classifications used for the study

Sector	Rows in the IO table for 2013–2014	Aggregated sectors
Agriculture	1–26	Paddy, wheat, jowar, bajra, maize, gram, pulses, sugarcane, groundnut, coconut, other oilseeds, jute, cotton, tea, coffee, rubber, tobacco, fruits, vegetables, other crops, milk and milk products, animal services (agricultural), poultry and eggs, other livestock production, forestry and logging, fishing
Mining	27–37	Coal and lignite, natural gas, crude petroleum, iron ore, manganese ore, bauxite, copper ore, other metallic minerals, limestone, mica, other non-metallic minerals
Manufacturing	38–105	Sugar; kshandsari; boora; hydrogenated oil (vanaspati); edible oils other than vanaspati; tea and coffee processing; miscellaneous food products; beverages; tobacco products; khadi; cotton textiles (handlooms); cotton textiles; woollen textiles; silk textiles; art silk; synthetic fibre textiles; art silk; synthetic fibre textiles; jute; hemp; mesta textiles; carpet weaving; readymade garments; miscellaneous textile products; furniture and fixtures—wooden; wood and wood products; paper; paper products and newsprint; printing and publishing; leather footwear; leather and leather products; rubber products; plastic products; petroleum products; coal tar products; inorganic heavy chemicals; organic heavy chemicals; fertilizers; pesticides; paints; varnishes and lacquers; drugs and medicines; soaps, cosmetics, and glycerine; synthetic fibres; resin; other chemicals; structural clay products; cement; other non-metallic mineral products; iron, steel, and ferro alloys; iron and steel casting and forging; iron and steel foundries; non-ferrous basic metals; hand tools, hardware; miscellaneous metal products; tractors and agricultural implements; industrial machinery (F & T); industrial machinery (others); machine tools, other non-electrical machinery; electrical industrial machinery; electrical wires and cables; batteries; electrical appliances; communication equipment; other electrical machinery; electronic equipment (including TV); ships and boats; rail equipment; motor vehicles; motorcycles and scooters; bicycles; cycle-rickshaws; other transport equipment; watches and clocks; medical, precision, and optical instruments; jem and jewellery; aircraft and spacecraft; miscellaneous manufacturing

Table A2 Continued

Sector	Rows in the IO table for 2013–2014	Aggregated sectors
Construction	106	Construction
Other industries	107–108	Electricity, gas, and water supply; other utilities
Trade, hotel, transport, and communication	109, 110, 111, 112, 113, 114, 115, 116, 117	Railway transport services; land transport, including via pipeline; water transport; air transport; supporting and auxiliary transport activities; storage and warehousing; communication; trade; hotels and restaurants
Business services	118, 119, 120, 123, 125, 126, 127	Banking, insurance, ownership of dwellings, business services, legal services, real estate activities, renting of machinery and equipment
Community, social, and personal services	121, 122, 124, 128, 129, 130	Education and research; medical and health; computer and related activities; O.com, social, and personal services; other services; public administration

Source: Input–output table (2013–2014).

3

The Indian Mining Industry

Challenges and Possible Pathways

3.1 Introduction

Chapter 2 examined the economic impact of the mining industry in terms of its effects on output, employment, and income. The results indicate the existence of the potential of mining to influence the growth path of the nation. However, the pragmatic realization of this potential may be obstructed by the many serious challenges that the industry faces. This makes it imperative to identify these challenges. This chapter aims to identify the various challenges faced by the industry in the context of mining.

India exhibits a fast-growing population, leading to greater economic needs and increased urbanization. This, in turn, augments the increase in demand for basic infrastructure, such as residential and industrial buildings, and the demand for basic infrastructure requires more mined materials and thereby becomes a fundamental driving force for the mining industry. Thus, mining plays a vital role in the progress of India's economic growth. India is the fourth largest mineral producer next to China, Russia, and the United States (IBEF, 2020), and the mining industry contributes around 2% of India's gross domestic product (GDP) (Singh et al., 2020). Besides its economic contribution, the mining industry also contributes to the growth of some other key sectors, such as power, cement, and steel. Though the mining industry plays a significant role in contributing to the economy, its adverse impact socially and in terms of the environment is enormous and always a key concern for the policymakers (Kinnunen and Kaksonen, 2019). This concern emanates from the problems associated with the industry due to the nature of its operation. The

The Indian Mining Industry. Meenakshi Parida and S. Madheswaran, Oxford University Press.
 DOI: 10.1093/9780198954392.003.0003

problems associated with the mining industry have become a concern for the world economy.

Many research works have been undertaken to provide solutions to overcome the challenges of the mining industry. The majority of the research work relates to environmental challenges and highlights the absence of community pressure and institutional governance as the key reasons for the emergence of such problems (Chand et al., 2020). A study related to Chile's mining industry showed that uncontrolled extraction was the major factor leading to the loss of biodiversity and high levels of pollution (Herrera-León et al., 2019). In another study, Nasih et al. (2019) pointed out that the extent of carbon emission by this industry was higher as compared with other sectors in Indonesia. Regulatory failure to implement stringent laws to preserve environmental conditions paved the way for lobbyists to take advantage of the loopholes, thereby hampering law enforcement (Hobbs, 2020).

The above observations reveal that the mining industry, though critical for the development of society, is beset by many challenges and problems that need to be addressed if it is to be sustainable in the future. This chapter aims to identify the key challenges and suggest possible solutions. The rationale for identifying the challenges concerning the Indian mining industry lies in its fast-paced growth rate, which is expected to increase exponentially in the coming years (Pandey et al., 2020; Sandberg et al., 2020). At the same time, as India is a developing country, this type of study will be helpful for other developing countries with similar socio-economic situations.

The remainder of the chapter is organized as follows: section 3.2 discusses the existing literature, and section 3.3 describes the methodology used for the study. In section 3.4, the findings of the study are reported. Section 3.5 presents the possible solutions to overcoming the challenges of this industry, and section 3.6 goes on to provide a discussion based on the findings. Section 3.7 provides a conclusion for the chapter.

3.2 Review of the Literature

Due to the primary nature of its operation, mineral resource extraction affects the economy and society as well as the environment. As such, this industry faces several challenges from these three aspects, which need to be addressed properly if the industry is to continue to operate. A majority of research work on this area differentiates between three types of challenges: operational, social, and environmental (Ramaganesh et al., 2021; Sutomo, 2020).

Primarily, the problems that hinder the operational activities of these plants are operational challenges. A majority of studies have indicated the absence of technical innovation as one of the impending factors that may halt the growth of the industry (Gruenhagen and Parker, 2020; Lööw et al., 2019; Warhurst and Bridge, 1996). These studies cited that as the mining industry is largely fragmented and belongs to the small and medium enterprise category, it lacked financial capital to invest in research and development (R&D) activities, which, in turn, hampered the progress of the industry. By developing a human and machine labour distribution model for their study, Lööw and Nygren (2019) showed that lack of financial availability was another important challenge that plagued the mining industry. Another study by Nikulin et al. (2019) pointed to the unavailability of advanced technology as the major challenge to mining operations. Nikulin, studying the Australian coal-mining industry, showed that the inability to incorporate modern technology was the major hurdle in managing mine fires. A few studies, such as those by Gruenhagen and Parker (2020), Roldán et al. (2019), and Zhang (2017), highlighted the lack of skilled labour as one of the major challenges faced by the mining industry. Gruenhagen and Parker (2020) pointed out that the unavailability of skilled labour impeded the progress of the mining industry by affecting the production process. In the same line of argument, Roldán et al. (2019) and Zhang (2017) discussed the fact that mining labour was mostly semi-skilled and not equipped with modern technical know-how. This incompetence of the labour force created a major hurdle in the production process of the mining industry. Govindan et al. (2014) attempted to find out the major determinants of corporate social responsibility in the mining industry. They found a lack of financial assistance to be the major problem hampering the corporate social responsibility (CSR) performance of the mining industry. Pactwa et al. (2020) found that mining waste was one of the problems faced by the mining industry of Poland. By investigating Poland's coal-mining industry, they found that the huge amount of waste resulting from the mining process became an important problem, creating obstacles in the waste management process.

In addition to operational challenges, the mining industry was also associated with many social and environmental challenges that have become roadblocks to mining sustainability. There is a plethora of study literature related to the socio-environmental challenges of the mining industry. The social challenges that the mining industry faces can be complex and varied. Shrivastava and Vidhi (2020)—studying two Fortune 500 mining companies, Alcoa and Rio Tinto—found that mining companies were embroiled in many problems, particularly around environmental concerns that, in turn, created problems for their continued business sustenance. According to them, protection of human rights, good working conditions, and reduced waste and emissions could help the companies achieve sustainable development. Failure to provide regional social protection schemes also constitutes one important challenge for the mining industry. Particularly, mining companies face problems creating reasonable protection systems for the workers to protect their health and mental ability (Asr et al., 2019; Frederiksen, 2018; Harris et al., 2021; Shannon and Parker, 2020). Maintaining good health and safety practices has become another challenge for this industry. Studying the mental health of mine workers through an intervention study, Shannon and Parker (2020) showed the need for establishing proper communication between the organization and the workers. Jiskani et al. (2020), studying coal mine companies, revealed that cognitive factors played a major role in workplace accidents. Their study showed that truck drivers were prominent in violating the safety norms and were thereby major contributors to workplace accidents. In a similar study, Zhang et al. (2020) found that violation of safety rules and regulations, absence of safety education, and restrictive roles of functional departments were some of the major causes of mine accidents.

The above literature shows that though much has been discussed in the literature on the challenges of the mining industry in general, there is a dearth of studies about the challenges faced by the Indian mining industry in particular. This chapter aims to fill this void by undertaking a detailed investigation of the issue.

3.3 Methodology

We use a systematic literature review (SLR) to identify the probable challenges faced by the mining industry in India. For this, we searched research articles published in leading databases such as Scopus, Google Scholar, and web science using keywords 'challenges in mining', 'barriers to mining industry operation', and 'challenges to sustainable mining'. We also used Boolean operators such as inhibitors to sustainability, challenges to environmental sustainability, challenges in environment practices, challenges in sustainable practices, obstacles in sustainability, problems faced by the mining industry or challenges faced by the mining industry. Initially, forty-five articles related to the subject matter were identified. Among these articles, some were found to be duplicates. After removing duplicated works, we finalized thirty-five articles for the literature review. Apart from the review of literature, we relied on some important podcast interviews of subject-matter experts for the identification of mining industry challenges. Key challenges that were found from the literature survey were also validated by the expert opinions. The next section presents the key findings related to mining industry challenges in India. We categorize all the challenges into three heads: operational, regulatory, and socio-environmental.

3.4 Findings

3.4.1 Operational Challenges

3.4.1.1 Inadequate information on mineral resources

Although India is well endowed with huge natural mineral resources, the reserves-to-production ratio of various minerals in India is low (Table 3.1), reflecting significant unexplored opportunities. There is an immediate need to speed up the exploration process. One of the probable reasons why exploration has taken a back seat in India is inadequate information on resources and the lack of investment in exploration.

The first and foremost step in mining is searching for ore deposits. However, India suffers from a lack of geophysical and geochemical

Table 3.1 Reserves-to-production ratio for India, 2015–2016

Mineral	Production as of 2015	Proved reserves as of 2015	R/P ratio
Bauxite (kt)	22,493.67	4,34,043	19.30
Diamond (crt)	62,144	9,59,500	15.44
Copper (kt)	3505.348	1,62,972	46.49
Gold (tonnes)	4,47,278	1,04,04,349	23.26
Iron ore (kt)	1,29,321	40,83,384	31.58

Source: GoI (2016a); author's analysis.

data—only 2–4% (MOM, 2011). In India, the generalization of baseline data to promote exploration activity, led by the Geological Survey of India (GSI), is far from complete due to lack of precision equipment such as gravimeters and total field magnetometers. Only 30–40% of India's total area has been covered by aeromagnetic surveys as against 90% of that of Australia since 1990 (McKinsey & Company, 2014).

3.4.1.2 Low exploration spend

Lack of investment in exploration activity has been a key deterrent in the mining sector's growth. Despite being a mineral-rich country, India accounts for a very low share of 0.3%[1] in the global exploration budget as against 19% and 12% that of Canada and Australia, respectively, resulting in a stagnant reserve base in all mineral categories. Exploration expenditure per square kilometre is one of the lowest in India among the major mining economies (Fig. 3.1). One of the major drivers for this low exploration spend is the rule of restricting mining exploration to a depth of 50–100 metres. Most of the total exploration expenditure, of about rupees 3.5 billion is incurred on coal only.[2] Thus, there is an increasing need to raise the investment and expedite the exploration process to keep reserve development in line with production, as only 5–10% of the available mineral resources have been explored in India to date.

Despite being a mineral-rich country, exploration expenditure per square kilometre is one of the lowest in India among the major mining

[1] Refer to the strategy paper for the Ministry of Mines (MoM 2011).

[2] As given by the Government of India's report of the High-Level Committee on National Mineral Policy (GoI 2008).

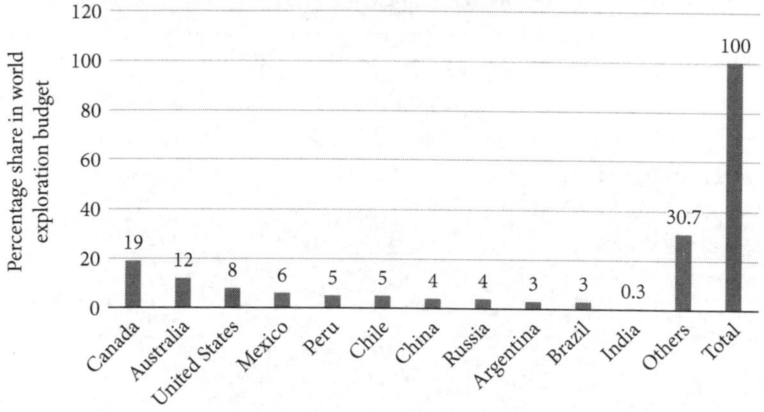

Fig. 3.1 Share of India in the global exploration budget, 2014
Source: Ernst & Young/ASSOCHAM (2011).

economies. India accounts for a very low share of 0.3% in the global exploration budget as against 19% and 12% for that of Canada and Australia, respectively. The rule of restricting mining exploration to a depth of 50–100 metres is one of the key drivers for this low exploration spend.

3.4.1.3 Inadequate infrastructure facilities

Lack of proper transportation and logistics facilities creates constraints for the growth of the mining industry in India, as a majority of mineral reserves are located in remote areas devoid of rail/road connectivity. For instance, railway connectivity in most key mining regions is poor and has inadequate capacity for greater volumes to be transported, leading to a higher supply chain cost, thereby creating a hindrance to the output growth of companies. The Indian mining sector loses around rupees 9,000 crore (5–6% of GDP) each year due to inefficiencies in logistics (Table 3.2).

3.4.2 Regulatory Challenges

A set of regulatory and administrative challenges create hurdles in the growth of mining in India. It has become extremely difficult under the present regulatory provisions to transfer the mining leases. Uncertainty prevails as to whether or not mining leases will be obtained, even if

Table 3.2 Extra costs spent on logistics in India

Sectors	Extra costs on logistics ('000 Rs)	% of gross output
Agriculture, forestry, and fishing	49–54	(5–6)
Mining and quarrying	9	(5–6)
Manufacturing	76–81	(2–3)
Electricity, gas, water	4	(2–3)
Construction	31	(2–3)
Other trades	22	(2–3)

Source: MoM (2011).

successful exploration is done by a mining company, as no transparency is maintained in allotting the leases, although the rule is to award them on a first-come, first-served basis. Further, obtaining all mining approvals is a long-drawn-out and tedious process as multiple agencies are involved, leading to substantial delays in the disposal of various clearances. Environmental clearance/forest clearance (EC/FC) takes a long time due to inefficiencies and ambiguous land records. At present, it takes more than five years to obtain mining licences (MLs)/prospecting licences (PLs) in India, while in mining economies such as Canada and Australia, it takes much less than two months (Fig. 3.2). A long processing time results in fewer applications for new mining rights. Finally, the private sector's incentive to invest in technology and equipment in mining projects is very low as the mining industry is heavily taxed in India. These regulatory challenges have adversely affected the investment in mining and exploration activities. Testimony to this fact is that even if it is one of the few sectors in India that allows for 100% foreign direct investment (FDI) (excluding atomic and fuel minerals), the actual amount of foreign investment inflow has been quite low (FICCI, Mines and Metals Division, 2013).

A long processing time to obtain mining rights is one of the key regulatory challenges creating hurdles in the growth of mining in India. Currently, it takes more than five years to obtain MLs/PLs in India, while in mining economies like Canada and Australia, it takes much less than two months for the same, resulting in fewer applications for new mining rights.

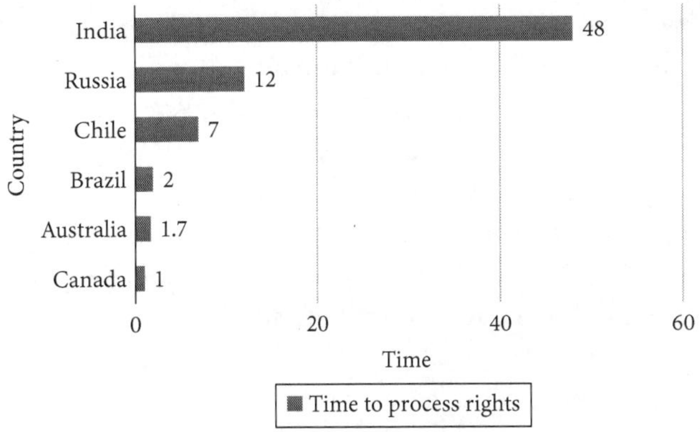

Fig. 3.2 Mining rights processing time in India as compared to other economies
Source: MoM (2011).

3.4.3 Social and Environmental Challenges

3.4.3.1 Sustainability

Mining activity has a tremendous impact on the environment as well as the socio-economic set-up. Therefore, it is of utmost importance to ensure that the adverse impacts of mining are minimized as far as possible so that mining can be carried out sustainably. The fact that a large number of mining projects do not get EC/FC proves how much importance is attached to sustainability. Besides obtaining EC/FC, the mining companies have to fulfil several requirements for the uplifting of the local community, which is very tedious as it involves multiple agencies. In addition, the mining firms have to obtain a 'social licence to operate' by taking people along with them. As mining firms disrupt social life, it is quite natural that these firms face resistance from the host community when it comes to extracting minerals from mines existing in their vicinity. Lack of trust and mutual understanding, lack of communication regarding the probable socio-economic impact of the investment in mines, and inadequate compensatory measures are some of the important reasons for this social unrest. The mining industry has been impacted greatly by this social conflict, leading to delays and suspension of some mining projects. For instance, Pohang Steel Company's (POSCO's) 11 billion US dollar investment plan for mining and steel production in the Jajpur district of

Odisha got suspended due to strong opposition from local people over land acquisition. Similarly, the Utkal alumina project, a 1 billion US dollar project between Ms Hindalco (India) and Allan (Canada) got delayed by more than a year due to challenges in land acquisition. Thus, the challenges the mining firms face from the host community/non-governmental organizations (NGOs) before they can operate are enormous. Though the Government of India has taken some steps to alleviate these problems, a lot remain to be addressed.

3.4.3.2 Occupational health hazards in mines

One of the key challenges the Indian mining industry faces is the occurrence of occupational health hazards in mines. Surveys conducted by the Directorate-General of Mines Safety in a few selected mines show that a significant number of persons employed in the mines suffer from occupational diseases: silicosis, pneumoconiosis, noise-induced hearing loss, etc. Due to the absence of occupational health inspectors, the occupational health status of mine workers is not completely available. However, it is evident from some surveys that persons employed in mines are exposed to several problems in the workplace, such as noise, dust, vibrations, heat, and humidity, which have a negative effect on their health. In this twelfth Five-Year Plan, the Government of India has declared occupational safety and health at workplaces as a priority area for formulation of activities, and therefore several initiatives have been undertaken to restore the safety and health of mine workers. Unfortunately, despite many initiatives, the standards of safety in mines have not yet reached a globally accepted norm of zero harm at the workplace. This calls for fresh initiatives in the areas of scientific data collection, use of modern technologies and tools, formulation of action plans on identified thrust areas, proper implementation, and effective monitoring of results.

3.4.3.3 Corruption

Given the complex process and little transparency, the Indian mining industry is constantly plagued with fraud and corruption, resulting in loss to the exchequer. According to Transparency International's Corruption Perceptions Index for 2014 (Transparency International 2014), India ranked 85 out of 175 countries, implying that India is perceived as a highly corrupt country. However, the government is taking positive measures to bring this ranking down by making the process transparent to the public, which is expected to reduce corruption to a large extent.

3.5 Possible Pathways

Given the challenges of mining in India, immediate action is called for on some of the key areas to ensure high growth of the sector. In this section, we attempt to provide some suggestions, based on expert opinions, that may help the industry overcome the above-mentioned challenges.

1. An integrated map for mining, output production, and usage of minerals should be created. Along with this, there should be investment in geophysical and geochemical baseline data generation, as this can stimulate exploration and lead to the discovery of new minerals.
2. As India has a low reserve base and scarce supply in some of the strategic minerals such as nickel, cobalt, and fertilizer minerals (MOM, 2011), it would be of value to acquire these minerals from the world market. This acquisition should be undertaken by a central body, whose prime responsibility would be to identify the key resources to be acquired by making a long-term (twenty-to-thirty-year) demand–supply analysis and prioritizing the regions to be targeted for resource acquisition. These regions should be targeted with the provision of financial support in their projects as well as with attractive incentives in terms of infrastructure development for their economies to attract a high-stakes deal.
3. India uses a resource allotment process which, although based on a first-come, first-served basis, does not serve any purpose as no transparency is maintained. There is an urgent need to adopt a progressive resource allotment mechanism embedding competitiveness and transparency following some of the global best practices as India's context is unique due to the existence of known and partially known minerals and a supply-demand imbalance. The known mineral resources should be allotted through competitive bidding to maximize the value of the product, whereas, for

partially known and unknown minerals, the extent of the mineralization should first be ascertained, after which the same allotment process could be followed as for the known minerals.

4. Mineral resources are non-renewable and finite in quantity. If the resources are exploited at the current rate, then it would lead to an unsustainable exploitation of reserves, which would ultimately result in the non-availability of minerals for future generations. Hence, its exploitation should be undertaken with the utmost care. In addition to this, new geographical areas should be explored to speed up the process of discovery of mineral resources.
5. At present, India needs to address the permit delays and delays in environment and forest clearance with vigour. It should establish a single-window clearance system at the state level, which could monitor the clearance process and ensure timely approvals to streamline the approval process, and at the Ministry of Mines level, one single window should be opened for processing environment clearance for mining projects. The new Mines and Minerals (Development and Regulation) (MMDR) Act (2015), should be facilitated at the earliest, which has a lot of provisioning for establishing a structural mechanism to reduce permit delays, such as a mining appellate for faster dispute resolution.
6. As the Indian mining sector loses around rupees 9,000 crores every year due to inefficiencies in logistics, it is of paramount importance to build infrastructure capacity to support the mining sector. For this, the way ahead is to collaborate with the transport (roads, railways, and ports) ministry to pursue the important infrastructure projects linked with the mining areas on a war footing. Some percentage of the District Minerals Fund (DMF) could also be used to develop the local socio-economic infrastructure. To overcome railway capacity constraints, the sea route could be seen as an option for transporting minerals from supply to demand centres, which could help reduce the transportation cost. However, this would require liaising with the Department of Shipping to develop key coastal corridors and expand port capacity.
7. The sustainable development of the mining sector calls for a skilled and efficient labour force. It is estimated that there could be an additional labour force requirement amounting to 1.5 to 2.5

times the current workforce by 2025 (MOM, 2011). To meet this future demand and overcome shortages in human capital in the mining sector, the way forward would be to work in tandem with the Ministry of Education of India (MHRD) to raise the number of mining engineering seats in the relevant institutes over the next fifteen years. The introduction of job-specific mining courses could also go a long way to improve the human capital shortage problem in this sector. At the same time, the capacity building of the institutes (industrial training and other technical institutes) should be enhanced so that they deliver to the maximum extent. Private-sector participation should be attracted by providing them with appropriate remuneration and incentives to do skill development programmes.

8. It is a well-established fact that India lacks improved mining technology. Thus, the need of the moment is to ensure improved technology application across the mining industry. The government should come forward to tackle the technology gap by making provisions for the clearance of imports and use of technology in the short term and creating a support system for R&D programmes of the GSI, India Private Limited (IBM), and academic institutions in the long term.
9. The mining industry in India is required to address the sustainability issues first and foremost, as mining is considered to have a huge socio-economic and environmental impact. Sustainability concerns could be addressed by enforcing all the vital components of sustainability (social, economic, and environmental) through regulatory changes. For this, mining companies must adopt measures such as integrating sustainability key performance indicators (KPIs) with productivity outcomes, monitoring emissions, and strict adherence to mine closure norms (provided in the India Sustainable Development Framework). Mine closure could be facilitated by increasing the financial amount attached to it and linking it with the post-closure rehabilitation cost.
10. There is significant scope for the Indian mining industry. The growing infrastructure sector and real estate sector have provided much impetus to mining industry expansion. Infrastructure projects continue to provide lucrative business opportunities for steel,

zinc, and aluminium. Iron and steel make up a core component of the real estate sector. Demand for these metals is expected to raise the growth expectations for the residential and commercial building industry. As the expectations of these sectors are set in positive notes, this ultimately would demand an increase in mining production. Thus, looking at the future scope of the mining industry, the expansion of the mining capacity in iron ore, bauxite, and coal is called for, along with future discoveries of subsurface deposits.

3.6 Discussion

India has a fairly large variety of mineral deposits, and its endowment is quite adequate, except a few deficient minerals such as petroleum, lead, copper, zinc, kyanite, rock phosphate, and fluorspar (Chapter 1). In recent years, the trend in production has seen a shift from minerals such as coal and iron ores to other important minerals such as petroleum, natural gas, lignite, lead, zinc, copper, silver, diamond, and rock phosphate.

When we look at the performance of the Indian minerals sector in terms of volume of production, contribution to output, employment, and foreign trade, a gloomy picture emerges (Chapter 1). India's mineral sector performance has been poor both on output and input parameters. On the output front, the contribution of the mining sector to India's gross value added (GVA) has been stagnant and low, at around 3% over the past decade. As far as employment is concerned, the mining sector employs a smaller percentage of India's population (0.3%) as opposed to the expectation from this sector (MOM, 2011). Also in terms of its contribution to foreign trade, this sector presents a dismal picture, which is reflected through stagnant mineral exports over the years, increasing mineral imports indicating a negative impact on the balance-of-payment situation of the country, and negative direction of trade as imports have always been greater than exports over the years. This trend presents a paradoxical situation in the Indian context: even though considered as a mineral resource-rich country, India is not self-sufficient in many minerals and has to depend on others to provide an impetus to the economic growth of the nation. Higher imports also point towards the lower productivity of the sector, which can be attributed a to variety of reasons, such as low level of mechanization, unskilled manpower, or low level of investment.

Despite enjoying the leverage of large mineral endowments in some of the mineral reserves, the mining industry has remained relatively small and stagnant and has not achieved its true potential. The contribution of mining to India's GDP has fallen from 3.2 to 2.2% from 2012 to 2016. This slow growth rate is due to several challenges faced by the industry. Low reserves-to-production ratio, lack of investment in exploration activities, inadequate infrastructure facilities, procedural and permit delays in mining operations, land acquisition issues, shortage of skilled human capital, corruption, sustainability, and the country's complex mining policy environment have all posed serious challenges to the growth of this sector.

Despite this scenario, the industry has a good starting position with abundant mineral reserves and the new MMDR Act (2015). A turnaround in the sector can be brought about if several important critical success factors, enablers, and building blocks are put in place. In this respect, a supportive government policy and framework to deal with land acquisition and other issues, adequate infrastructure facilities, raw material security, supply-chain optimization techniques, and sustainability and environment reforms could go a long way to bringing glory to this sector and making it a game changer.

3.7 Conclusion

This chapter attempts to identify the key challenges faced by the Indian mining industry by using an extensive literature survey and referring to expert opinions. The findings indicate that even though India is abundant in some of the mineral deposits, its contribution to the national economy is rather meagre. This poor contribution can be attributable to the many challenges/problems that this industry faces. The chapter identifies factors such as low reserves-to-production ratio, lack of investment in exploration activities, inadequate infrastructure facilities, procedural and permit delays in mining operations, land acquisition issues, shortage of skilled human capital, corruption, sustainability, and the country's complex mining policy environment are the key challenges that the mining industry is currently facing. Along with identifying the problems, this chapter also attempts to put forward some possible pathways to overcoming these challenges. The chapter concludes by mentioning that several critical success factors, enablers, and building blocks in the form of supportive government policy, adequate infrastructure facilities, raw material security, supply-chain optimization techniques, and sustainability and environment reforms can help overcome the challenges.

4

The Indian Mining Industry

Total Factor Productivity, Trends, and the Effect of Ownership

4.1 Introduction

After examining the impact of the mining industry on three macroeconomic variables and identifying the challenges faced by this industry, this chapter aims to estimate the productivity performance of the mining industry in the context of India.

Productivity is unarguably a key concept for all economic sectors as it is central to a nation's general well-being. Productivity is an indicator of efficiency, and as such, productivity growth improves the standard of living of the nation. As rightly mentioned by Paul Krugman (1994), 'Productivity isn't everything, but in the long run it is almost everything. A country's ability to improve its standard of living over time depends almost entirely on its ability to raise its output per worker.' Moreover, the notion of productivity has particular significance for the mining industry as it belongs to the natural resource industry, which is associated with resource depletion. Thus, the real challenge here is productivity growth, which has to first offset the effects of this resource depletion before it makes any further progress. Considering the importance of productivity in the economic prosperity of a nation, this chapter intends to estimate the total factor productivity growth of the Indian mining industry. Further, with the liberalization process that started around 1991, private-sector participation was allowed into the mining sector in India, which fully opened up to the global economy in 2006. This increasing participation of the private-sector in an industry that had been under the total control of the government may have an impact on mining productivity. In this context, the question that arises is does ownership have a bearing

The Indian Mining Industry. Meenakshi Parida and S. Madheswaran, Oxford University Press.
 DOI: 10.1093/9780198954392.003.0004

on mining productivity? Consequent upon this, the moot question is, 'Who extracts minerals more productively, the state-owned firm or the privately owned firm?' Therefore, this chapter also aims to examine this ownership and productivity link. Many empirical studies have attempted to examine the impact of ownership on factor productivity. However, no common consensus has been reached, which is evident from the two schools of thought: one based on property rights (Alchian, 1965; Alchian and Demsetz, 1972), public choice (Buchanan, 1978; Niskanen, 1971; Olson, 1965), and agency theory (Fama, 1980; Jensen and Meckling, 1976; Williamson, 1964), which advocates the presence of ownership effects on productivity, and the other line of arguments that sees no significant effect (Averch and Johnson, 1962; Laffont and Tirole, 1993; Stigler, 1971). Empirical studies, too, do not provide any conclusive evidence, which makes this a constantly emerging empirical issue. This chapter aims to assess these two issues: first, to estimate the total factor productivity and examine how this factor productivity has moved (the trend) over the period covered in the Indian mining industry, as well as across its component subsectors; second, to study the effect of ownership on productivity in the context of the mining industry.

Productivity can be defined as the output per unit of representative units of resources (Abramovitz, 1956) and is measured as a ratio of output(s) to input(s). Productivity can be of two types: single-factor (or partial) productivity or total factor productivity (TFP). Single-factor productivity is measured by the ratio of output to single-factor input. TFP, unlike partial productivity, is defined as the ratio of output to the weighted sum of all inputs and is seen as a measure of technological change that has taken place in the industry. It is important to note here that, as productivity is an indicator of efficiency, we use TFP synonymously with productive efficiency or extraction efficiency. Since single-factor productivity takes into account a single input, it fails to provide the true picture of productivity growth. For instance, labour productivity would improve if the labour requirement per unit of output declined. However, this reduction in labour requirement may be due to a large requirement of capital or other inputs, thereby not reflecting actual productivity growth. So, we have used the concept of TFP, which assumes equal importance to all the scarce inputs and recognizes that productivity growth results from the combined savings over all inputs, not just one. Thus, this chapter attempts to estimate the TFP (productive efficiency) of the mining industry and its component subsectors: metallic, non-metallic, coal, and petroleum. Further, the trends in TFP growth have been examined to assess the direction of change of the TFP growth for the whole mining industry over the period. Thereafter, we have studied the effects of ownership on TFP for the mining industry and its component subsectors. To examine the ownership effects, we have compared TFP levels and growth rates of public and private mining firms in the four subsectors of the Indian mining industry. Along with productive efficiency, we have estimated the technical efficiency of one of the component subsectors of the mining industry (coal). This choice of subsector is because of its importance in the contribution to the production volume of the whole mining industry. We present the technical efficiency estimation part in Chapter 5. The reason for not calculating the technical efficiency of the entire mining industry is that the Indian mining industry is an amalgamation of different subsectors. The techniques of production used in these subsectors are different from one another. If we used the whole industry data for technical efficiency estimation, it might result in biased results. Thus, we have refrained from estimating the technical efficiency for the entire mining industry and instead focus on one of the major subsectors of the mining industry for technical efficiency estimation, that is, coal.

The rest of the chapter has been organized as follows: section 4.2 briefly discusses the review of literature; section 4.3 enumerates the methodology; section 4.4 introduces the data sources, measurement of variables, and time period of the study. Empirical findings are presented in section 4.5. Section 4.6 discusses the results and finally, section 4.7 concludes the chapter.

4.2 Studies on Productivity and Efficiency

4.2.1 Theoretical Literature

The discussion of productivity and efficiency estimation is always done in the case of a specified production function. The production function provides a technical relationship between output and all the input variables, given the technology. Thus, the concept of productivity and efficiency is explained from the perspective of a production function approach, which provides a fundamental theoretical framework for estimation. The insights drawn from all the theoretical literature about this production function approach in the context of productivity and efficiency estimation are comprehensively presented in Chapter 1. Thus, here we concentrate on the empirical literature and subsequently attempt to draw insights from the literature.

4.2.2 Empirical Literature

The literature on the productivity and efficiency performance of the mining and mineral industry is not extensive. There have been very few studies on the performance analysis of the mining industry, and studies are even more sparse in the case of the Indian mining industry. The majority of the productivity and efficiency studies focus on the Indian coal-mining subsector.

The study of Kulshreshtha and Parikh (2001) was an attempt made to do an in-depth analysis of the productivity growth in the Indian coal subsector during the period 1980–1992. TFP was calculated from the output and input indices for Coal India Ltd. Results of the analysis indicated that a labour productivity increase of around 37.6% was achieved. A study of the individual subsidiaries indicated that companies with a larger share of underground mines had shown slower productivity growth. The underutilization of capital, surplus labour, power shortages in the underground mines, inability to adapt to modern technologies, and the pricing structure of coal were the reasons for the poor performance of Coal India Ltd.

In their study, Wang, Tran, and Nguyen (2015) attempted to measure the productive efficiency of twenty-three listed companies in India covering the period 2010–2014. The data were collected from the websites of Bombay Stock Exchange and Money Control, which contain the financial details of individual Indian mining companies. They employed the message passing interface (MPI) model to see the performance of these companies in the past–present period and the four-year future period (2015–2018) by using forecasting results of the Grey System theory. The results revealed that from the past to future period, the National

Mineral Development Corporation, Hindalco Industries Limited, and Coal India always kept their highest rankings among twenty-three decision making units (DMUs) regarding performance scores.

Kasap et al. (2007) conducted a study that examined the effects of non-controllable factors as well as input parameters on the efficiency performances of eight enterprises within Turkish Coal Enterprises (TCE) from 2005 to 2007. For each enterprise, the outputs included the production sold and the total income; the controllable inputs consisted of investment expenditure, overburden stripping, and number of staff; and the non-controllable inputs consisted of total reserve and low heat values. Considering the non-controllable inputs as a result of the analyses conducted with the three-stage data envelopment analysis (DEA) model, it was determined that the average efficiency value of TCE increased from 87.5 to 92.3%.

In the study of Xue et al. (2008), the authors used an input-orientated model to measure the energy consumption productivity change of fourteen industry sectors in China from 1999 to 2008 as decision-making units. The results showed that there were only four sectors that experienced effective energy consumption throughout the whole reference period. The other ten sectors experienced inefficiency in some two-year time periods and the productivity changes were not steady. The DEA-based Malmquist Productivity Index provided a good way to measure energy consumption.

Fang et al. (2009) attempted to compare the technical efficiency performance of listed coal-mining companies in China and the United States using Charnes, Cooper, and Rhodes (CCR) and behaviour change communication (BCC) models in the advanced DEA linear programming. The results showed that the level of relative efficiency in Chinese coal-mining enterprises, regardless of total technical efficiency or decomposed pure technical and scale efficiency, was much lower than that in US coal firms.

Das (2012), in his research study, attempted to examine the performances of mining firms in the public and private sectors in three dimensions: productivity, environmental compliance, and social compliance. He defined social compliance as the compensation provided by the mining firms for direct and indirect losses caused to the land-surrendering households as per the promises made during the land acquisition. Using the data provided by the Centre for Monitoring the Indian Economy (CMIE) in its Prowess data for the period 1988–1989 and 2005–2006, he tried to find the productivity differences between public- and private-sector mining firms for the four subsectors of the mining industry—metallic, non-metallic, coal, and petroleum.

Parry (1997), in his study, examined multifactor productivity trends in the US petroleum, coal, copper, and logging industries since 1970. Using growth accounting theory, the study found that measures of multifactor productivity growth were negative for all four industries during the 1970s. The decline in measured multifactor productivity in that decade appeared to be explained by a number of special factors that generally had a transitory rather than a permanent effect on productivity growth. For example, the rise in natural resource prices encouraged the entry of relatively inefficient producers. New environmental and health and safety regulations were phased in during the period, which also reduced measured multifactor productivity.

Neingo and Tholana (2016), in their study, attempted to analyse the performance of the South African gold mining industry from 2006 to 2014. This study discussed only labour productivity trends for the African gold mining industry. The findings revealed that labour productivity declined for the above period.

Stoker et al. (2005), in their study, presented an empirical analysis of labour productivity in US coal mining from 1972 to 1975. Using panel regression models, the authors tried to find out productivity indices on the basis of fixed effect and time effect. The fixed-effect index showed that the average fixed-effect values for mines in operation increased uniformly, which indicated that there was progress embodied in capital available for mines. The scale effect reflected the productivity gains associated with the increase in output scales. This study found that there was a rapid labour productivity increase between 1978 and 1995. However, the weak point of the study was that it used a very simple model that was associated with several potential problems. As it used goodness-of-fit criterion in the model and assumed that output was predetermined, there was a greater chance of the endogeneity problem occurring.

Lovell and Lovell (2013), in their study attempted to measure the decline in productivity in the Australian coal-mining subsector from 2000–2001 to 2006–2007. Using both value added and gross output framework and index number methodology, this study found a considerable decline in the estimated TFP. The study also went one step further to explore the possible financial consequences of the productivity decline. However, the weak point of the study was that it did not say anything about the sources of productivity decline.

The review of the above empirical literature indicates that the majority of the research work undertaken in the context of mining has been restricted to only one specific subsector. With the exception of one or two studies (e.g. Das, 2012), hardly any literature examined the mining industry from a holistic perspective. And the study that attempted to do so only examined the industry by giving a public- and private-sector comparison and was thereby lacking in many respects.

4.2.3 Studies on the Effect of Ownership on TFP

The subject of firm ownership and productivity or extraction efficiency is always controversial. Who extracts minerals more productively is always a matter of concern. Theoretical and empirical literature abounds on this topic. However, the literature stands highly divided in its conclusions. While one set of literature argues for the superiority of private firms over public firms (Li and Xia, 2008; Majumdar, 1998; Stiglitz, 1988), the other set views it differently (Caves and Christensen 1980). This section presents a summary of selected literature on the effect of firm ownership on productivity.

4.2.3.1 Insights from theoretical literature

The differences in productivity can result from the characteristic of firm ownership. The public choice theory and the property rights theory discuss this extensively. According to public choice theory, ownership difference results in productivity difference due to two kinds of problem—the agency problem and the incentives problem. With agency problem (also referred to as the principal–agent problem), public-sector firms perform inefficiently as compared with private firms. In the case of public-sector enterprises, there is a difference in ownership (principals) and management (agents). Because of this difference, the major challenge here is to ensure that the agents work for the interests of the owners rather than fulfilling their own vested interests by grabbing other people's resources. As the agents have more, and better, information about the resources than the owners, they have the advantage of being able to use these resources for their own benefit. In the absence of proper monitoring by the owners, managers often misuse their status for personal gain at the expense of the investor's interest (Li and Xia, 2008). This information asymmetry enables the managers to undertake wasteful projects in their own self-interest.

In the same way, public-sector firms also perform inefficiently due to the lack of two types of incentives—organizational and individual. There are no organizational incentives for public-sector firms to improve their productivity. Unlike private firms, the managers of public firms are seldom concerned about organizational improvement. They show the least concern about the bankruptcy and competitiveness of their companies. The losses of these firms are very often adjusted through budgetary support, giving the public firm managers least incentive to perform efficiently. Most of the time, the objective function of the public-sector firms is distorted by political interference (Sheshinski et al., 2003). Public managers incorporate their political career objectives into the objective function of public-sector firms, thus giving importance to employment generation at the cost of efficiency, and, on the individual front, fixed tenures and determined pay scales do not provide much incentive to increase the efficiency of managers of public-sector firms. As the salaries of public-sector firms are not linked to profit, they do not put in their best efforts to maximize the profits of public-sector firms. Similarly, fixed tenure does not provide any incentive to work hard.

As with property rights theory, public firms are more inefficient than private firms. Property rights theory proponent Alchian (1965) held the view that property rights were more visible in a public firm than in a private firm. This is because ownership in the case of public firms is diffused among all members of society, and no member has the right to sell his or her property. Given this aspect of public ownership, there is little incentive for owners to monitor the behaviour of managers. On the contrary, the ownership of private firms is concentrated among fewer individuals, and each individual has the right to sell his or her property shares. This gives owners the incentive to keep a watch on the management to ensure better productivity.

4.2.3.2 Empirical literature

The literature abounds with a vast number of empirical studies concerning the performance of public and private firms. Some studies have shown the superiority of private firms over public firms (Das, 2012; Faria et al., 2005; Li and Xia, 2008; Majumdar, 1998), whereas other studies show either superior or neutral status of public firms over private firms (Boardman and Vining, 1989; Caves and Christensen, 1980; Ehrlich et al., 1994). In his study, Das (2012) found out that private mining firms were more productive than public firms in three subsectors (metallic, non-metallic, and coal), while for the petroleum subsector, the public firms showed better productivity than private firms. Li and Xia (2008), in a study of Chinese state firms and non-state firms, established that non-state firms were more efficient than the state firms. Studying the Brazilian private and public companies providing water and sewerage utilities, Faria et al. (2005) showed that the private companies were only marginally more efficient than the public ones. Majumdar (1998) studied three types of firms in his study of the government-owned, mixed, and private-sector enterprises in India for fifteen years between 1973–1974 and 1988–1989, and his results pointed out that enterprises owned by central and state governments were less efficient than mixed or private-sector enterprises, while mixed enterprises were less efficient than those in the private sector.

One of the studies that showed the superior performance of public firms was that of Caves and Christensen (1980). In their study of Canadian railroads, they showed no significant inferior performance by the public ownership. According to them, public ownership was not inherently more inefficient than private ownership; rather, the inefficiency arose from the fact that public firms were not subject to healthy competition. Boardman and Vining (1989) pointed out that the efficiency difference between public and private firms varied from sector to sector. They further showed that public firms were more efficient in that sector, where there was limited competition or regulations were imposed on private firms such as electricity and water. Private firms were more efficient in the delivery of services where the government subcontracted to the private sector. Greater efficiency of the private sector is also observed in health-related literature. Boardman and Vining (1989) argued that the comparison between public and private firms would be inappropriate as most of the comparative studies were undertaken either for natural monopolies or regulated duopolies.

Ehrlich et al. (1994) considered that a comparison between public and private firms would be inappropriate and may lead to inconclusive results, depending on the age structure of the firm. Hence, age can be a major determinant in deciding the difference in productivity and efficiency between public and private firms. Their study showed that, in the long run, private firms showed more productivity growth than state-owned enterprises.

From the above review of literature, it can be concluded that studies on ownership and productive efficiency present varied results for different sectors. Hence, it would be wrong to spell out the superiority of one type of ownership over another. Rather, it remains an empirical issue that needs further investigation. In this context, this book will be an addition to the existing literature of impact of ownership on productivity.

4.3 Methodology

To estimate the TFP, and also to compare the productivity between public and private mining firms, we use the Levinsohn and Petrin (2003) method, a semi-parametric approach. We first estimate the firm-level TFP and then the TFP of each subsector by taking the weighted mean of TFP levels using the share of each firm in the specific subsector as weights.

TFP can be estimated by broadly two methods: the growth accounting method and the econometric or production function method. We use the latter approach for our estimation purposes. For our present study, we estimate TFP as a residual in the production function, which can be written as

$$\ln P_{it} = \ln q_{it} - \ln x'_{it}\beta \tag{1}$$

where P_{it} is firm-specific productivity, $q_{it} = p_{it} x'_{it}\beta$, x_{it} is the vector of inputs, and β is the vector of input coefficients. We are first required to find out the input coefficients from a production function, which is expressed in Cobb–Douglas form. For the *i*th firm in period *t*, the production function can be expressed as follows.

$$q_{it} = a_0 + a_c\, c_{it} + a_l l_{it} + a_e e_{it} + u_{it} \quad (2)$$

Productivity is estimated as

$$p_{it} = q_{it} - a_c\, c_{it} - a_l l_{it} - a_e e_{it} \quad (3)$$

where q_{it} is the log of gross output in the year *t*, c_{it} is the log of capital stock, l_{it} is the log of wage bill, e_{it} is the log of energy expenses (comprising power and fuel), and u_{it} is an error term. P_{it} is the log value of firm-specific productivity.

We use the production function method (or econometric approach) for estimating the TFP as, unlike the growth accounting method, this method is free from unrealistic assumptions such as constant returns to scale, competitive market, and uniform price and technology. However, it is associated with problems such as simultaneity and endogeneity.[1] The endogeneity problem arising in a production function can be explained as follows. In equation (2) the error term can be divided into two parts—errors arising due to productivity component i.e. ω_{it} and other errors occurring because of errors in estimation and data, etc., that is, η_{it}. Thus, $u_{it} = \omega_{it} + \eta_{it}$.

The simple ordinary least squares (OLS) estimates of the above production function (equation (2)) would result in biased and inconsistent estimates, as unbiased OLS estimates require that the stochastic error term and the inputs should be uncorrelated. However, in practice, this condition is not met as the error term ω_{it} and inputs are correlated. Inputs are chosen by the firms, given some optimality conditions, and would be affected by the productivity shock. Productivity could be contemporaneously and serially correlated with the inputs. For instance, contemporaneous correlation occurs if the firm hires more workers on the basis of

[1] For more information on the problems associated with the estimation of production function and the evolution of methodologies to address the problems, refer to Griliches and Mairesse (1998).

its current productivity in anticipation of future profitability. In the case of a single-input production process, serial correlation between productivity and hiring decisions will result in an upward bias in the coefficient and in a multi-input process, the direction of bias is less pronounced (Griliches and Mairesse (1998). Thus, in the presence of endogeneity, the application of the OLS method would result in biased and inconsistent estimates. Marschak and Andrews (1944) pointed out that since inputs are chosen by the firm and not known to the econometrician, there is endogeneity in the estimation equation, which would make the OLS estimates inconsistent.

The simultaneity problem can be addressed by a number of methodologies that have evolved over time. The first one is the application of within transformation. However, the major predicament with this method is that it does not solve the simultaneity problem properly, leading to other problems, such as errors in variables. Chamberlain (1982) suggested the first differences (or longer differences) of the available panel data, instead of applying within transformation for resolving the simultaneity problem. According to him, if the error term and the inputs are correlated and the error term gets transmitted to the current period variable inputs, then the difference in variable inputs needs to be instrumented to ward off the simultaneity problem. However, as the number of instruments depend on the length of the panel data and changes from one cross-section to another, the estimation becomes tedious and calls for the use of general method of moments (GMM) estimators (e.g. Arellano and Bond, 1991). The problem with the instrumental variables (IV) method is that these internal instruments (past levels for current differences and past differences for current levels) are likely to be quite poor and possess less resolving power (Griliches and Mairesse, 1998). Hence, they recommended bringing in more information (such as external instruments, more theoretical restrictions on the structure, and/or more equations) to solve the problem in a better way. Further, the simultaneity problem can be addressed by using a proxy for the unobserved transmitted component ω_{it} (Olley and Pakes, 1996) The advantages of using a proxy ω_{it} over the usual within estimators or the Chamberlain or GMM estimators can be many—for instance, it is free from the assumption that ω_{it} reduces to fixed firm effect, which is a cost-effective solution to omitted variable bias and/or simultaneity problem as it leaves more identifying variance in variables and fixed inputs, so it is more informative (Griliches and Mairesse, 1998). The Olley and Pakes (OP) method turns out to be more reliable and effective if productivity shocks are more persistent (Van Biesebroeck, 2007).

The problem with the OP method is that it sues the investment function as a proxy for the productivity error component. It assumes that a firm's investment function is strictly increasing with productivity shocks, implying that better productivity in the current period would lead to better productivity in the future, thereby leading to capital accumulation. However, in practice, there are firms that make intermittent investment, and for them, their zero investment observations would be truncated from the estimation procedure. As a result of this, a substantial number of firms would be deleted from the analysis. However, this issue can be taken care of by using intermediate inputs as a proxy. Levinsohn and Petrin (2003) further refine the technique of Olley and Pakes and use intermediate input (raw materials) as a proxy to control for the simultaneity problem.

This chapter uses Levinsohn and Petrin (2003), a semi-parametric[2] method to estimate the TFP, as this is considered the most appropriate method for estimating productivity that takes care of simultaneity. Following Levinsohn and Petrin, intermediate input (namely energy consumed) is used as a proxy to deal with the simultaneity problem. The choice to use energy as a proxy is justified by the primary nature of the mining industry and the minimal use of raw materials.

We can rewrite our equation (2) as

$$q_{it} = a_0 + a_c\, c_{it} + a_l l_{it} + a_e e_{it} + \omega_{it} + \eta_{it} \tag{4}$$

It is assumed that the firm's energy demand function $e_{it} = e_t\,(\omega_{it}, c_{it})$ is monotonically increasing in productivity, given its capital stock. The inverse of the energy demand function becomes $\omega_{it} = \omega_t\,(e_t, c_{it})$. As the ω_{it}

[2] Refer to Griliches and Mairesse (1998) for a comprehensive idea about the superiority of the semi-parametric method over other methods, such as IV and GMM. Also, see Biesebroeck (2007) for the details of alternative methods of measuring TFP.

depends on the observable variables c_{it} and e_{it}, we can substitute this value into equation (4) to derive a partial linear model as follows:

$$q_{it} = a_l l_{it} + \phi_t(e_{it}, c_{it}) + \eta_{it} \tag{5}$$

where,

$$\phi_t(e_{it}, c_{it}) = a_0 + a_c\, c_{it} + a_e e_{it} + \omega_t(e_{it},\, c_{it}).$$

Now equation (5) can be estimated in two stages. In the first stage, as the error term in equation (5) η_{it} is uncorrelated with the input, the coefficient for labour (a_l) can be estimated by including ϕt (.) in the estimation procedure. In this, ϕt (.) is approximated by a third order polynomial with full set of interactions. This is allowed to be different in three sub-periods corresponding to the three distinct phases of the mining industry.

In the second stage, ω_{it} is assumed to follow the first-order Markov process:

$$\omega_{it} = E\left[\omega_{it}\ x\ \omega_{it-1}\right] + \xi_{it} \tag{6}$$

where ξ_{it} is the innovation in productivity over the last period's expectation. a_c and a_e are identified by two-moment conditions. The first-moment condition to identify a_c assumes that capital does not respond to ξ_{it}, and is given as

$$\mathrm{E}\left[(\xi_{it} + \eta_{it})c_{it}\right] = \mathrm{E}\left[\xi_{it}, c_{it}\right] = 0 \tag{7}$$

The second-moment condition to identify a_e, which assumes that the previous period's energy choice is not correlated with ξ_{it}, is

$$\begin{aligned} &\mathrm{E}\left[(\xi_{it} + \eta_{it})e_{it-1}\right] = \mathrm{E}\left[\xi_{it}, c_{it}\right] = 0 \\ &E\left[\xi_{it} + \eta_{it})e_{it-1}\right] = E\left[\xi_{it} e_{it-1}\right] = 0 \end{aligned} \tag{8}$$

The residuals used in the moment conditions in equations (7) and (8) are given by equation (9):

$$\xi_{it} \hat{+} \eta_{it}\left(a^*\right) = q_{it} - \hat{a}_l l_{it} - a_e^* e_{it} - a_c^* c_{it} - E\left[\omega_{it} \hat{|} \omega_{it-1}\right] \tag{9}$$

where the residuals are expressed as a function of the two parameters $a^{*} = a_{c}^{*} a_{e}^{*}$.

$E[\omega_{it} | \omega_{it-1}]$ is estimated by regressing $\widehat{\omega}_{it}$ on fourth order polynomial $\widehat{\omega}_{it-1}$. $\widehat{\omega}_{it}$ and $\widehat{\omega}_{it-1}$ are obtained from the following two equations using the estimates from the first stage (labour coefficient) and the OLS estimates of production function (2):

$$\omega_{it} \hat{+} \eta_{it} = y_{it} - \hat{a}_l l_{it} - a_c^{*} c_{it} - a_e^{*} e_{it} \tag{10}$$

$$\widehat{\omega}_{it-1} = \widehat{\Phi}_{t-1}(.) - a_c^{*} c_{it-1} - a_e^{*} e_{it-1} \tag{11}$$

To test the unbiasedness of the estimated coefficients of the choice variables such as labour, capital, and energy, three additional moment restrictions are used, which are given below:

$$E[\xi_{it}\, l_{it-1}] = 0, \quad E[\xi_{it}\, c_{it-1}] = 0, \quad E[\xi_{it}\, e_{it-2}] = 0 \tag{12}$$

These over-identifying moment restrictions are valid under the null hypothesis that the coefficient estimates are unbiased. Thus, we have a total of five population moment conditions given by the vector of expectations:

$$E[(\xi_{it} + \eta_{it})\, Z_{it} = 0 \tag{13}$$

where Z_{it} is the vector given by

$$Z_{it} = \{c_{it}, e_{it-1}, c_{it-1}, e_{it-2}, l_{it-1}\} \tag{14}$$

Finally, we obtain estimates $(\hat{a}_c, \hat{a}_e)$ by minimizing the GMM criterion function:

$$Q(a^{*}) = \min a^{*} \sum_{h=1}^{5} (\sum_{i} \sum_{t=Ti0}^{Ti1} (\xi_{i,t} \hat{+} \eta_{i,t}(a^{*})) Z_{i,h,t})2 \tag{15}$$

where i and h refer to the firms and five instruments, respectively; T_{i0} and T_{i1} index the second and last period firms i is observed.

The estimated production function coefficients are used to estimate the TFP (P_{it}). TFP levels for each firm are estimated as follows:

$$P_{it} = \exp\left(lnq_{it} - ln\, c \times a_c - lnl \times a_l - lne \times a_e\right) \quad (16)$$

Using the firm-level TFP, the industry-level TFP has been estimated as the weighted mean of firm-level TFP estimates where weights are each firms' output share in the industry. Using a similar estimation procedure, the TFP levels for all four subsectors (namely, metallic, non-metallic, coal, and petroleum) have been estimated. Again, by dividing each subsector into two ownership groups (public and private), the TFP has been estimated for eight subsectors. For grouping the firms under the four subsectors, we have followed the National Industrial Classification (NIC) codes at five-digit level. Similarly, for ownership classification, we have enlisted all the government—central and state—enterprises under the public sector and the rest under the private sector.

4.4 Data and Measurement of Variables

The study uses firm-level data from the Prowess database of the CMIE.[3] Our data set contains yearly information on Indian mining firms from 2000 to 2016. The reason for taking 2000 as the initial year is that the Indian economy witnessed structural reforms in the early 1990s, which subsequently brought in vast changes in the mining sector policy, and the results of this sectoral reform process were realized in the late 1990s. Another reason is that data on all variables, price indices, and deflators for all variables are systematically available from this year. Our sample

[3] Prowess is an online database provided by the CMIE, which covers financial data for over 23,000 companies operating in India. Most of the companies covered in the database are listed on stock exchanges, and the financial data includes all information that operating companies are required to disclose in their annual reports. The accepted disclosure norms under the Indian Companies Act (1956) make it compulsory for companies to report all heads of income and expenditure, which account for more than 1% of their turnover. The Prowess database provides quantitative information on variables, such as output, sales, raw materials, and energy.

includes firms mainly from four important subsectors: coal, metallic, non-metallic, and petroleum. We have selected firms primarily based on the availability of data. Firms having data for at least four years in sequence have been included in the analysis. Thus, we have a sample of firms consisting of a total of 976 observations on 69 firms. In 2000, the data represented 84% of the total value of mining output and subsequently a higher percentage in the following years. In 2004–2005, the data set represents around 92% of the total value of the output of the mining industry (Table A4.1 in Appendix A4), which is the highest value recorded during sample tenure, whereas in 2012–2013, the total value of the output of the mining industry is about 75.17%, which is the minimum value recorded during the sampling period. Therefore, the range from 75.17–92% is quite significant and representative of the current mining scenario in India. The data set used for this analysis is an unbalanced panel. The summary estimates of the data are presented in Table A4.2 in Appendix A4.

4.4.1 Construction of Variables

The first step in estimating the production function is to convert all the values into real terms as the Prowess database provides the values in nominal terms. This can be done by deflating the nominal values with the appropriate price indices. For this, we collected the values of price indices from the 'Index numbers of wholesale prices in India, base 2004–2005 = 100' published by the Economic Advisor, Ministry of Commerce and Industry, Government of India. The time series variables are measured at 2004–2005 prices. The detailed procedure is explained below.

4.4.1.1 Output

The value of the output series for each firm is obtained by deflating the current year's values. As the mining industry is divided into four subsectors, and the price deflators of each subsector are different, disaggregated price deflators have been used for the four subsectors—coal, metallic, non-metallic, and petroleum. For the mining industry as a whole, the Wholesale Price Index (WPI) for Minerals has been used to deflate the current year's values to convert it into the real output.

4.4.1.2 Labour

The labour input is measured in terms of wages and salaries. While constructing the variable (labour input), we deflated the total wages and salaries of labourers to the standard Consumer Price Index for Industrial Workers to arrive at the real wages and salaries of labourers. Here, a question may arise that such wage rates are seldom paid in actual practice. In actual practice, the wage rate (nominal) may vary depending on several factors such as location, supply, or skills. This large variation in wage rate is difficult to capture for any kind of econometric analysis. In this context, a standard All-India Consumer Price Index (CPI) for Industrial Workers is of great help, which reflects the purchasing power of the industrial workers. The data for the latter is obtained from the Labour Bureau, Ministry of Labour and Employment, Government of India. To ensure that the CPI reflects the true changes happening in consumer prices, the Government of India makes appropriate changes in the consumer basket from time to time to capture the real changes in consumption, the latest being in 2010. Hence, it cannot be denied that the CPI reflects the true CPI for Industrial Workers. By deflating the total wage bill with the CPI for Industrial Workers, taking the 2001 = 100 as a base, we obtain our variable labour input.

4.4.1.3 Energy

The energy variable is constructed by deflating the energy cost (power and fuel) by the Composite Price Index of Fuel, Power, Light, and Lubricants. This composite price index has been collected from the Office of the Economic Advisor (OEA), Ministry of Commerce and Industry, which has been publishing the price index since 1942.

4.4.1.4 Capital

The capital variable is estimated using the perpetual inventory method. The detailed procedure is provided in Appendix A4.

4.5 Empirical Findings

This section presents our results. First of all, we have shown the production function estimates from two different methodologies, namely the OLS and

Levinsohn and Petrin (LP) method. Thereafter, we have presented the TFP levels of mining firms. We have refrained from comparing the TFP levels of mining firms across subsectors, as any such attempt may lead to misleading results. This is because the four subsectors of the mining industry exhibit different pricing mechanisms. For instance, in the case of coal and petroleum, the administered price mechanism is followed, wherein the price of coal and crude petrol is determined by the central government and not the market forces. Therefore, it does not reflect the true market price. On the other hand, in the case of the metallic and non-metallic subsectors, the price is (by and large) determined by the market forces. Thus, productivity estimates for the subsectors where the administered price mechanism is followed would show a downward bias as against the subsectors where price is market-determined. In this kind of scenario, it would be misleading to compare the productivity estimates across subsectors. However, a comparison of productivity estimates within the subsectors (intra-subsector) would not cause any such bias, as all the firms within the subsector would be facing the same pricing mechanism. Hence, given this kind of possibility, we have attempted to provide an intra-subsector comparison of TFP levels and across subsectors. We have compared only the growth rates. In the end, we have tested the productivity gap between the public and private firms through a multivariate regression model controlling for initial productivity levels and age of the firms.

The production function estimates from two different methodologies (namely, the OLS and LP methods) are presented in Table 4.1.

Table 4.1 Production function estimates

Inputs	OLS	LP
Labour	0.463* (0.027)	0.512* (0.098)
Capital	0.398* (0.024)	0.406* (0.078)
Energy	0.231*(0.023)	0.221* (0.069)
P(Q)	–	0.624
No. of observations	976	976

Notes: For the LP method, the bootstrap standard errors are provided in parentheses. Number of replications is 500. For OLS, ordinary standard errors are given. P (Q) is the P value of the over-identification test. *Indicates the significance of variables at a 1% level of confidence.

Source: Author's estimation.

The results show that the OLS estimates for labour and capital are biased downwards and that of energy is biased upwards as against the estimates of the LP. The value of P (Q) for the LP method indicates the P value of the over-identification test under the null hypothesis that over-identification restrictions are valid. A valid null hypothesis implies that the proxy is taking care of all the changes in the inputs correlated with unobserved productivity. In other words, the proxy, which is the energy variable here, is taking care of the simultaneity problem. Table 4.1 demonstrates that the null is accepted at a reasonable significance level. The results of the estimates from these two different methodologies reveal that the LP method is a better method than OLS for this particular study.

Having determined that the LP method estimates are better than OLS estimates, we then proceed to show the results of productivity estimates and compare TFP levels between the public and private sectors.

4.5.1 Measured TFP

4.5.1.1 TFP of the mining industry

In this section, we present the TFP levels that we obtain directly from the LP method for the whole industry and its four subsectors (Table 4.2).

The TFP levels of the Indian mining industry have grown more than one-and-a-half times from 5.6 in 2000 to 8.64 in 2016. Sector-wise analysis shows that the highest TFP levels have been achieved by the non-metallic subsector, followed by the metallic, petroleum, and coal subsectors.

Table 4.3 highlights the total factor productivity growth (TFPG) between mining industry and its four subsectors from 2000–2001 to 2016–2017.

Table 4.3 shows that during the entire period of our analysis, the mining industry grew by 2.72% per annum. During the second phase of liberalization (i.e. from 2000 to 2005–2006), the industry grew to the maximum (3.03%). However, after this phase, the growth rate of this industry slowed down to 2.55%. This may be due to the many challenges faced by the industry, which are listed in Chapter 1. Although the mining industry was completely opened up during 2006, the benefits of this policy decision have not been reflected in the productivity growth performance of the industry

Table 4.2 Weighted average of the TFP levels for the Indian mining industry and its four subsectors

Years	Mining industry	Metallic	Non-metallic	Coal	Petroleum
2000–2001	5.6	6.46	6.79	4.92	5.52
2001–2002	5.88	6.71	6.71	5.21	6.05
2002–2003	5.98	6.95	7.37	5.26	6.12
2003–2004	5.84	6.67	7.83	5.06	6.29
2004–2005	6.5	7.12	8.87	5.19	6.88
2005–2006	6.58	6.84	9.15	5.49	7.11
2006–2007	6.7	6.87	9.18	5.52	7.57
2007–2008	6.85	7	9.5	5.6	7.92
2008–2009	6.82	6.84	10.07	5.56	7.97
2009–2010	6.8	6.86	10.18	5.71	8.11
2010–2011	7.41	6.99	10.71	5.83	8.43
2011–2012	7.55	7.02	11.34	5.86	9.07
2012–2013	8.01	7.67	11.87	6.29	9.83
2013–2014	8.54	8.04	12.42	6.34	10.51
2014–2015	8.51	8.02	12.85	6.46	10.98
2015–2016	8.62	8.33	12.97	6.47	11.46
2016–2017	8.64	8.66	13.53	6.52	12.04

Source: Author's estimation.

Table 4.3 Average annual growth rates in the four subsectors of the Indian mining industry

Periods	Total mining industry	Metallic	Non-metallic	Coal	Petroleum
2000–2001 to 2005–2006	3.03	1.68	6.35	1.44	5.3
2006–2007 to 2011–2012	2.37	0.44	3.67	1.1	4.17
2012–2013 to 2016–2017	2.78	4.33	3.60	2.19	5.88
2006–2007 to 2016–2017	2.55	2.21	3.6	1.6	4.93
2000–2001 to 2016–2017	2.72	2.02	4.59	1.54	5.06

Source: Author's estimation.

after 2006, as the industry has registered a smaller growth rate of 2.37% per annum over the period 2006–2011. Nonetheless, from 2012 to 2016, the industry recovered to register a growth rate of 2.78%, although the overall TFP growth rates of the whole mining industry seem to register a low productivity rate, a mere 2.72%. Thus, it can be said that in India, the TFP growth rate of the mining industry is low and shows a declining trend. The fall in TFP growth was more pronounced during the period 2006–2011. This could have been due to a surge in commodity prices, which had a major influence on the industry. These higher prices have led to an increase in the value of output. However, this increase in the output value has not been accompanied by a simultaneous increase in the output volume. Attracted by the high profit margins, the mining firms have increased their usage of inputs substantially. This has elevated input costs but has not been accompanied by the same increase in the volume of output, resulting in a fall in the TFP. Besides it is also observed that during this period, the demand for crude oil registered a high increase, which was met through imports rather than domestic production (RBI, 2014). This increased input cost might have been reflected in a fall in the TFP growth of the industry.

4.5.1.2 TFP of the subsectors within the mining industry

Figure 4.1 shows the TFPG of four important subsectors of the Indian mining industry. Disaggregated analysis for the mining subsectors shows that the petroleum subsector registered the highest growth rate of 5.06% per annum over the entire period (2000–2016), followed by non-metallic (4.59%), metallic (2.02%), and coal (1.94%). But a different picture was observed during the second phase of liberalization (2000–2006). The non-metallic subsector registered the highest growth rate, followed by petroleum, metallic, and coal subsectors. The probable reasons for this could be greater investment by private players in the non-metallic subsector owing to the liberalization process. However, during the mining boom phase, the petroleum subsector grew more rapidly than other subsectors. A completely different picture was observed during the recovery phase, where after the petroleum subsector, metallic mining registered the second-highest growth rate (Fig. 4.1). Thus, it can be observed that there is no particular trend in TFP growth rates across the subsectors of the mining industry.

Figure 4.1 depicts that over the entire period of analysis, the TFP growth rates of the subsectors coal and metallic are less than the industry

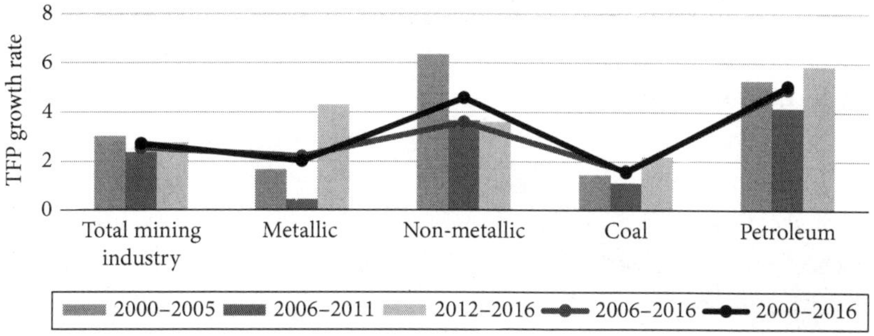

Fig. 4.1 TFP growth rates in the mining industry and its subsectors (annual average growth rates)
Source: Author's estimation.

average, whereas those of non-metallic and petroleum are more. This suggests that there exists year-to-year variability in the subsector productivity measures. This may be due to the presence of some small subsectors, and their estimates can be affected by changes occurring within a small number of individual mines. For instance, the inclusion and exclusion of large mines can influence the results, as can the investments made by the large mines.

From Table 4.3 and Fig. 4.1, it can be seen that there are differences among the four subsectors in terms of their level of TFP and their productivity growth rates over time. As can be seen from Table 4.3, the overall TFP growth has declined over time. Probably, the changes in the composition of the mining industry have been the contributing factor to this decline in aggregate productivity since 2000–2001. Compositional changes can have an adverse impact on the factor productivity if low-productive sectors expand more against the more productive sectors and if resources are allocated favourably to the sectors experiencing a sharp fall in productivity, making the resource allocation inefficient. Thus, the overall decline in mining productivity can be largely explained by the falling productivity in large subsectors such as non-metallic, coal, and petroleum.

4.5.2 Ownership and Productivity Link

An important question regarding the mining industry that needs to be investigated is whether or not ownership influences TFP and which type of firm is more productive. Here, we intend to empirically answers the above questions in the context of the Indian mining industry.

For this purpose, we compare the TFP levels of public and private mining firms in the four subsectors of the Indian mining industry. To make the comparison a feasible and smooth process, we have converted the absolute TFP levels in index form for public and private mining firms in the four subsectors. The TFP indices have been constructed by assuming the initial year TFP value of the public sector as 100. This serves as the reference point, and the TFP values of subsequent years and the private sector are estimated against this. Thereafter, under each subsector, TFP indices of private firms are compared with those of firms in the public sector.

Table 4.4 shows the TFP levels in index form for public and private firms in the four subsectors of the mining industry in India. It reveals that over the entire analysis period, the TFP levels of private firms were higher than their public-sector counterparts in three subsectors: metallic, non-metallic, and coal. However, for petroleum mining, the situation was quite different. For this subsector, the TFP levels of the public sector exceeded that of the private sector. In the initial years (from 2000–2001 to 2008–2009, the productivity levels of private firms were dominant over public firms. In the other years (from 2009–2010 to 2016–2017), the productivity levels of public firms outweighed those of their private counterparts except for the years 2010–2011, 2011–2012, 2014–2015, and 2016–2017.

To work out to what extent private mining firms are more productive than public mining firms, we have taken the ratios of productivity levels of private firms to that of public mining firms. Table 4.5 shows the ratios of private firms to that of public firms. A value larger than 1 indicates the multiples by which private firms are more productive than public firms, a value less than one signifies the multiples by which private firms are less productive than public firms, and a value equal to one exhibits no difference in productivity between the public and private mining firms.

It can be seen from Table 4.5 that the non-metallic-mining subsector records the highest productivity gap between public and private firms. The private firms in this subsector were approximately two times more productive than the public firms. For the metallic and coal subsectors, private firms are more productive than public firms by approximately

Table 4.4 Comparison of TFP between public and private mining firms in the four subsectors of the Indian mining industry, 2000–2016

Years	Metallic		Non-metallic		Coal		Petroleum	
	Public	Private	Public	Private	Public	Private	Public	Private
2000–2001	100.00	173.00	100.00	201.00	100.00	138.00	100.00	312.00
2001–2002	106.60	176.96	126.30	257.65	108.10	156.75	152.10	463.91
2002–2003	110.80	157.34	139.80	248.84	105.40	159.15	147.10	425.12
2003–2004	108.90	145.93	147.50	302.38	105.80	217.95	143.70	421.04
2004–2005	118.10	171.25	162.40	280.95	111.20	280.22	157.80	312.44
2005–2006	111.30	158.05	165.30	274.40	109.30	181.44	170.90	300.78
2006–2007	120.60	165.22	171.10	236.12	108.30	148.37	205.10	299.45
2007–2008	112.40	134.88	178.30	317.37	114.10	151.75	180.90	198.99
2008–2009	121.70	143.61	168.40	308.17	112.10	143.49	190.30	213.14
2009–2010	138.90	183.35	156.90	283.99	107.50	150.50	195.50	187.68
2010–2011	147.20	197.25	164.80	306.53	110.10	173.96	218.40	268.63
2011–2012	137.40	169.00	170.90	281.99	112.00	153.44	176.30	195.69
2012–2013	152.70	187.82	173.10	283.88	107.40	155.73	196.50	192.57
2013–2014	158.80	235.02	168.70	251.36	106.90	157.14	224.30	186.17
2014–2015	167.40	232.69	159.40	250.26	109.80	164.70	189.50	191.40
2015–2016	169.90	265.04	178.20	313.63	115.80	167.91	180.20	180.20
2016–2017	160.80	250.85	181.20	337.03	118.90	170.03	233.20	237.86

Source: Author's estimation.

Table 4.5 Ratio of TFP levels of private to public mining firms in the four subsectors of the Indian mining industry

Years	Metallic	Non-metallic	Coal	Petroleum
2000–2001	1.73	2.01	1.38	3.12
2001–2002	1.66	2.04	1.45	3.05
2002–2003	1.42	1.78	1.51	2.89
2003–2004	1.34	2.05	2.06	2.93
2004–2005	1.45	1.73	2.52	1.98
2005–2006	1.42	1.66	1.66	1.76
2006–2007	1.37	1.38	1.37	1.46
2007–2008	1.2	1.78	1.33	1.1
2008–2009	1.18	1.83	1.28	1.12
2009–2010	1.32	1.81	1.4	0.96
2010–2011	1.34	1.86	1.58	1.23
2011–2012	1.23	1.65	1.37	1.11
2012–2013	1.23	1.64	1.45	0.98
2013–2014	1.48	1.49	1.47	0.83
2014–2015	1.39	1.57	1.5	1.01
2015–2016	1.56	1.76	1.45	1
2016–2017	1.56	1.86	1.43	0.93

Source: Author's estimation.

one-and-half times. However, so far as the petroleum subsector is concerned, the productivity of public firms is close to, or exceeds, that of private firms from 2007 to 2016. This is partly due to the sharp decrease in the productivity levels of private firms. The public firms in the petroleum subsector experienced a steady rise, while a sharp decline in productivity levels was observed by private firms.

Since liberalization, the Indian mining industry has opened up to private-sector participation. This has effectively created a competition between public and private firms to enhance their productivity growth to survive in the market. In this context, it is imperative to provide a comparative picture of difference in productivity growth rates of public and private firms. Table 4.6 shows the average annual TFP growth rates of private and public firms in the four subsectors of the Indian mining industry for the period 2000–2016.

Table 4.6 Average annual TFP growth rates (%)

Time period	Metallic		Non-metallic		Coal		Petroleum	
	Public	Private	Public	Private	Public	Private	Public	Private
2000–2005	−0.31	0.63	3.68	7.02	1.38	1.46	6.11	3.23
2006–2011	−0.28	0.76	3.47	6.36	1.45	1.53	6.5	2.57
2012–2016	2.03	2.35	4.01	7.09	1.02	1.37	5.85	3.11

Source: Author's estimation.

The results in Table 4.6 show that over the entire period of analysis, the TFP growth of private firms was higher than that of public firms, except in the case of the petroleum subsector. The entire period is divided into three sub-periods: 2000–2001 to 2005–2006, 2006–2007 to 2011–2012, and 2012–2013 to 2016–2017. The first period (2000–2001 to 2005–2006) is considered as the second phase of liberalization, the first phase being 1992–1993 to 2000. The second phase (2006–2007 to 2011–2012) is the period during which the mining boom happened due to rising commodity prices, and also this period has significance as the world witnessed the financial crisis of 2008. The final phase (2012–2013 to 2016–2017) indicates the phase of recovery. Over the entire analysis period, the TFP growth of private firms in the metallic, non-metallic, and coal subsectors was higher than that of the public firms. However, for the petroleum subsector, the situation was quite contradictory. During this phase, the public mining firms' TFP growth was higher than that for private mining firms. It shows that in the petroleum subsector, public firms have consistently shown higher productivity than private firms. On the other hand, as far as the coal subsector is concerned, the public firms showed poor productivity growth. One of the possible reasons why the public firms have performed better than the private firms in terms of productivity growth in the petroleum subsector could be due to the persistence of limited competition and the high regulation of private firms.

The above discussion points to the existence of a productivity gap between public and private firms. This productivity gap may have arisen due to factors such as differences in age and initial productivity level of firms. The age of the firms might cause differences in the productivity of public and private firms (Ehrlich et al., 1994). To confirm this, we have estimated a multivariate regression model where TFP levels are expressed as dependent variables and lagged values of TFP level, age, and ownership of firm as independent variables. The regression model is shown in equation (17):

$$P_{it} = \alpha_p P_{i,t-1} + \alpha_A A_{it} + \alpha_o O_i + \eta_i + v_{i,t} \quad (17)$$

$$\text{For } i = 1 \ldots N \text{ and } t = 2 \ldots, T$$

where P_{it} is the log value of TFP levels of firm *i* in period *t*, and *O* is the dummy variable for ownership of firms. The dummy variable takes the value 1 for private-sector firms and zero otherwise. Hence, a positive and significant value for *O* implies that private-sector firms are more productive than their public counterparts. A_{it} is the log value of the age of the firm *i* in period t, $\eta_i + \mathbf{v}_{i,t} = \mathbf{U}_{it}$ is the fixed-effects decomposition of the error term. The above model is autoregressive as the lagged dependent variable has been included as one of the independent variables on the right-hand side of the equation. As we are well aware, in an autoregressive model, the endogeneity problem is the major problem. To address this, we adopt the Blundell and Bond (1998) method, a GMM estimation, which uses lagged differences of P_{it} as instruments for equations in levels along with lagged levels of p_{it} (from second to fifth) for equations in differences. Equation (17) is estimated for the whole mining industry as well as for the four subsectors of the industry separately. The results of this dynamic panel regression are shown in Table 4.7.

From Table 4.7, it can be visualized that the Sargan test statistics imply that the over-identification restrictions are valid, which in turn validates the instruments used. Similarly, the statistics for AR (2) indicate the absence of serial correlation of order two. This satisfies the prerequisite for instrument validity when the second lag has been included in the instrument set. The results reveal that at the industry level, the private mining firms' TFP levels are significantly higher than that of public firms, as the coefficient of Ownership variable (O_i) is positive and significant. A sectorwise analysis also confirms the difference in the metallic, non-metallic, and coal subsectors. However, for the petroleum subsector, TFP levels of the public sector are more than that of the private sector. The results also show that at the industry level, the age of the firm does not significantly

Table 4.7 Results of dynamic panel regression analysis

Dependent variable: P_{it}					
Independent variables	**Model 1**	**Model 2**	**Model 3**	**Model 4**	**Model 5**
	Total industry	**Metallic**	**Non-metallic**	**Coal**	**Petroleum**
$P_{i,t-1}$	0.521* (0.011)	0.281* (0.015)	0.374* (0.03)	0.25* (0.02)	−0.06 (0.27)
A_{it}	0.007 (0.03)	0.32* (0.015)	0.38* (0.07)	0.30* (0.012)	0.36* (0.05)
O_i	0.14** (0.06)	0.18* (0.04)	0.24* (0.05)	0.17* (0.05)	−0.59 (0.31)
Constant	0.91* (0.16)	0.108* (0.001)	0.47* (0.13)	0.15* (0.01)	0.29* (0.11)
Sargan	64.56 (0.85)	0.000 (1.000)	0.000 (1.000)	0.000 (1.000)	0.000 (1.000)
AR (2)	−1.114 (0.259)	0.92 (0.341)	−1.056 (0.276)	−1.043 (0.28)	−0.8 9 (0.381)
Number of observations	972	173	357	329	113

Notes: Standard errors of the two-step GMM estimators have been corrected for small sample bias as in Windmeijer (2005) and are presented in parentheses. Sargan test P-values are in parentheses. *, ** indicate significance at 1% and 5% level, respectively.

Source: Author's estimation.

affect the TFP levels. At the sectoral level, however, the age of the firm positively and significantly affects the TFP levels. As far as lagged TFP levels are concerned, these have a positive and significant influence on the TFP levels of the mining industry as a whole, whereas at the sectoral level, this is true for coal, metallic, and non-metallic mining.

4.6 Discussion

The above findings show that productivity in the mining industry has deteriorated over the years to 2.72% since 2000. The proximate causes of this fall in productivity could be comparatively strong growth in inputs coincident with less output growth. Compositional changes and the poor performance of individual subsectors could be additional factors contributing to this decline in productivity.

Mining, unlike other industries, depends on non-renewable resources as inputs into production. At the same time, it also demands heavy capital investments in building new mining plants, which can take a long time to build and become operational. These two factors may lead to a reduction in factor productivity if not adjusted properly. Therefore, traditional productivity estimates must be interpreted with caution.

Typically, the TFP is interpreted as an indicator of efficiency with which capital and labour inputs are used to generate output of goods and services. Several factors (such as technology, management, skills, and work practices) determine the efficiency of production. However, TFP in mining also is determined by another factor—the input of natural resources. While natural resources are implicitly considered as a major input into mining production, changes in their quality are often ignored in the estimation of standard productivity measurement. This exclusion would not create any issue had the supply of mineral deposits been infinite and quality been homogenous—that is, available without constraint at the same unit cost of extraction. In reality, however, the mineral resources are neither infinite in supply nor of homogenous quality. Rather, non-renewability constrains their supply as the mineral deposits get depleted by continuous extraction. And with the depletion of mineral resources, the accessibility and quality of the remaining resources fall. Initially, in expectation of greater returns, miners focus on high-quality and easily accessible mineral deposits, which costs them less. But as the reserves get depleted, the remaining reserves, which may be of low quality and deeper underground, having more impurities and being in more remote locations, may require large investments in complex extraction techniques.

With the decline in quality and accessibility of mineral deposits, greater efforts are required to extract them in the form of more capital and labour. The additional capital and labour needed per unit of output bring about a fall in the measured productivity. Thus, the conventional measure of TFP that does not consider resource depletion and accounts for only labour, capital, and other inputs provides only a limited measure of productivity. However, it can be said that there exist interdependencies among the natural resource input and other inputs such as physical capital, labour, and other intermediate inputs. The number of inputs required to produce one unit of output varies depending on the accessibility and quality of mineral deposits. For instance, the amount of physical capital, labour, and intermediate inputs required to produce one tonne of iron ore is much lower if the deposits are near the surface than when deposits are deeper underground. Because of this interdependence, variations in quality and characteristics of mineral resources may lead to variations in the TFP. Thus, in particular with the decline in the quality of deposits, the TFP, as conventionally measured, will also decline as more of the purchased units of inputs are required to produce one unit of output. Further, the decline in TFP does not reflect a decline in the technical efficiency of the use of purchased inputs in mining. Instead, it would imply that exogenous factors, such as economic circumstances (higher output prices), make it justified to commit proportionally more input resources to production.

As our study also uses the conventional method of TFP measurement, the measured productivity does not give a true picture. However, if the effects of resource depletion were taken into consideration (i.e. removed) in the measurement, the corresponding measure of TFP would show an improved result in the form of better productivity. The declining trend we have observed in our study over the period (2000–2016) could be less. So, our results in the absence of resource depletion data could provide an overstated figure for the TFP measure.

Apart from the quality of mineral deposits, there is another factor that can influence the TFP estimates. There is generally a long lead time between the mining investment (either in new mine construction or mine expansion) and the output generation. Empirical and other data suggest that the lead time for new mining projects is, on average, around three years. This new investment in mines is immediately registered in the TFP calculation in the form of capital inputs, but lag in output responses can have an immediate negative effect on the TFP. However, this can be nullified by a concomitant positive effect that can occur in future. Moreover, these changes in the TFP brought out by long lead times are temporary and bring in short-term fluctuations, and as such, long lead time does not have a significant effect on our productivity estimates.

4.7 Conclusion

In this chapter, we sought to estimate the TFP of the whole mining industry and its coal, petroleum, metallic, and non-metallic subsectors. The results show that over the entire period of analysis, the TFP growth for the whole industry exhibit a declining trend. The decline in TFP growth is more visible during the period 2006–2011, considered as the mining boom phase. During this phase, the industry witnessed a higher commodity price owing to the mining boom. This increased commodity price could be one of the likely reasons that would explain the reduction in the TFP growth.

This chapter further attempted to examine the effect of ownership on the TFP for the period 2000–2016. The results reveal that private firms were more productive than public firms in three subsectors of the mining industry—metallic, non-metallic, and coal—whereas for the petroleum subsector, the public firms showed superior productivity. The highest productivity difference was recorded in the non-metallic subsector, wherein private firms were two times more productive than the public firms. Metallic and coal subsectors followed suit, where private firms registered more than twice as high productivity than the public firms. It would be worth mentioning here that the findings of this work conform to that of the study made by Das (2012). Though the studies resemble each other in their methodological approach, the novelty of this study lies in its study period, sample, and the variables construction. Use of the same methodology helped us work out that the old model is fully compatible with the new set of updated, latest, and larger data. The results suggest that even after a decade (Das's study was from 1989 to 2005), the productivity gap between the public and private sectors has undergone little change, indicating inherent implications for policymakers. The continuing productivity differential defies the purpose of opening up the mining industry to private-sector participation as it fails to create a healthy competitive environment to give a boost to the public sector.

This productivity gap between the public and private sectors raises questions about the stability of state ownership over time. This is so because the superior performance of the private sector, in terms of productivity, may create the impression that only when a firm is privatized does its productivity become enhanced, as suggested by the public choice and property rights theory. In the long run, this would motivate policymakers to further the privatization process by divesting in the public-sector firms. This is evident from the recent trend concerning the privatization of state-owned enterprises. While such a trend is currently high on the economic reform agenda of the Indian Government for other sectors, it has been extended to sectors like mining as well, as is evident from the recent deregulation of coal-mining companies, which once enjoyed monopoly power. Thus, the stability of the state ownership of mining firms is at stake as public-sector mining firms are experiencing low productivity growth as indicated by our analysis. Unlike the private sector, the public sector is guided by profit and also societal welfare motive. Hence, the role of the public sector vis-a-vis the private sector cannot be negated. However, as the public-sector mining firms show low productivity and currently the Government of India is on a disinvestment and privatization spree, this poses a serious threat to the very existence of the public sector. It cannot be denied that both public- and private-sector mining firms have their predicaments. While the public-sector mining firms are marred by rampant corruption, the private-sector firms indulge in large-scale illegal mining, which ultimately brings down the productivity of the whole mining industry. Nevertheless, notwithstanding the challenges of both sectors, if the best practices employed by both sectors were to be followed, then the Indian mining industry would experience a high growth rate. Thus, this chapter calls for the attention of the decision-makers involved in mining policymaking to implement the best practices of both sectors to gain maximum leverage from this industry. However, as our results suggest that the public-sector mining firms are experiencing low productivity growth, this necessarily calls for the policymakers to take appropriate and requisite steps to strengthen the public-sector firms by identifying the causes of their slow productivity.

The probable reasons for the low productivity of public-sector firms could be found in the public choice and property rights theory. According to the public choice theory, public-sector firms perform inefficiently due to the agency problem, which states that there is a difference in ownership (principals) and management (agents) in the case of a public-sector enterprise. As managers have more, and better, information than owners, there is every chance that they can take undue advantage of this information asymmetry and undertake wasteful projects in their own self-interest. In the absence of proper monitoring by the owners, managers misuse their status for personal gain at the expense of the investor's interest (Li and Xia, 2008). Inefficient performance can also result from a lack of incentives at the organizational and individual levels. At the organizational level, unlike private firms, the managers of public firms are seldom concerned about organizational improvements. The losses of these firms are very often adjusted through budgetary support, giving the public firm managers least incentive to perform efficiently. Often, to accomplish their political career objectives, public-sector managers give importance to employment generation at the cost of efficiency. On the individual front, fixed tenure and pay scale do not provide much incentive to public-sector managers to perform efficiently. As their salaries are not linked to profit and they have an assurance of a fixed tenure, they do not put in much effort to improve organisation. Besides incentives and agency problems, the low productivity of public-sector firms can stem from property rights. As ownership in the case of public firms is diffused through all members of society, and no member has the right to sell his or her property, there is little incentive for owners to monitor the behaviour of managers. On the contrary, the ownership of private firms is concentrated among fewer individuals, and each individual has the right to sell his or her property shares. This gives the owners the incentive to keep a watch on the management to ensure better productivity. Apart from the above-mentioned issues, several other reasons (such as inadequate and unskilled manpower, absence of upgraded technology, inadequate infrastructural facilities) could be contributing to the low productivity of public-sector mining firms.

The reasons may vary from firm to firm and sector to sector. Since our findings point to the large productivity difference between public and private firms, as the previous study did (Das, 2012), it implies that the findings of the previous research have not been effectively implemented to bridge the gap between the two types of firm. Thus, all these pertinent causes provide us with enough impetus to call for policymakers to take the necessary steps in the form of giving incentives to the public firms, improving infrastructural facilities, upgrading manpower by providing training and learning opportunities, facilitating better and improved technologies so that they can improve their productivity levels, and thereby allowing them to stand up to the private firms in terms of competitiveness.

Appendix A4

Measurement of Capital

The database provides a firm's gross fixed asset (GFA) at historical cost. In many of our studies, especially in productivity-related studies, we use capital as a variable. However, it is a herculean task to estimate capital accurately. Generally, capital stock is valued at historic cost, which is known as the book value of capital. However, we need the present value of capital stock at constant prices for analysis. One of the methods to obtain this present value is by applying the perpetual inventory method (PIM), which is used in this book to estimate data on capital stock. As a first step to this, given GFA values are revalued at the replacement cost with 2009–2010 as the benchmark year. For estimating the revaluation factor, we have followed the method used by Srivastava (1996). This book uses the GFA rather than the net fixed asset because depreciation charges in the Indian industry are highly arbitrary, fixed by income tax authorities and hardly representing actual consumption. The detailed methodology of capital stock estimation (GFA) is presented below.

Estimation of Capital Stock Using the PIM

To estimate the capital stock from GFA, we have assumed the following:

1. **Selection of the Base year**
   For our data, the base year is 2009 (our study period is from 2000 to 2016). This is due to the availability of a greater number of observations in this year. We assume that the earliest vintage in the capital occurs from 1984, or the year of incorporation if it is after 1984. This specific year was chosen because the life of machinery and tools is assumed to be twenty-five years for the mining industry.
2. We assume that the price of capital changes at a constant rate $\Pi = P_t / P_{t-1}$ from 1984 or the year of incorporation up to 2009. The values of Π are arrived at from a series of price deflators constructed from the Central Statistics Office's (CSO's) data on gross fixed

capital formation (GFCF) published in various issues of *National accounts of statistics* (NAS).

3. Similar to the price of capital, we also assume that the price of investment changes at a constant rate $g = I_t / I_{t-1}$. The growth rate of fixed capital formation at 2004–2005 constant prices, taken from various issues of NAS, is applied to the case of all the firms.
4. Based on the value of $\prod$ and g, we estimate the 'revaluation factor', R^G, defined by Srivastava (1996) as

$$R^G = \frac{[(1+g)^{t=1} - 1](1+\prod)^t[(1+g)(1+\prod) - 1]}{g\{[(1+g)(1+\prod)]^{t+1} - 1\}} \quad (18)$$

5. After the revaluation factor is estimated, we multiply the capital stock in the base year (2009) by this factor to convert the base year capital into capital stock at replacement cost at current prices.
6. The value of capital stock in the benchmark year is then converted to constant prices using the WPI for machinery with the year 2004–2005 as the base.
7. Capital stock in the subsequent year is then estimated by adding the subsequent year's investment, $GFA_t - GFA_{t-1}$ (at constant prices) to the existing stock of capital stock at each point of time using the perpetual inventory method.

Table A4.1 Percentage share of prowess output in the total value of mining output

Years	Total value of output in mining industry, rupees in crores	Total value represented by CMIE data, rupees in crores	% representation by prowess
2000–2001	6,0931	5,1305	84.2
2001–2002	66,878	53,253	79.63
2002–2003	71,382	64,768	90.73
2003–2004	75,018	67,840	90.43
2004–2005	98,934	91,563	92.55
2005–2006	113,354	102,085	90.06
2006–2007	131,023	115,220	87.94
2007–2008	154,622	121,385	78.5
2008–2009	174,133	143,077	82.17
2009–2010	192,108	165,523	86.16
2010–2011	266,623	221,689	83.15
2011–2012	284,149	226,792	79.81
2012–2013	280,006	210,471	75.17
2013–2014	277,413	232,918	83.96
2014–2015	290,588	221,416	76.2
2015–2016	282,966	245,188	86.65
2016–2017	371,100	316,093	85.18

Note: The data used in this table are taken from various issues of the Indian Bureau of Mines (IBM) Publication *Indian Mineral Industry—at a glance*. The data published by the Central Statistical Organisation (CSO) in its Annual Survey of Industries provides only a part of the total value of mineral production.

Source: Author's estimation.

Table A4.2 Summary statistics of the variables used in the analysis

Years	Real output value in crore		Labour		Fuel and energy in crores		Capital stock crores	
	Average	SD	Average	SD	Average	SD	Average	SD
2000–2001	393.9	2993.4	37.9	220.7	11.3	53.2	1,044.6	10754.7
2001–2002	431.1	3387.6	44.6	250.1	11.1	49.9	1,015.5	10182.2
2002–2003	409.2	3209.5	37.5	222.1	10.5	51.8	1,028.4	10185.4
2003–2004	555.3	4700.3	41.7	236.8	10.7	48.0	992.8	10129.0
2004–2005	557.3	4354.1	41.4	231.9	9.8	43.0	996.8	9846.9
2005–2006	354.6	2899.2	42.5	236.7	9.0	39.4	915.5	8676.1
2006–2007	339.0	2691.3	43.0	243.1	9.1	41.6	1,070.4	11218.0
2007–2008	325.2	2691.7	43.6	248.4	47.9	273.2	973.0	9886.5
2008–2009	338.4	2534.4	48.5	285.5	10.2	46.5	982.1	9914.8
2009–2010	304.3	2236.5	50.8	282.8	10.5	51.6	1,026.4	10289.4
2010–2011	290.7	1966.0	50.7	273.6	12.0	55.4	1,280.4	13726.2
2011–2012	273.3	1789.5	52.5	282.7	9.8	47.0	1,124.7	11382.4
2012–2013	250.8	1619.9	60.5	319.6	11.6	54.6	1,117.7	11382.3
2013–2014	259.5	1635.8	56.3	290.5	13.4	64.7	1170.0	11492.6
2014–2015	268.4	1671.8	58.4	308.4	16.1	76.8	1,194.1	12288.5
2015–2016	303.1	1861.9	58.0	306.5	20.0	96.5	1,214.3	11559.6
2016–2017	413.1	2582.5	140.5	780.3	14.2	71.4	2,98.0	1488.5

Source: Author's estimation.

5

Technical Efficiency Estimation of the Coal-Mining Sector

5.1 Introduction

The concept of technical efficiency dates back to neoclassical economics. The basic concept of measuring technical efficiency is concerned with defining a production technology.

As such, there are four different production technologies—isoquants, production functions, cost functions, and profit functions—that provide four different tools for measuring technical efficiency.

Although the analytical procedure for the above four different functions is different, the basic approach underlying them is the same, and ideally, the results emerging out of them are expected to converge.

The basic premise underlying the technical efficiency measurement is that there is a gap between a firm's actual and potential level of technical performance. Thus, technical efficiency is defined as the ability and willingness of a firm to produce the maximum possible output from a given level of input and technology (Kalirajan and Shand, 1999).

This chapter intends to measure the technical efficiency of coal-mining firms and find out the factors that influence the technical efficiency of coal-mining companies.

The choice of the coal-mining subsector is due to its volume of contribution to the production of the whole mining industry. The reason behind not calculating the technical efficiency of the entire mining industry is that the Indian mining industry is an amalgamation of different subsectors, and the production technologies used within these subsectors are different from one another. If we were to use the entire industry data for technical efficiency estimation, it might result in biased results. Thus, we have refrained from estimating the technical efficiency for the entire

The Indian Mining Industry. Meenakshi Parida and S. Madheswaran, Oxford University Press.
 DOI: 10.1093/9780198954392.003.0005

mining industry, instead focusing on one of the major subsectors of the mining industry for technical efficiency estimation, that is, coal.

The rest of the chapter is organized as follows. Section 5.2 provides a detailed description of the methodology, while section 5.3 discusses the data. Section 5.4 presents the empirical findings, and section 5.5 concludes the chapter.

5.2 Methodology

For estimating the technical efficiency (TE), this chapter uses the stochastic frontier analysis (SFA) approach. The detailed methodology is described below.

Drawing on Aigner et al. (1977) and Meeusen and Van den Broeck (1977), a stochastic frontier production function can be expressed as

$$\mathbf{Y}_{it} = f\left(x_{it}, \beta, t\right) exp\left(v_{it}\right) exp\left(-u_{it}\right) \qquad (1)$$

where $\mathbf{Y}_{it}$ is the output of the ith firm ($i = 1, 2, 3 \ldots, N$) in the t th period ($t = 1, 2, 3 \ldots T$); $f(.)$ is the production function; x is an input vector; and three inputs (labour, capital, and energy) are used in the production process. It is noteworthy here that due to the systemic unavailability of data for raw materials across subsectors and over time, this variable is not included in the production process. It is the time trend index that is the proxy for the technological change, and $\boldsymbol{u} \geq 0$ is the output-orientated technical inefficiency. Thus, this model is able to capture the technical inefficiency present in a production unit through the error term $\boldsymbol{u}_{it.}$ Technical inefficiency is the inability of a production unit to produce the maximum level of output due to factors under the control of the unit. The technical inefficiency error term can take the value of either zero or some positive value. When the technical inefficiency error is zero, it means that the production unit is fully efficient for achieving the maximum feasible output. This model can also capture the stochastic nature of the production process through the error term $\boldsymbol{v}_{it}$, which arises due to factors beyond the control of the production unit, such as climate conditions, natural disasters, and weather conditions. These two error terms—$\boldsymbol{u}_{it}$ and $\boldsymbol{v}_{it}$—independently and identically distributed to each other and the inputs.

From the above model, the TE is estimated as follows:

$$TE_{it} = exp\left(-u_{it}\right) \tag{2}$$

The TE is derived by taking the ratio of actual output to the maximum possible output, which is shown by the above term.

5.2.1 Functional Form

For our estimation purposes, we have considered the time-varying stochastic production frontier, originally proposed by Aigner, Lovell, and Schmidt (1977) in translog form as

$$lny_{it} = \alpha_o + \sum_j \alpha_j lnx_{jit} + \alpha_t t + \frac{1}{2}\sum_j \sum_i \beta_{ji} lnx_{jit} lnx_{lit}$$
$$+ \frac{1}{2}\beta_{tt} t^2 + \sum_j t\beta_{tj} lnx_{lit} + v_{it} + u_{it} \tag{3}$$

where y_{it} is the observed output of the ith firm in the t th period. $\boldsymbol{x}$ represents the input vector with the parameter α. In equation (3), t represents the time trend. The two error components are represented by v_{it} and u_{it}, respectively. Among the two error terms, u represents production loss due to observation-specific technical inefficiency. Thus, it is always greater than or equal to zero, and v_{it} is also assumed to be independently and identically distributed as $N\left(0, \sigma_v^2\right)$.

v_{it} represents the error that is beyond the control of production unit and captures the error due to the omitted variable, wrong functional form, and measurement errors in the specified model.

The translog frontier production function as specified in equation (3) is rewritten for three inputs—labour, energy, and capital—in the following form:

$$lnY_{it} = \alpha_o + \alpha_l lnL_{it} + \alpha_k lnK_{it} + \alpha_e lnE_{it} + \frac{1}{2}\beta_{ll}(lnL_{it})^2 + \frac{1}{2}\beta_{kk}(lnK_{it})^2$$
$$+ \frac{1}{2}\beta_{ee}(lnE_{it})^2 + \beta_{lk}(lnL_{it})(lnK_{it}) + \beta_{ke}(lnK_{it})(lnE_{it})$$
$$+ \beta_{le}(lnL_{it})(lnE_{it}) + \beta_{tl}(lnL_{it})t + \beta_{tk}(lnK_{it})t + \beta_{te}(lnE_{it})t$$
$$+ \alpha_t t + \frac{1}{2}\beta_{tt} t^2 + (V_{it} - U_{it}) \tag{4}$$

where Y_{it} is the gross value of the output of the *i*th firm over a time period *t*. *K*, *L*, and *E* are the input variables such as capital labour and energy, respectively. The above specification of the model allows for estimating both technical progress and time-varying TE. The translog specification of the production frontier allows for non-neutral technical progress (TP). TP will be neutral if all β_{tj}'s are equal to zero, and the production function will be reduced to the Cobb–Douglas function with neutral TP if all the β's are equal to zero.

The technical inefficiency term, U_{it}, is assumed to be non-negative truncation of the normal distribution $N(\mu, \sigma_v^2)$, and can be modelled (following Battese and Coelli, 1992; Greene, 1997, p. 119) to be the product of an exponential function of time as

$$U_{it} = \eta_t u_i = exp\left[-\eta(t-T)\right]u_i \quad \text{i}=1\ldots\text{N};\ \text{t}=1\ldots\text{T} \qquad (5)$$

In equation (5), the unknown parameter, η, represents the rate of change in technical inefficiency, and the non-negative random variable u_i, is the technical inefficiency effect for the *i*th production unit in the past year of the data set. Thus, the technical inefficiency effects in previous periods are deterministic exponential functions of the inefficiency effects for the corresponding forms in the final period (i.e. $u_{it} = u_i$), given the data for the *i*th production unit are available in the final period. So, the production unit with a positive η value tends to improve its TE over a period and vice versa. However, a zero value η implies that the technical inefficiency is time-invariant.

In the above mode, the TE can be observed through the ratio of the actual output to the potential output as determined by the production frontier. So, the TE of the *i* th firm in the *t* th period can be estimated as

$$TE_{it} = exp(-u_{it}) \qquad (6)$$

The technical efficiency change is the change in TE.

Similarly, technological progress can be estimated by taking the partial differentiation of the production function concerning time:

$$TP_{it} = \frac{\partial \boldsymbol{lnY}_{it}}{\partial \boldsymbol{t}} = \alpha_t + \beta_{tl}(lnL_{it}) + \beta_{tk}(lnK_{it}) + \beta_{te}(lnE_{it}) + \beta_{tt}t \qquad (7)$$

For estimating the TE of coal-mining firms, we employ the SFA. In the SFA method, the production function reflects the maximum possible output a production unit can achieve with the available inputs and technology.

5.3 Data

We estimate the TE for the coal-mining subsector. The data for this is collected from the same source, that is, the Centre for Monitoring the Indian Economy (CMIE) Prowess database. Our sample includes firms from the coal-mining subsector. We selected firms primarily on the basis of the availability of data. Firms having data for at least four years in sequence were included in the analysis. The study is based on the available data from twenty-one coal-mining firms operating in mineral extraction activities from 2000 to 2016.

5.4 Results

The present chapter estimates the TE in the context of Indian coal-mining companies from 2000–2001 to 2016–2017. All the estimations in the study were undertaken using Frontier 4.1 and the statistical software STATA 15. Using Frontier 4.1, the maximum likelihood estimates for the parameters of the stochastic frontier model were estimated.

As we know, accurate productivity growth results would emerge when modelling the inefficiency effect is appropriate. Wrong modelling of the inefficiency effect would lead to biased results, thereby misguiding the researcher in its interpretation and analysis. To overcome this problem, we tested alternative possible specifications of the production frontier and inefficiency effect. Following Battese and Coelli (1992), we estimated seven alternative models to validate the modelling of the inefficiency effect. The unrestricted model 1.0 and seven restricted models were estimated to choose the appropriate functional form to check the validity of the technical inefficiency effects and technical change captured by a time trend. Model 1.0 consists of all parameters and is based on a stochastic translog frontier production function in which technical inefficiency effects, u_{it}, have the time varying structure that follows a truncated normal distribution. Model 1.1 is the stochastic Cobb–Douglas frontier production function with Hicks-neutral technical change and time-varying technical inefficiency effects. Model 1.2 is the stochastic translog frontier production function with the absence of technical change and having time-varying inefficiency effects. Model 1.3 is the stochastic translog frontier production function with Hicks-neutral technical change and time-varying inefficiency effects. Model 1.4 is the traditional specification of translog production frontier with zero inefficiency effects; that is, production is assumed to be fully efficient. Model 1.5 is a special case of model 1.0 in which the inefficiency term, u_{it}, follows a half-normal distribution. Model 1.6 is also a special case of Model 1.0 in which the inefficiency term is time-invariant (Battese and Coelli, 1995; Battese et al. 1989). Model 1.7 is another special case of Model 1.0 wherein the u_{it} is time-invariant and follows half-normal distribution. All the models explained above were estimated using Frontier 4.1, and the results are presented in Table 5.1.

The selection of the appropriate model from all the above models was done through likelihood-ratio (LR) tests. Table 5.2 reports the test statistics of various null hypotheses. The null hypotheses were tested using LR tests. The test statistic for the LR test is $\lambda = -2[L(H_0) - L(H_1)]$, where $L(H_0)$ and $L(H_1)$ become the values of the log-likelihood function under the null hypothesis and alternative hypothesis, respectively. If the null hypothesis is true, then λ has a chi-square distribution (or mixed chi-square) distribution with degrees of freedom equal to the number of restrictions. Given the specifications of the functional form of the production frontier and the results of LR statistics, the selected model is Model 1.5. It can be seen from Table 5.2 that most of the coefficients obtained in Model 1.5 were significant at the 1% level.

The results presented in Tables 5.1 and 5.2 reveal that the stochastic frontier production function is time-varying. Also, the non-fulfilment of the Hicks neutrality test reveals that the technical change in the Indian coal-mining industry involves a technical bias. It can be observed from Table 5.1 that the coefficients of $t(lnL)$ and $t(lnK)$ are positive, while that of $t(lnE)$ is negative and significant at the 1% level. This implies that technological progress in the Indian coal-mining industry involves

Table 5.1 Panel frontier models with different specifications

Variable	Model 1.0	Model 1.1	Model 1.2	Model 1.3	Model 1.4	Model 1.5	Model 1.6	Model 1.7
Const	-6.85*	5.11*	-2.73***	-8.11*	-8.72*	-8.72*	-6.11*	-5.44**
	(-5.15)	(16.21)	(-1.87)	(-6.12)	(-7.89)	(-5.76)	(-3.44)	(-4.11)
Ln L	-0.34	0.38*	-0.21	-0.31	0.83*	0.67	-0.13	-0.05
	(-0.84)	(7.89)	(-0.59)	(-0.87)	(4.02)	(3.25)	(-0.53)	(-0.27)
Ln E	0.82*	0.62*	0.81*	0.54**	-0.25	0.71*	0.76*	8.62*
	(3.45)	(13.69)	(3.14)	(2.04)	(-1.03)	(3.53)	(4.06)	(5.15)
Ln K	3.51*	-0.17*	2.31*	3.48*	3.27*	3.44*	2.98*	3.10*
	(8.26)	(-2.64)	(5.11)	(9.25)	(9.98)	(8.68)	(6.40)	(6.19)
(Ln L)2	0.08	–	0.11***	0.13*	-0.17*	0.07	0.08	0.07
	(1.57)		(1.79)	(2.66)	(-2.97)	(1.50)	(1.52)	(1.56)
(Ln E)2	-0.31*	–	-0.28*	-0.17*	-0.02	-0.21*	-0.34*	-0.04*
	(-4.35)		(-6.78)	(-3.53)	(-0.30)	(-2.98)	(-5.99)	(-5.91)
(Ln K)2	-0.84*	–	-0.61*	-0.82*	-0.61*	-0.75*	-0.68*	-0.76*
	(11.96)		(-6.89)	(-12.1)	(-11.49)	(-11.89)	(-8.98)	(-9.57)
lnLlnE	-0.15*	–	-0.17*	-0.16*	0.02	-0.15*	-0.11*	-0.12*
	(-3.34)		(-4.98)	(-5.82)	(0.49)	(-3.36)	(-3.71)	(-3.99)
lnLlnK	0.12*	–	0.13*	0.13*	0.01	0.12*	-0.08***	0.08***
	(2.65)		(3.41)	(2.79)	(0.16)	(3.10)	(1.96)	(1.79)
lnElnk	0.27*	–	0.28*	0.21*	0.15*	0.23*	0.30*	0.28*
	(6.41)		(5.98)	(5.67)	(2.87)	(5.56)	(6.81)	(7.01)
t	0.01	0.001	–	0.05*	-0.03	0.002	-0.03	-0.03
	(0.43)	(0.08)		(4.01)	(-1.02)	(0.33)	(-1.08)	(-1.31)
t2	-0.005	–	–	-0.003	-0.003**	-0.004	-0.004***	-0.006
	(-1.13)			(0.76)	(-2.26)	(-1.36)	(-1.87)	(-1.65)
(lnL)t	-0.003	–	–	–	0.006	0.003*	-0.004***	0.004
	(-0.06)				(0.69)	(-2.85)	(1.78)	(1.49)
(lnE)t	-0.006*	–	–	–	-0.006***	-0.002*	-0.003*	-0.002*
	(-2.87)				(-1.59)	(-2.87)	(-2.79)	(-3.01)
(lnk)t	0.02*	–	–	–	0.01*	0.01*	0.01*	0.01*
	(2.56)				(3.05)	(2.62)	(3.35)	(3.34)
σ2	1.00***	0.51*	0.40*	0.69*	0.31	1.52*	0.67***	1.06**
	(1.78)	(5.52)	(5.43)	(2.96)		(3.12)	(1.78)	(2.05)
γ	0.92*	0.76**	0.79*	0.87*	–	0.96*	0.91*	0.94*
	(25.1)	(2.56)	(13.96)	(27.76)		(51.9)	(20.79)	(23.98)
μ	0.50	1.13*	1.03**	1.48*	–	0.000	0.82**	0.000
	(0.82)	(8.11)	(2.48)	(4.02)			(2.01)	
η	-0.004*	0.01**	0.05**	-0.02*	–	-0.03*	0.000	0.000
	(-4.06)	(1.96)	(2.07)	(-3.54)		(-5.10)		
log-likelihood	-97.63	-189.21	-135.32	-103.73	-298.67	-97.89	-106.76	-107.65

Note: (1) The dependent variable for frontier estimation is $\ln y_{it}$ and a total number of observations is 330. (2) The values in parentheses below the coefficients show the t-statistics. (3) *, **, and *** show the 1%, 5%, and 10% level of significance, respectively.

Source: Author's estimation.

Table 5.2 Tests of hypothesis for modelling inefficiency and appropriate functional forms

Models	Null hypothesis	Test statistics (λ)	χ^2 0.01	χ^2 0.05	Decision
Model 1.1	All $\beta_s = 0$	183.16	23.2	18.3	Reject H0
Model 1.2	$\alpha_t = \beta_{tt} = \beta_{tL} = \beta_{tE} = \beta_{tK=0}$	75.38	15.08	11.07	Reject H0
Model 1.3	$\beta_{tL} = \beta_{tE} = \beta_{tK} = 0$	12.2	11.34	7.81	Reject H0
Model 1.4	$\gamma = \mu = \eta = 0$	402.08	10.5	7.04	Reject H0
Model 1.5	$\mu = 0$	0.52	6.63	3.84	Accept H0
Model 1.6	$\eta = 0$	18.26	6.63	3.84	Reject H0
Model 1.7	$\mu = \eta = 0$	20.04	9.21	5.99	Reject H0

Source: Author's estimation.

labour and capital use but energy-saving bias. As per the definition of the direction of technical change given by Berndt (1990), technological change is input *i*-saving (or input *i*-using) if the proportional savings on the *i*th input is greater than (or less than) the average proportional savings over all inputs.

Technological progress is input *i*-neutral if the proportional savings on the *i*th input just equals the average proportional savings over all inputs (Berndt, 1990). Thus, according to this definition, capital-using technological change does not mean that capital per unit of output has increased due to this capital-using technical change; rather, it implies that the relative use of capital compared with other inputs has increased and, as a consequence, proportional saving in capital has been less than average proportional savings over all inputs.

Further, the results reveal that the Indian coal-mining industry involves a labour-using bias. The possible explanation for this could be due to the advent of the National Mineral Policy (NMP) 2008; most of the coal-mining companies were going for technological upgradation that required skilled labour in the form of engineers and trained personnel. Thus, firms were spending a huge amount on human capital by paying higher salaries. As we measured labour input in terms of wages and salaries, this higher spending may have led to labour-using technical

Table 5.3 Direction of technological change in the Indian coal-mining industry, 2000–2001 to 2016–2017

Input	Direction of technological change
Labour	Using
Energy	Saving
Capital	Using

Source: Author's estimation.

change. Table 5.3 summarizes the direction of technical change concerning each input.

5.4.1 TE of Coal-Mining Companies

By using the Battese and Coelli (1995) specification of Model 2, we estimated the average TE scores for coal-mining companies to show the trends in TE over time. The estimated average TE scores, which were directly given by the Frontier 4.1 programme, are presented in Table 5.4.

Table 5.4 indicates that the estimated average TE of the mining companies is as high as 0.75. This implies that the companies are operating at 75% of their potential output, which is determined by the Frontier technology. Table 5.4 also represents a low average efficiency score for 2000 compared with 2015 and 2016. The major reason behind the low average efficiency for 2000 in comparison to 2015 and 2016 was due to low output production by each firm. The statistical test suggests that the TE of mining companies is time-variant; that is, over time, technical efficiency change (TEC) is statistically significant. However, it can be seen from Table 5.4 that although the coal-mining companies are operating at as high as 75% of their potential output, none of them can follow the best practice technique and thereby attain 100% efficiency. Possible reasons for this could be the unavailability of advanced machinery and equipment; most of the machinery and equipment used by these coal-mining companies are borrowed from abroad. On the other hand, because of the poor infrastructure of the coal-mining companies, limited research and development (R&D) facilities, lack of adequate technology support

Table 5.4 Average TE estimates for coal-mining companies

Years	Average efficiency scores (%)
2000	70
2001	69
2002	72
2003	73
2004	75
2005	78
2006	76
2007	67
2008	67
2009	65
2010	64
2011	79
2012	86
2013	82
2014	82
2015	86
2016	89
Average (2000–2016)	75

Note: The efficiency scores are rounded off to zero decimal points.

Source: Author's estimation.

services, and lack of skilled personnel, the borrowed technology is not properly absorbed and adapted by the coal-mining companies, as a consequence of which the machines and equipment cannot be properly utilized to attain the maximum feasible efficiency of production.

However, as these companies are operating at 75% of their potential output, there is every possibility that the TE can be improved once the obstacles to achieving 100% efficiency are mitigated. It requires appropriate government policy action in the form of building good infrastructure (such as roads and other transportation facilities), inviting investment (both public and private) for improving the R&D facilities of these firms, and devising a long-term training programme for facilitating the local personnel with the appropriate skill sets to equip them with the requisite knowledge.

5.4.2 Distribution of Coal-Mining Firms Based on TE Scores

We also classified the coal firms into three types based on their TE scores obtained from the stochastic frontier model. Firms with less than 50% TE were termed as inefficient, with 50–75% TE categorized as medium efficient, and firms having more than 75% TE scores considered highly efficient. Table 5.5 shows the classification of firms as per their TE performance.

It can be observed from Table 5.5 that the coal subsector is dominated by the presence of medium and highly efficient firms over the entire period of analysis. The presence of inefficient firms is less in proportion as compared with the other two categories.

To visualize the situation properly, we present the pictorial representation of Table 5.5 in Fig. 5.1. It illustrates that the percentage of inefficient firms is significantly lower than the other two categories. The distribution

Table 5.5 Distribution of firms according to TE scores, 2000–2016

Years	Inefficient	Medium efficient	Highly efficient
2000–2001	4.1	72.8	23.1
2001–2002	2.2	65.1	32.7
2002–2003	2.7	81.3	16
2000–2004	1.3	79.6	19.1
2004–2005	0	82.4	17.6
2005–2006	2.4	52.5	45.1
2006–2007	7.2	41.7	51.1
2007–2008	3.2	50.8	46
2008–2009	8.1	57.3	34.6
2009–2010	7.9	75	17.1
2010–2011	8.6	77.2	14.2
2011–2012	5.6	32.3	62.1
2012–2013	6.8	31.7	61.5
2013–2014	4.7	28.6	66.7
2014–2015	3.6	34.4	62
2015–2016	2.1	42.8	55.1
2016–2017	6.8	39.1	54.1

Source: Author's estimation.

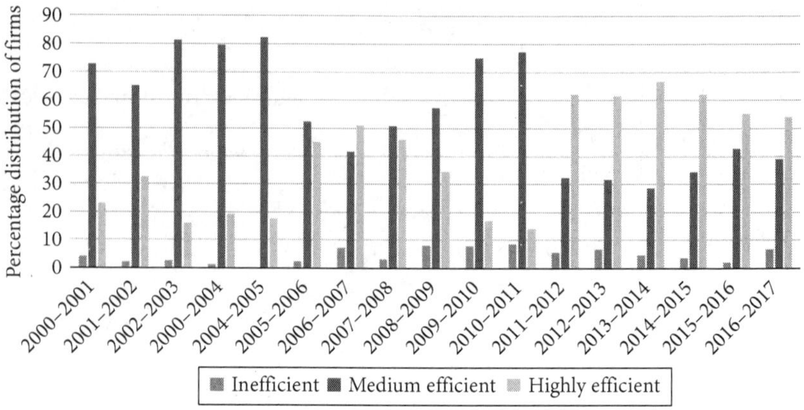

Fig. 5.1 Distribution of coal firms (%) based on technical efficiency
Source: Author's estimation.

of medium and highly efficient firms does not follow any specific pattern. Rather, in some years, medium-efficient firms are high in proportion, while in other years, the proportion of highly efficient firms is greater. It is clear from Fig. 5.1 that a considerable proportion of firms falls under the medium-efficient category, indicating thereby that there is a lot of scope for firms to improve their efficiency and move up the ladder to the highly efficient category. The presence of inefficient firms over the years also calls for the attention of policymakers to adopt appropriate strategies to level up their efficiencies (Fig. 5.1). Percentage distribution of coal firms based on technical efficiency.

5.4.3 Distribution of TE Based on Size

Further, we attempted to understand the distribution of TE based on the size of the firms (Table 5.6). We found that most of the small-size firms were inefficient. We defined all the firms into three sizes—small, medium, and large. The firms having a fixed asset value of less than rupees 50 crore were considered small-size firms, while firms having a fixed asset value of rupees 50–100 crore were classified as medium-size firms. Finally, firms with a fixed asset value of more than rupees 100 crore were termed as large-sized firms. This classification was made based on the available value of fixed-asset data for the year 2000. We found that most of

Table 5.6 Average TE scores based on the size of the firm

Size	TE
Small	0.46
Medium	0.74
Large	0.81

Source: Author's estimation.

the small-sized firms were inefficient. The distribution of the average TE of coal-mining firms based on the size is given in Table 5.6.

It can be seen from Table 5.6 that large firms have a higher TE (81%) than medium and small-sized firms. This may be because large firms can diversify their business into many areas by taking advantage of economies of scale and scope. This allows them to be more efficient in their performance as against smaller firms. Large firms may utilize their resources (financial and non-finance) more efficiently in the production process. Thus, we found a positive correlation between the size and efficiency of firms. Almost all the firms having an inefficiency score of less than 0.50 belonged to the small-size group, with a small scale of operation. On the contrary, most of the medium and large firms were either medium or highly efficient.

5.4.4 Factors Leading to Inter-Firm Variations in TE

This chapter also attempted to estimate the observed variations in TE across firms during our study period. For this, we employed regression analysis, where TE was considered as the dependent variable and various firm-specific factors were taken as independent variables. The major firm-specific variables considered for this book are described below.

5.4.4.1 Size

One of the important factors that leads to inter-firm variations in efficiency is the size of the firm. The size of the firm is an important determinant in the sense that large-sized firms can expand their business, diversify it in many areas, and thereby exploit the economies of scale and scope. By taking advantage of this, they can make their operation more effective, which ultimately allows them to create superior performance relative to the smaller firms (Penrose, 1959). On the contrary, size is correlated with market power (Shepherd, 1986), which enhances the possibility of generating X-inefficiency in production, leading to relatively poor performance (Leibenstein, 1976). Hence, the theory is inconclusive and ambiguous concerning the relationship between firm size and its performance. In this context, it is therefore worth examining how firm size affects the productive efficiency of coal-mining companies. For this purpose, we considered the value of output as a proxy for a firm's size.

5.4.4.2 Age

Another factor that may significantly influence the performance of firms in terms of efficiency is age. However, the theory does not provide any unique relationship between age and the performance of the firm. Some studies suggest that older firms exhibit better performance than younger ones due to their experience (Stinchcombe, 1965). On the other hand, some studies have found that older firms suffer from inertia and cannot rapidly adapt to changing economic circumstances, as a result of which they show poorer performance than the younger firms (Marshall, 1920). In this book, we have measured a firm's age by taking the difference between that particular year and the firm's incorporation year.

5.4.4.3 Labour productivity

The quality of the labour force may affect the performance of a firm to a great extent. To measure the labour quality, we used the variable labour productivity (LPROD), which is given by output per unit of wages and salaries. It is expected that a higher-quality labour force would lead to better performance of the firm in terms of more productivity and efficiency.

5.4.4.4 Capital–energy ratio

Sometimes, energy saving and the resultant improved productivity may become a capital-intensive process, and hence, in that sense, a higher capital–energy ratio would be associated with higher productivity. However, the literature is quite unclear about the relationship between capital and energy. In some cases, capital and energy act as substitutes, whereas in some other cases, they complement each other. Thus, we included the capital–energy ratio (KE) as an independent variable that could have either a positive or negative coefficient.

5.4.4.5 Ownership

Ownership patterns may also have an impact on the efficiency performance of the firm. To examine whether or not private-sector firms are more efficient than public sector firms, we used a dummy variable (D_1), which takes the value '1' for private-sector firms and zero otherwise. A positive and significant coefficient of D_1 indicates that private-sector firms are more efficient than public-sector firms.

5.4.4.6 Policy dummy

To examine whether or not the policy change in the form of complete openness of the mining sector in India in 2006 had any possible impact on the productive efficiency of mining firms, we used another dummy variable (D_2), which takes the value zero for all the years before 2006 and 1 otherwise. A positive and significant coefficient of D_2 implies an improvement in TE after 2006.

To determine those factors from among the ones above that most influenced productive efficiency, a panel data regression model was considered. This was because the panel data model is a powerful tool to help control dependencies of unobserved independent variables, which can lead to biased estimators in simple linear regression models.

A panel data model was specified hypothesizing a functional relationship between productive efficiency and its various determinants, as explained above. The panel data model was used to control for individual heterogeneity of the firms. Moreover, the panel data model provided more information, greater variability, a greater degree of freedom, and greater efficiency. The panel data model is specified in equation (8):

$$\left(TE_{it}\right) = \alpha + \beta \boldsymbol{X}_{it} + \mu_i + \lambda_t + \epsilon_{it} \tag{8}$$

where *TE* is considered the dependent variable; αs and βs are the parameters to be estimated; x_{it} is the vector of explanatory variables, which includes the dummy variables; μ_i is the time-invariant, firm-specific factors that influence efficiency; and λ_t is the firm-invariant, time-specific factors that affect efficiency. ε_{it} is the disturbance term, which is assumed to be homoscedastic and non-auto-correlated.

Firms are denoted by subscript $i = 1, 2 \ldots 21$ and time by $t = 1, 2 \ldots 17$.

After doing the model specification, we estimated the two-panel data models and fixed-effect and random-effect models to find out which was best suited for our objective. Out of these two models, the appropriate model was chosen based on the Hausman test (Hausman, 1978). The Hausman test is used to differentiate between fixed-effect and random-effect models in panel analysis, where random effects (RE) are preferred under null hypothesis due to greater efficiency. Since the *p*-value of the Hausman test is more than that of the significance level, we accept the null hypothesis and conclude that random-effect estimators are efficient.

The results of the regression analysis have been provided in Table 5.7. It can be seen from the results that the size variable has a positive and significant coefficient, which implies that the larger the firm size, the greater the performance in terms of efficiency. The age of the firm does not significantly influence the efficiency of the firm. The capital–energy ratio is positive and significant, implying that energy saving, and thereby the resultant energy efficiency, is a capital-intensive process. LPROD has a positive and significant coefficient, implying that firms with greater quality of labour are more efficient. The dummy variable D_1 also has a positive and significant coefficient, indicating that private coal-mining firms are more efficient than their public counterparts. Finally, a positive

Table 5.7 Random effect panel Tobit regression for estimating intra-firm variations in efficiency

Parameter	Coefficients
Intercept	1.7894 (0.96)
Age	–0.03987 (–0.61)
Size	0.5687* (6.32)
Size sq.	–0.0564*(–4.11)
K/E	0.0920*(3.56)
LPROD	0.0552* (4.23)
D_1	0.0670* (3.11)
D_2	0.0592* (3.09)
Log likelihood	182.0645

Note: (1) Figures in parentheses are standard error. (2) * Implies significance at 1% level. (3) Number of observations = 330; chibar2 = 509.75; log likelihood = 182.0645; prob > chi2 = 0.02.

Source: Author's estimation.

and significant value of the variable D_2 denotes that the economic reform in the form of a complete opening up of the mining sector has had a profound impact on achieving more efficiency.

5.5 Conclusion

This chapter estimated the TE of the coal-mining industry using the SFA. The results indicate that the estimated average TE of the mining companies is as high as 0.75, implying that companies are operating at 75% of their potential output, which is determined by the Frontier technology. Thus, there is scope for improving the TE of coal-mining companies in India. The reasons for not achieving 100% efficiency could be explained by the lack of availability of advanced machinery, poor infrastructure of the coal-mining companies, limited R&D facilities, lack of adequate technology support services, and lack of skilled personnel. In this context, we suggest appropriate government policy action in the form of building good infrastructure (such as roads and other transportation facilities), inviting investment (both public and private) for improving R&D facilities of these firms, and devising a long-term training programme for facilitating the local personnel with the appropriate skill sets to equip them with requisite knowledge as prerequisites for improving the technical efficiencies of Indian coal firms.

6

Energy Efficiency of the Indian Mining Industry

6.1 Introduction

In Chapter 5, we examined the productivity performance of the Indian mining industry at the industry as well as the subsectoral level. Along with productivity, energy efficiency is considered a key performance dimension when it comes to the performance measurement of any industry. This is because improvement in energy efficiency can have a positive influence on the overall efficiency performance of the industry. So, this calls for an empirical examination of the energy efficiency of the mining industry to search for the energy-saving potential. Thus, the chapter aims to estimate the energy efficiency of the mining industry at four subsectoral levels—coal, petroleum, metallic, and non-metallic mining.

Energy is one of the key factors of production in many industries and, as such, necessitates that it should be used efficiently for the overall growth of the industry. The rapid growth of the globalization process and increase in international competitiveness have created much pressure on the industrial sectors to reduce their production costs and thereby energy-related costs. Besides, a large amount of energy use results in environmental pollution via CO_2 emissions from fossil fuel, which has become a cause of concern for governments all over the world. Therefore, achieving energy-use efficiency assumes the utmost importance in the present scenario. To achieve this, the Government of India enacted the much-needed Energy Conservation Act in 2001. It is envisaged that a unit saved is more than a unit of energy produced, as it saves on production, transportation, transmission, and distribution losses (Mukherjee, 2008). Thus, this undoubtedly calls for an in-depth examination of the nature and magnitude of energy-use inefficiency in various end-use sectors.

The Indian Mining Industry. Meenakshi Parida and S. Madheswaran, Oxford University Press.
 DOI: 10.1093/9780198954392.003.0006

In recent years (excluding the COVID-19 pandemic years of 2020/2021), the Indian economy has grown at an impressive pace. According to World Bank figures, the Indian economy exhibited an economic growth rate of 8% and 8.26% in the years 2015 and 2016, respectively. However, the trajectory of this growth rate was halted by the unprecedented COVID-19 pandemic. Nevertheless, with the receding of the impact of this pandemic, the Government of India aims to bring back the same glorious growth rate of the Indian economy in the immediate future.

However, energy being a key component of production, fulfilment of this goal calls for a large supply of energy by the industrial sectors. Various estimates show that India would have to increase its energy supply by at least three or four times, and its electricity generation by five to six times by 2031 in order to achieve the growth it desires.

According to the Integrated Energy Policy Report (by the Planning Commission), an 8% gross domestic product (GDP) growth rate requires India's total energy to be in the range between 1,536 million tonnes of oil equivalent (MTOE) and 1,887 MTOE by 2031. The non-fulfilment of this energy need would pose a formidable challenge in maintaining sustainable growth. In the wake of this concern over the ever-increasing demand for energy and shortage of fossil fuels in the near future, the goal of achieving improvement in industrial energy efficiency has taken an even greater significance.

In formulating its growth strategy, the Government of India has placed greater emphasis on the growth of the mining industry (as evident from the Make in India Campaign) due to the primary nature of the industry as a basic raw material provider to the manufacturing industry. The prime objective is to achieve growth targets by accelerating the growth of the industrial sectors. This 'industry-driven growth' requires massive energy consumption as India's industrial sector consumes a large proportion of total primary energy, accounting for 4.5% of industrial energy use worldwide (Gielen and Tailor, 2009). With the rapid expansion of this industry, this share is expected to rise further. Such a scenario entails improving the energy-use efficiency to meet the growing energy demand.

Improving energy efficiency is important from various policy perspectives. An important objective is to conserve energy derived from fossil fuels to prevent their depletion in the near future. Improving energy efficiency will also enhance the nation's energy security. Further reduction in energy use, especially from burning fossil fuels, is essential to prevent further deterioration of environmental quality. Another objective for achieving energy efficiency is driven by the underlying economic objective of cost minimization. From a cost-effectiveness standpoint, it is important to reduce energy use during periods of high energy prices and also to suitably substitute other inputs for energy.

Improved energy efficiency is a vital factor for climate change mitigation and sustainable development processes. The connection between climate change, energy efficiency, and sustainable development is circular. There exists a two-way relationship between climate change and sustainable development. On the one hand, climate change impacts key natural and human living conditions and, consequently, the basis for social and economic development. On the other hand, society's priorities on sustainable development influence both the greenhouse gas (GHG) emissions that are causing climate change and vulnerability. Increased GHG emissions are one of the major drivers of the climate change crisis. Energy efficiency is a key and valuable tool to reduce the GHC emissions driving the climate crisis. Energy efficiency is a cost-effective way to obtain decreased energy consumption and carbon emissions, which will lead to climate change mitigation and thereby help create the desired change needed for a better and sustainable future. Thus, it can be said with certainty that the connection between energy efficiency, climate change, and sustainable development makes a full circle.

In the literature, energy efficiency is often analysed in terms of intensity, the ratio of energy to output. This method requires that a suitable aggregate measure of output be defined for the denominator of this ratio, as well as a measure of energy. A fall in the energy intensity implies an improvement in efficiency. Several empirical studies point out energy intensity as an inappropriate measure as it is largely influenced by the aggregation of output and shifts in the composition of that output (Ang and Liu, 2001; 2007; Ang et al., 2004; Boyd and McClelland, 1999; Boyd and Roop 2004; Boyd et al., 1988; Greening et al., 1997; Liu et al., 1992), which influences the measurement in trends of this intensity. A variety of techniques have been applied to decompose the energy intensity into trends of the composition shift and real change in intensity (for details, see Ang and Liu, 2001).

Our study departs from other studies in respect of its different perspectives. In our study, instead of looking at the evolution of the energy intensity (energy/output) ratio over time, we seek to estimate energy efficiency relative to the best practice benchmark, which is the lowest observable energy use in our case. Two approaches are suggested in the literature to identify the benchmark—a theoretical function specified by engineers and an empirical function based on the best observable performance (Farrell, 1957). In this chapter, we employ the second approach suggested by Farrell, an empirical estimate of the best observable industry practice.

Energy is considered as a key component of the production cost of the mineral ores. However, our aim here is to analyse the technical energy efficiency and not to examine the issue of cost-efficiency, so we take a production rather than cost or profit function perspective. It is presumed that a particular level of energy use by a firm implies that it is cost-effective at some relevant price by the firm. Our analysis focuses on monetary measures of outputs and inputs instead of physical measures. This is found to be consistent with a production function interpretation of technical efficiency.

Mining is a process that primarily uses electricity and fuels for production. Since the extraction of ores requires both diesel and electricity for the different processes (blasting, hauling, extraction, and so on), use of combined electricity and diesel is common in this industry. Therefore, it would not be appropriate to measure the efficiency of fuel and electricity use separately, as both energy sources are entangled in a complex manner in the extraction of ores. This is also evident from the aggregate data, which provides the total energy consumption (both electricity and fuel) by individual plants instead of disaggregated figures of energy use. Our study also considers this data as it is and does not attempt to disaggregate the energy use by type, referring to it as the total primary energy (TPE) consumption for the extraction of minerals.

The remainder of the chapter is organized as follows. Section 6.2 explains how the mining industry uses energy. Section 6.3 presents insights from the theoretical and empirical literature. The methodological details of the stochastic frontier approach and its interpretation as an input demand function used for energy efficiency estimation is presented in section 6.4. Empirical results are presented in section 6.5, and finally, section 6.6 discusses the results with concluding remarks.

6.2 How the Mineral Industry Uses Energy

The mining and minerals industries worldwide use impressive amounts of energy, perhaps as much as 4–7% of global energy use (Rábago et. al., 2001). Energy used in mining operations accounts for approximately 3–7% of the mining and minerals sector's total energy use but represents about 17% of the total cost of supplies. About one-third of energy requirements are met by electricity, one-third by fuel/diesel oil, and the remaining one-third by coal, natural gas, and gasoline. Energy requirements vary widely for each mined commodity and depend upon the type of ore being mined and whether it is underground or surface. Underground mining operations require significantly greater amounts of energy than surface mining operations because of the increase in hauling requirements, ventilation, water, and pumping. The majority of energy used in surface mining is diesel fuel for haulage. Electricity is a major energy source for underground mining, to hoist the ore to the surface and for ventilation. The majority of electricity is used in milling and processing operations. Within the excavation process (roughly one-third of mining energy demand), removal accounts for about one-half of energy use; haulage for one-quarter; and drilling, blasting, ventilation services, and in-mine processing for the remainder. Within the processing stage (roughly one-third of mining energy demand), comminution (crushing and grinding) accounts for an estimated 85% of energy requirements. Smelting/refining accounts for 10% and separations and agglomeration for the remainder. Energy use tends to increase with declining ore grade and with finer mineral grain size (Rábago et al., 2001).

6.3 Studies on Energy Efficiency and the Mining Industry

6.3.1 Theoretical Literature

Like productivity and efficiency, the theory related to energy efficiency estimation is given by production theory, which specifically gives an energy demand or consumption function. The energy-demand function provides a functional relationship between the energy used and the various factors that influence the energy use. Thus, energy efficiency can be explained from a production theoretic perspective.

In the extant literature, energy intensity is defined as the quantity of energy required per unit of output or activity. If a given level of output is produced with less amounts of energy over time, energy efficiency is considered to have improved. Hence, if E_t/Y_t (where E_t is the total energy consumed and Y_t is the total output produced at time t) declines over time, it is concluded that energy efficiency has improved. Energy efficiency gains can result from decreasing energy (fuel) consumption per unit of output or increasing output per unit of energy consumption. In the context of the industrial sector, a rich body of research has emerged, which examines the energy intensity changes over time to understand the changes in energy efficiency. In this respect, the mining industry is no exception.

Energy efficiency is defined as the ratio of useful work done (energy output) to energy input. For mining, the amount of product (e.g. tonnage of rock, grams of metal) is often used as a proxy for useful work done. These proxies can include payload or the product of payload and distance travelled (Motlogelwa and Minnitt, 2013; Odhams et al., 2010). In some cases, proxies are used to describe the energy input as well. For instance, the volume of diesel fuel is commonly used in truck haulage as a measure of energy input (Awuah-Offei et al., 2011; Motlogelwa and Minnitt, 2013).

6.3.2 Empirical Literature on Energy Efficiency in Mining

Energy efficiency initiatives in mining have been documented in the literature since the early 1970s. These early energy efficiency programmes included waste heat recovery, training employees, adequate and timely maintenance, and demand management (Levesque et al., 2014). A review of the literature shows that energy efficiency initiatives have targeted all aspects of mining operations and the mining sector as a whole. These initiatives can be classified into mining, processing, and support activities as well as energy sources and government policy analysis.

Most of the research on the effect of government policies on energy efficiency of mining focuses on electricity demand, although some studies are more comprehensive. The published research indicates that government policies, as a whole, often have contradictory effects on energy efficiency in mining (Henriksson et al., 2014; Hu and Kavan, 2014). For example, one government policy may expressly encourage industry to invest in energy efficiency projects while another may deprive industry of the required financing to carry out such investments (Hu and Kavan, 2014). In most cases, government policies aimed at achieving national energy efficiency goals are a combination of new taxes and tax incentives. Such policies must balance the need to discourage energy-intensive activities with the need for national or regional competitiveness in an increasingly global economy. Otherwise, an unintended outcome of such policies may be a weakening economy (resulting from, for example, capital flight as mines close and the product is mined elsewhere) and its attendant problems. Another key issue that informs such government policy is whether or not electricity (or energy) demand in the mining sector is sensitive to electricity (energy) prices. (If mining energy demand is elastic concerning prices, then higher government taxes on electricity will reduce consumption.) There appears to be some contradiction in the literature, with regards to this question. While Henriksson et al. (2014) show that electricity demand in the Swedish mining sector is price elastic, Kohler (2014) does not find statistically significant elasticity in the South African sector. It appears this contradiction is explained by whether the model allows for substitution or not.

The majority of the energy efficiency studies in mining have emphasized demand management, by mines, so as to bring down electricity consumption and costs. Managing electricity consumption for ventilation and cooling systems has received a lot of attention lately (Chatterjee et al., 2015; Van Greunen et al., 2014). Mine drainage systems have also received attention (Sahoo et al., 2014).

Another area that has gained extensive attention in energy efficiency research is mining processing. In mining processing, comminution is considered energy inefficient (Napier-Munn, 2015; US DoE, 2007). Thus, this aspect of mining has received much research attention, with many researchers attempting to understand specific energy, undertaking benchmark studies, or suggesting more energy-efficient alternatives (Nadolski et al., 2014; Palaniandy et al., 2015; Pothina et al., 2007). However, no visible changes are seen in the industrial performance concerning comminution, and it still represents the area where perhaps there lies huge potential for energy savings in mining (when compared with theoretical limits) (Napier-Munn, 2015; US DoE, 2007).

Some of the energy research has also focused on examining the climate change impacts of processing (Haque and Norgate, 2014; Nimana et al., 2015; Norgate and Haque, 2010). For instance, the energy-intensive nature of oil sands processing has received attention even in society at large and is at the centre of debates on the role of oil sands in energy policy.

Most of the research in mining energy efficiency has also been conducted on the energy efficiency in loading and hauling operations, which are considered the core energy-intensive portions of mining activities. The energy efficiency of loading and hauling operations depends on the efficiency of the equipment units, operating conditions (including those imposed by mine planning and design), and consumption.

From the above review of literature, it is clear that although the energy-use efficiency study in mining has covered all aspects of mining, yet no one has attempted to quantify the energy efficiency in this industry from a production theoretic framework. In most of the studies, energy intensity is considered as a proxy for energy-use efficiency. And, in the context of the Indian mining industry, research based on energy efficiency is almost non-existent. This book aims to fill the gap.

6.4 Methodology

6.4.1 Modelling

This section outlines the methodology that we use to estimate the energy efficiency of mining firms. For this, we use a two-step procedure: first, we estimate the overall energy efficiency values for each firm and consequently the average efficiency scores for each subsector in the sample. Thereafter, we use these efficiency estimates as dependent variables to examine the factors causing interfirm heterogeneity in energy efficiency.

6.4.2 Deriving Energy Efficiency Using stochastic frontier analysis

In the economics of production theory, energy demand is considered a derived demand. For producing outputs, firms use a mix of both energy and non-energy inputs. Thus, the derived energy demand depends on several independent variables such as prices and quantities that vary based on a firm's objectives (profit maximization or cost minimization). Therefore, it is essential to define energy demand from an economic perspective in the industrial context. In this context, the efficient use of energy implies the ability of the producing firm to produce a given level of output at a minimum cost (Lundgren et al., 2016). In this chapter, we use the input demand frontier suggested by Schmidt and Lovell (1979) and further described in, for example, Kumbhakar and Lovell (2000) to depict the energy demand.

Considering energy, which is used as an input in the production process, as a dependent variable while modelling for the energy consumption frontier has become a debatable point. However, in the literature, a majority of studies that estimate energy efficiency, either at the country level or firm level, provide sufficient justifications for the use of energy consumption as a dependent variable (Boyd and Lee, 2019; Evans et al., 2013; Filippini and Hunt, 2011, 2012; Filippini et al., 2014; Lundgren et al., 2016). The explanation is based on the economic perspective of energy consumption. In other words, plants demand for energy is a derived demand based on a number of factors, such as the amount of output produced, energy prices, technology, and other input prices. Thus, energy consumption can be expressed as a function of a number of other independent factors.

Energy = F (output, price, labour, capital, and so on).

Since energy consumption is a derived concept, it would not be misleading to model it in a production theoretical framework. Literature has sufficient witnesses that model energy consumption as a dependent variable for the estimation of energy efficiency.

Lundgren et al. (2016) constructed an energy-demand frontier for analysing the energy efficiency of fourteen Swedish manufacturing industries using firm-level data for the years 2000–2008. They use a parametric stochastic approach and the 'true random effects' model given by Greene (2005a, 2005b) for the same purpose that allows for firm-specific heterogeneity. Their results reveal the presence of considerable inefficiencies in fuel use in comparison to electricity use. In another study, Boyd and Lee (2019) constructed the same energy-demand frontier to estimate the energy efficiency of five metal-based. durable manufacturing industries in the United States. Their results also indicate significant energy inefficiencies and consistently lower fuel efficiency compared with electrical efficiency. On the same subject, many other studies (Lutz et al, 2017; Petrick et al., 2011) also use a similar kind of approach for energy efficiency estimation.

Going by this evidence from the literature, in this chapter, we also follow the same procedure of modelling energy consumption as dependent variable in the construction of the energy-demand frontier. In the absence of absolute energy-demand figures for each firm, we use the energy consumption as the proxy for constructing an energy-demand frontier.

Following Filippini and Hunt (2010), we construct an energy-demand frontier for power (fuel and electricity) for the mining industry for the estimation of energy efficiency. The energy-demand frontier shows the minimum amount of energy consumed to produce a given level of output, given the production technology, input prices, and non-energy inputs, etc.

Energy efficiency is estimated from the energy-demand frontier by taking a difference between the actual energy consumption and the optimal energy demand given by the estimated energy-demand frontier. It is important to note here that this energy efficiency represents both technical and allocative efficiencies (Filippini and Hunt, 2015). The technical inefficiency shows how much energy could be saved for a given output level, and the allocative efficiency indicates how efficiently the energy and other inputs are combined to achieve cost minimization. So, our energy efficiency estimate signifies the overall energy efficiency based on production theory and estimates how far a firm's energy consumption is from the best-practice energy demand.

As energy efficiency is a useful indicator to evaluate a firm's energy performance and plays an important role in climate and energy policy formulation, it is necessary to formulate an appropriate energy-demand frontier since the empirical model specification could potentially result in different estimates of inefficiency. There are various empirical stochastic frontier analysis (SFA) models for energy efficiency. A comprehensive summary of different SFA models can be found in Filippini and Hunt (2015).

The most commonly used Stochastic frontier models used for energy efficiency estimation are the pooled model (PM) (Aigner et al., 1977), the random effects model (REM), and the true random effects model (TREM). For our purpose, we use Green's true random effect frontier model for estimating energy efficiency because it has advantages over other models.

The PM does not exploit the possibility given by panel data to control for time-invariant unobserved heterogeneity variables. Therefore, the unobserved heterogeneity bias can be present in this model. On the other hand, the REM, introduced by Pitt and Lee (1981), considers the typical panel data individual random effects as inefficiency rather than unobserved heterogeneity as in the literature on panel data econometric methods. The REM produces efficiency indicators that do not vary over time (persistent efficiency). One problem with the REM is that unobserved time-invariant variables are captured by the individual effects and, therefore, considered as inefficiency. As an alternative to the REM, Greene (2005a, 2005b) proposed the TREM, whereby the PM is extended by adding fixed and random individual effects, respectively. The TREM produces values of the level of efficiency that vary over time (transient efficiency). In these models, the individual fixed or random effects take into account all unobserved variables that are time-invariant. In the TREM, any time-invariant or persistent component of inefficiency is completely absorbed in the state-specific constant terms. Therefore, if the production of energy services is characterized by persistent inefficient use of energy (for instance, by the presence of old production machines, old buildings, or an old road system or systematic behavioural failures such as adjusting the room temperature or frequently opening the windows), the TREM will produce relatively high levels of estimated energy efficiency.

Greene (2004, 2005a, 2005b) pointed out that firm-level heterogeneity is an important issue to be addressed while using panel data. If the issue of heterogeneity is not properly accounted for, it may produce biased estimated energy efficiency scores. The true random effects SFA model takes into account this heterogeneity problem and can be considered as an appropriate model for plant-level energy efficiency estimation. In the light of the above discussion, and to provide a comprehensive estimate of firm-level energy efficiency, we prefer to use Greene's TREM.

We provide below the true random effects specification of the short-run energy-demand frontier for firms i, in period t, as follows:

$$\boldsymbol{lnE}_{it} = \beta_o + \alpha_i + \beta_y lnY_{it} + \beta_p lnP_{it} + \beta_l lnL_{it} + \beta_k lnK_{it} + \alpha_t T + v_{it} + u_{it} \quad (1)$$

where Y refers to the output values and L and K are non-energy inputs defined as quasi-fixed labour and capital inputs, respectively. For estimating energy efficiency, we assume capital and labour to be quasi-fixed in the short run. The assumption of capital to be fixed in the short run is obvious; however, assuming labour to be fixed in the short run may be controversial. In the case of India, this is not unreasonable because, as per the Indian Employment Act, the term of notice is one to three months and can exceed this period in practice. Thus, along with capital, labour varies slowly as against energy use in production. The same assumption has been made by many other studies in the context of energy-use efficiency (Lundgren and Markland, 2015), which validates our assumption. Energy prices are denoted as p_e, and following Greene (2004), we allow for Hicks-neutral technological change, in our case by including a trend variable T. This specification is a derived demand for energy estimation assuming cost minimization and a Cobb–Douglas technology with flexible (power and fuel) and quasi-fixed inputs (capital and labour). The firm-specific random component α_i captures the unobserved time-invariant heterogeneity. The residuals include a statistical noise term v_{it} and, input-orientated, time-variant technical inefficiency u_{it}.

The distribution of statistical noise is assumed to be normally distributed with a zero mean and standard deviation σ_v, that is, $v_{it\ i}$~$N(0, \sigma_v^2)$N $(0, \sigma_v\ 2)$. The distribution of inefficiency effects, u_{it}, is taken to be a non-negative truncation of the normal distribution $N(\mu, \sigma_v^2)$. Thus, the term u_{it} represents energy inefficiency. An indicator of inefficiency is $\lambda = {}^{\sigma_u}/\sigma_v$. The larger the value of this indicator, the greater is the inefficiency component. We also run a test on λ to test for the significance of inefficiency.

The energy efficiency of firm i at time t (EE_{it}) is defined as the ratio of actual energy consumption to the optimal energy demand given by the energy-demand frontier and can be written as follows:

$$\left(EF_{it}\right) = exp\left(-u_{it}\right) \quad (2)$$

6.5 Data Consolidation

The data source for this book is the Prowess database from the Centre for Monitoring Indian Economy (CMIE), which provides all kinds of financial information for companies from their annual balance sheet. The data consists of an unbalanced panel that covers sixty-nine firms across four Indian mining subsectors from 2000 to 2016. The four industry subsectors are coal-, metallic-, non-metallic-, and petroleum-mining companies. The data spans the implementation of the Energy Conservation Act (2001), which is important from the perspective of examining the impact of this regulation on energy efficiency. The data contains information about inputs and outputs used to estimate the energy-demand functions as specified in equation (1). Descriptive statistics are shown in Table 6.1.

The data for all the variables (such as the value of output, labour, capital, and energy) are in nominal terms. Using the appropriate price index series, these nominal values have been converted into the real values at 2004–2005 prices. The period chosen for the study is 2000–2001 to 2016–2017, and an unbalanced panel of sixty-nine firms has been constructed for the study. The gross value of output has been used as an index of output in place of gross value added (GVA) as in the production

Table 6.1 Descriptive statistics of variables in the energy demand function

	Output	Labour	Energy	Capital stock	Number of observations (n)
Coal	465.8 (1,896.3)	78.6 (412.1)	17.3 (78.2)	1,215.8 (12514.2)	329
Metallic	378.9 (1,614.2)	58.2 (291.7)	16.1 (75.3)	1,117.6 (1,1332.5)	173
Non-metallic	290.7 (1,967.5)	43.6 (273.1)	14.3 (68.9)	1,084.8 (10,132.6)	357
Petroleum	345.9 (1,234.4)	47.3 (270.1)	16.5 (74.8)	1,185.7 (10,187.2)	113
N	–	–	–	–	972

Note: All figures in parentheses represent standard errors. N represents the total number of observations; n represents subsector-wise observations.

Source: Author's estimation.

process; we have included energy, which is an intermediate input. At the same time, GVA is negative for a large number of firms, which reduces the sample size to a large extent. The nominal value of the gross value of output has been converted into real values at 2004–2005 prices by using the Wholesale Price Index for Minerals.

Of the inputs, labour is entered in terms of expenses in wages and salary and energy as expenses for power and fuel, respectively. Labour input is deflated by the total wage bill (salary and wages) with the Consumer Price Index for Industrial Workers, taking the 2001 = 100 as a base. The energy input is deflated by the composite price index of fuel, power, light, and lubricants. Capital stock has been constructed using the gross fixed asset (GFA). The reason behind using the GFA, rather than net fixed asset, is due to the arbitrary depreciation charges in the Indian industries, fixed by income tax authorities, which hardly represent actual consumption. We use the perpetual inventory method, as given by Srivastava (1996), to construct the capital stock, with 2009–2010 as the benchmark. In the absence of information regarding input prices for individual firms, all-India price indexes for the inputs are used as a proxy for input prices. Here, it is worth mentioning that in a perfectly competitive input market, all firms are facing the same input prices.

The sectoral share of total energy consumption for all four subsectors is shown in Table 6.2.

Coal, petroleum, and metallic subsectors account for a large part of total energy consumption in Indian industry. Table 6.2 reveals that these subsectors consumed more than 80% of the total energy consumption in 2000–2016.

Table 6.2 Sector shares of energy in relation to total industrial energy use, 2000–2016

Sector	Share of energy (%)
Coal	32.1
Metallic	23.2
Non-metallic	19.4
Petroleum	25.3

Source: Author's estimation.

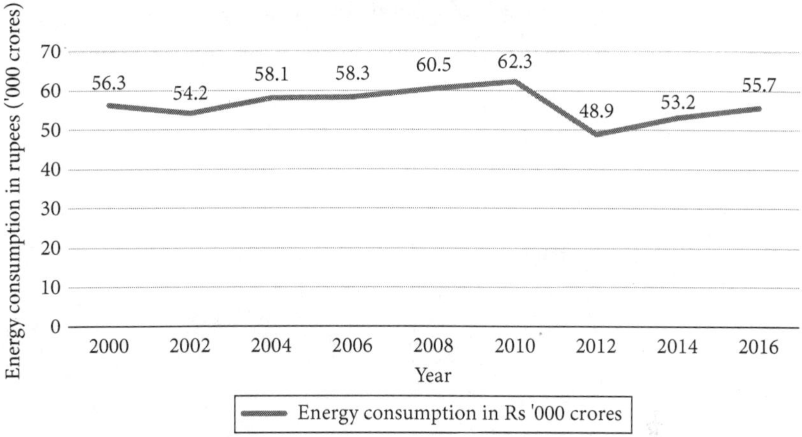

Fig. 6.1 Energy consumption in the Indian mining industry, 2000–2016
Source: Author's estimation.

The total energy consumption for the mining industry as a whole is illustrated in Fig. 6.1.

We present the energy intensities for the Indian mining industries in all four subsectors, calculated by total energy use/output in Fig. 6.2. The energy intensity is considered as a proxy for energy efficiency in most of the energy studies. Figure 6.2 shows that the mining industry's energy intensity was the same in most years, with small variations in some of the years. The mean values of energy intensity for each sector during 2000–2016 are shown in Table 6.3.

Higher values indicate a larger energy demand to produce one unit of output. Metallic mining was the most energy-intensive subsector, whereas non-metallic was the least intensive one. The coal and petroleum subsectors were also energy intensive.

As we have mentioned above, energy intensity is often considered as a proxy of energy efficiency. Based on the calculation of energy intensity and energy efficiency, we expect a negative correlation between them from the cost minimization point of view. As per the definition of energy intensity, a smaller intensity indicates less energy demand and thereby higher energy efficiency. Therefore, as per the energy-demand frontier defined in equation (1) and the energy intensity definition, intensity should be negatively correlated with efficiency.

Table 6.3 Sectoral energy intensity, mean values, 2000–2016

Sector	Energy intensity (energy/output)
Coal	0.286
Metallic	0.291
Non-metallic	0.063
Petroleum	0.274

Source: Author's estimation.

6.6 Empirical Findings

In this section, we present the results from the estimated energy-demand stochastic frontier along with the energy efficiency scores. In Table 6.4, we show the main estimation results. The first five columns show the estimated values of parameters of the energy-demand frontier, and the last two columns show the variance parameters of σ_u and λ, where ($\lambda = \sigma_u/\sigma_v$). The estimates of λ indicate how much contribution the variance in energy inefficiency (σ_u) has made relative to the variance of error (σ_v) If the estimated λ is statistically significant, it implies that there is energy inefficiency in the respective subsector.

Table 6.4 shows expected signs for the short-run elasticities from an economic perspective. The estimated parameter values for all the variables (labour, capital, and output) show positive signs. This is in line with the theoretical expectation. The positive signs for labour, capital, and output indicate that, given the technology, an increase in these variables would lead to an increase in energy demand for consumption. The results also show positive signs for the time trend, which is highly significant, implying that, over time, all the subsectors in the industry have increased their energy consumption. This ranges from 0.028 in the non-metallic subsector to 0.065 in the coal subsector. This shows that there is an increase in energy use from 2.8 to 6.5% across the subsectors.

Furthermore, our results also show an economically reasonable relationship between energy prices and energy demand (i.e. a negative relationship between energy prices and energy demand), indicating that with

Table 6.4 Estimation results for the energy demand from the frontier

Sectors	Parameters					Variance parameters	
	Y	P	L	K	T	σ_u	$\lambda = \sigma_u/\sigma_v$
Coal	0.432*	−0.679*	0.568*	0.501*	0.065*	0.768*	5.108*
Metallic	0.289*	−0.419*	0.567*	0.615*	0.033*	0.439*	2.584*
Non-metallic	0.251*	−0.393*	0.553*	0.416*	0.028*	0.211**	0.856**
Petroleum	0.376*	−0.534*	0.618*	0.593*	0.057*	0.532*	4.830*

Note: *, ** indicates significance level of 1% and 5%, respectively.
Source: Author's estimation.

an increase in energy prices, the energy demand reduces. In our study, the price elasticities of energy demand varied from −0.39 to −0.67. As our study does not distinguish between different types of energy use, we are unable to disentangle the energy efficiency for the different categories due to the nature of our data.

Our model gives two indicators of energy efficiency. The first one is given by λ, which is shown in the last column of Table 6.4. This column shows that λ is statistically significant in all the four subsectors of the Indian mining industry. This signifies the presence of energy inefficiency in most of the sectors. This propels us to reject the null hypothesis of $\lambda = 0$; that is, there are time-variant differences in energy efficiency between the firms within the respective subsector. The variance of the energy inefficiency term σ_u is significantly greater than zero.

Our second indicator is the energy efficiency scores. These scores are presented in Table 6.5.

A score of 1 indicates the maximum possible score, implying that there is no potential for improving time-variant energy efficiency in the respective subsector. The mean energy efficiency scores in our analysis vary from 0.511 in the non-metallic-mining subsector to 0.853 in the coal-mining subsector. This implies that, on average, the coal-mining subsector exhibits a better energy efficiency performance than other sectors (in relation to the subsector's own benchmarking technology). These results suggest that there exists the potential to improve energy efficiency in the context of the Indian mining industry.

Table 6.5 Energy efficiency scores for the four subsectors of the Indian mining industry

Subsectors	Mean
Coal	0.853
Metallic	0.792
Non-metallic	0.511
Petroleum	0.822

Source: Author's estimation.

A comparison between Tables 6.3 and 6.5 reveals that the metallic subsector exhibits high energy intensity and low energy efficiency scores. Energy intensity is the amount of energy required to produce one unit of output. Higher energy intensity for the metallic subsector indicates a larger amount of energy use. Efficiency requires either to produce the same amount of output with less inputs or more output with the same inputs. Unlike the coal subsector, the high energy intensity and low efficiency of the metallic subsector imply that this larger input use is not translating into a more than proportionate increase in the output, thereby yielding a low efficiency for the metallic subsector.

We present the year-wise average efficiency scores for four subsectors of the mining industry in Table 6.6.

It can be enumerated from Table 6.6 that the average energy efficiency of firms under study during the sample period are 0.8536, 0.7924, 0.5116, and 0.8215 for coal, metallic, non-metallic, and petroleum mining, respectively. These efficiency scores imply that there exists scope to improve energy efficiency by reducing energy consumption. For instance, in the case of coal mining, it would be possible to reduce the energy consumption by 14.64% and still produce the same amount of output. Table 6.6 shows that the highest amount of energy-saving potential lies with the non-metallic-mining subsector as it operates with the least energy efficiency.

We present the trends of energy efficiency in the four subsectors of the mining industry in Fig. 6.2. It is clear from Fig. 6.2 that there

Table 6.6 Year-wise average energy efficiency scores for the four subsectors of the Indian mining industry

Year	Energy efficiency scores			
	Coal	Metallic	Non-metallic	Petroleum
2000–2001	0.8538	0.8537	0.7019	0.8203
2001–2002	0.8212	0.8354	0.6943	0.8212
2002–2003	0.8208	0.8125	0.651	0.8208
2003–2004	0.8913	0.7986	0.5812	0.8351
2004–2005	0.8735	0.8087	0.5463	0.7989
2005–2006	0.8215	0.7988	0.4928	0.8123
2006–2007	0.8120	0.7913	0.4923	0.8234
2007–2008	0.8234	0.7754	0.4911	0.8226
2008–2009	0.8733	0.7844	0.4765	0.8113
2009–2010	0.8574	0.7856	0.4513	0.8342
2010–2011	0.8561	0.7791	0.4409	0.8213
2011–2012	0.8643	0.7659	0.4416	0.8107
2012–2013	0.8789	0.7798	0.4414	0.8228
2013–2014	0.8913	0.7745	0.4465	0.8289
2014–2015	0.8564	0.7683	0.4438	0.8465
2015–2016	0.8572	0.7756	0.4517	0.8316
2016–2017	0.8602	0.7828	0.4519	0.8043
2000–2017	0.8536	0.7924	0.5116	0.8215

Source: Author's estimation.

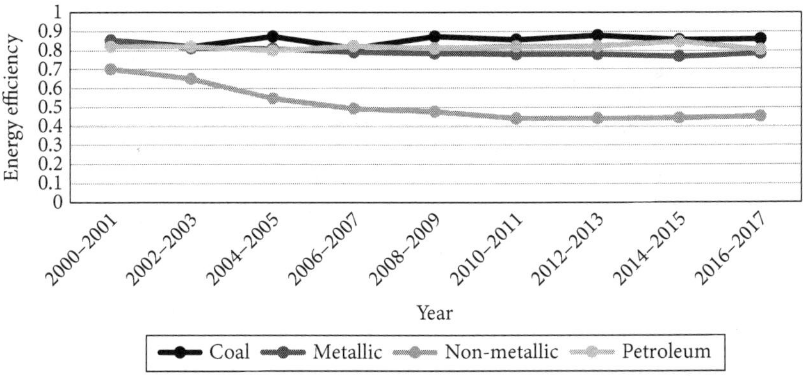

Fig. 6.2 Trends in energy efficiency in the four subsectors of the mining industry

Source: Author's estimation.

exists little difference in energy efficiency scores of coal-, metallic- and petroleum-mining firms. On the other hand, the energy efficiency scores of non-metallic mining have shown a continuous declining trend starting from 2000 up to 2010–2011, and since 2012–2013, it shows a marginal increasing trend. This implies that amongst all the four subsectors, the non-metallic-mining subsector contributes more to carbon emissions as this subsector is showing the least energy efficiency. This makes the subsector a cause of concern. As more energy consumption leads to more carbon emissions, this high level of energy inefficiency implies that non-metallic mining contributes more to carbon emissions as against other subsectors.

6.6.1 Determinants of Energy Efficiency

To assess the various factors that influence energy-use efficiency and thereby explain the possible inter-firm variations in energy-use efficiency across subsectors during our sample period, we perform a second-stage regression analysis. In the second-stage regression analysis, we consider the energy efficiency scores that we obtain from estimating the model equation (1) as our dependent variable. As regards the independent variables, we choose several factors derived from the literature that are expected to influence energy efficiency. Overall, we analyse the relationship of these different determinants with the energy efficiency development of firms in four subsectors of the Indian mining industry. This section briefly describes the determinants used in our analysis and presents the possible relationships drawn from the literature.

An important factor that can influence energy efficiency is the firm's size. The size of the firm can affect its performance in many ways. Larger firms have the advantage to diversify their business, exploiting economies of scale and scope and specialization in particular products. These features allow them to show better performance relative to the smaller ones (Penrose, 1959; Prescott and Vischer, 1980). On the contrary, in the case of larger-sized firms, managerial coordination becomes difficult (Downs, 1976). Also, as was mentioned by Shepherd (1986), size determines the market power and therefore increases the possibility of x-inefficiency in production, which can lead to inferior performance (Leibenstein, 1976).

Thus, we do not obtain any conclusive evidence regarding the relationship between size and the firm's performance. Hence, it remains an empirical issue to examine this relationship in the context of the mining industry. Following Lundgren et al. (2016), we use the value of output as a proxy for firm size. We categorize firms into three groups—small, medium, and large firms—based on their production value. Small, medium, and large firms refer to the first, second, and third quantiles of the value of produced output. Thus, three dummies are used for the size of firms, the small firms being the reference category.

Another important determinant of energy efficiency is the capacity utilization rate (CUR). This is because the CUR is considered a proxy for the productive capability of firms or to account for the business cycle (Lundgren et al., 2016). The CUR can be measured as the ratio of the output of a firm for a particular year to the maximum value of output for that firm over the years.[1] The literature does not provide any obvious relationship between capacity and firm performance. However, a positive sign can be expected on the assumption that high utilization would lead to high efficiency.

Another important factor that can influence the firm's energy performance is age. Some researchers hold the view that older firms, being equipped with obsolete technology, managerial inertia, and inability to adapt to the rapid changes in the economic environment, are more likely to exhibit low performance as compared with the younger and more dynamic firms (Marshall, 1920). In contrast, some other researchers think that older firms, being more experienced, tend to invest more in research and development compared with younger ones, resulting in higher energy efficiency. Thus, there is an inconclusive relationship between age and firms' energy performance, which requires to be tested empirically in the context of the mining industry. For this, age is included as one of the independent variables in the estimation procedure. Age for a particular firm in a specific year is estimated by subtracting that period from the firm's incorporation year.

[1] For a given mining sector, the CUR for firm k in period t is calculated as follows: Capacity $k_t = y_{kt}/maxy_k$, where $maxy_k$ is the highest observed value of output produced by a firm in the sector during the period.

Apart from size and age, labour quality can also impact energy efficiency among firms within the same sector (Walton, 1981). For estimating labour quality, labour productivity (LP) is used as the proxy. The LP is measured by dividing the output by one unit of wages and salaries. A positive relationship between LP and the firm's energy performance is expected as a high-quality labour force tends to be associated with improved efficiency performance.

Another driver that influences energy efficiency is the firm's capital–energy ratio. Energy saving and thereby improving energy efficiency may be a capital-intensive process and, in that case, a higher capital–energy (KE) ratio would result in greater energy efficiency (Mandal and Madheswaran, 2011). However, there is no definite relationship between capital and energy. Thus, this variable is included in the estimation process to assess the empirical relationship.

The other determinant that may have a role in assessing energy efficiency is type of ownership. Literature differs widely with respect to this variable (Chapter 5). Some studies show a superior performance of the private-sector firms over the public-sector firms, whereas others reveal either neutral or superior performance of public-sector firms. Looking at the unambiguous relationship between ownership and energy performance, this variable is chosen as an independent variable for our estimation. Further, the dummy variable D_1 is added, which takes the value 1 for private-sector firms and zero otherwise to assess the impact of ownership.

Finally, the Energy Conservation Act (2001) is included as a regulation dummy to express the impact of the implementation of this Act on the energy efficiency behaviour of firms. D_2 is the regulation dummy that takes the value 0 for all the preceding years to 2001 and a value 1 for all the years after 2001.

A panel data model is specified assuming a functional relationship between energy use and its various determinants as mentioned earlier. The use of the panel data model is due to its advantage in controlling individual heterogeneity of the firms. Apart from this, the panel data model is preferred as it provides greater information, greater variability, and a greater degree of freedom. Here, we specify the following panel data model for estimating determinants of energy efficiency:

$$\left(EF_{it}\right) = \alpha + \beta \mathbf{x}_{it} + \mu_i + \lambda_t + \epsilon_{it} \tag{3}$$

where *EF* is the energy efficiency score considered as the dependent variable; αs and βs are the parameters to be estimated; $\mathbf{x}_{it}$ is the vector of explanatory variables, which includes the dummy variables; μ_i is the time-invariant firm-specific factors that influence efficiency; λ_t is the firm-invariant, time-specific factors that affect efficiency; and ε_{it} is the disturbance term, which is assumed to be homoscedastic and non-auto-correlated. Firms are denoted by subscript *i* and time by *t*.

After the model specification was done, we estimated two-panel data models and fixed-effect and random-effect models. Out of these two sets of models, the appropriate model was chosen based on the Hausman test.

6.6.2 Estimation Method for Regression

To determine the factors that influence energy efficiency and, in turn, cause inter-firm heterogeneity in energy efficiency among firms within each subsector, a second-stage panel regression is used. Specifically, we use panel Tobit regression for this purpose. We consider the Tobit model as the appropriate method for this purpose due to the nature of our dependent variable, as our dependent variable energy efficiency is censored. Our energy efficiency scores lie between 0 and 1 (zero indicating least efficient and 1 implying 100% efficiency), and as the scores cannot go beyond 1, the dependent variable is right censored at 1.[2] For censored data, the Tobit regression is considered appropriate.

6.6.3 Regression Results

The regression results for all the four subsectors of the mining industry are presented in Tables 6.7, 6.8, 6.9, and 6.10. It can be seen from the results that energy efficiency is dependent on the firm's size. In our case, the

[2] Right censoring takes place when cases with a value at or above some threshold all take on the value of that threshold so that the true value might be equal to the threshold, but it might also be higher. In other words, the efficiency scores are right censored at 1 as when the actual score is <1, the observed efficiency score is equal to the actual (latent) score, and when the actual score is ≥ 1, the observed efficiency score is equal to 1.

Table 6.7 Random effect panel Tobit regression for explaining energy efficiency in the coal-mining subsector

Parameters	Coefficients
Intercept	0.7208* (0.0289)
Age	–0.0035 (0.0019)
CUR	0.0135 (0.0021)
Size (mid)	0.4361* (0.0013)
Size (large)	0.3754* (0.0018)
LP	0.0026* (0.0005)
KE	0.0023* (0.0007)
D1	0.0231* (0.0079)
D2	0.0375 (0.0045)
Log likelihood	223.0658

Note: (1) Figures in parentheses are standard errors. (2) * indicates significance at 1% level.

Source: Author's estimation.

Table 6.8 Random effect panel Tobit regression for explaining energy efficiency in the metallic-mining subsector

Parameters	Coefficients
Intercept	0.7189* (0.0138)
Age	0.0025 (0.0002)
CUR	0.0873 (0.0024)
Size (mid)	0.3356* (0.0015)
Size (large)	0.4165* (0.0021)
LP	0.0018* (0.0002)
KE	0.0012* (0.0004)
D1	0.0235* (0.0079)
D2	0.0381 (0.0045)
Log likelihood	355.043

Note: (1) Figures in parentheses are standard errors. (2) * indicates significance at 1% level.

Source: Author's estimation.

Table 6.9 Random effect panel Tobit regression for explaining energy efficiency in the non-metallic-mining subsector

Parameters	Coefficients
Intercept	0.8132* (0.0138)
Age	0.0042 (0.0002)
CUR	0.0657 (0.0032)
Size (mid)	0.4262* (0.0007)
Size (large)	0.3815* (0.0019)
LP	0.0023* (0.0005)
KE	0.0031* (0.0015)
D1	0.0197* (0.0068)
D2	0.0416 (0.0036)
Log likelihood	283.063

Note: (1) Figures in parentheses are standard errors. (2) * indicates significance at 1% level.

Source: Author's estimation.

Table 6.10 Random effect panel Tobit regression for explaining energy efficiency in the petroleum-mining subsector

Parameters	Coefficients
Intercept	0.6518* (0.0253)
Age	0.0038 (0.0011)
CUR	0.0598 (0.0046)
Size (mid)	0.4135* (0.0032)
Size (large)	0.3621* (0.0011)
LP	0.0053* (0.0014)
KE	0.0042* (0.0032)
D1	0.0219 (0.0034)
D2	0.03891 (0.0027)
Log likelihood	311.115

Source: Author's estimation.

size variable has a positive and significant effect on all four subsectors. In all the four subsectors (coal, metal, non-metallic, and petroleum), the medium- and large-sized firms have positive and significant impacts about the small-sized firms. So, the general assessment is that size matters in the case of energy efficiency. For most of the sectors, the larger the size, the more efficient the firms are in terms of energy use. Our results do not support the viewpoints of bigger size inefficiency due to lack of managerial coordination; rather, it supports the argument that bigger firms are capable of diversifying, tapping opportunity to exploit economies of scale and explore specialization. These firms tend to become more efficient as against the smaller ones.

As regards the age variable, our results show that, in all the subsectors, age is not a significant determinant of energy efficiency in the firms. This could be due to the presence of an equal combination of old and young firms. The older firms, being disadvantaged with outdated technology, managerial inertia, and inability to adapt to the rapid changes in the economic environment, are more likely to exhibit low performance as compared with the younger and more dynamic firms (Marshall, 1920). The low energy efficiency shown by older firms balances out the high energy efficiency performance by younger ones, thereby making the variable insignificant. However, the coal subsector shows a negative relation between age and efficiency performance. This may be due to the dominance of public-sector firms in this subsector, which are subjected to managerial slack and inertia.

Our results also indicate that the CUR has no significant effect on energy efficiency performance. For all four subsectors, this variable has a neutral effect. The coefficient of LP is positive and significant for all the subsectors, indicating that higher-quality labour contributes positively to energy efficiency. The KE ratio variable has a positive and significant influence on energy-use efficiency, implying that enhancing energy-use efficiency is a capital-intensive process. The coefficient of the ownership dummy is positive and significant for the three subsectors coal, metallic, and non-metallic, whereas for petroleum, ownership type has little impact on efficiency performance. This result corroborates our findings of productive efficiency performance, which shows that private-sector firms are more productive in three of the subsectors of mining, while the public sector performs better in the petroleum subsector. The coefficient of the regulation dummy is insignificant in all four subsectors, implying that the implementation of the Energy Conservation Act (2001) does not have much impact on energy efficiency. This is a matter of concern and would suggest an urgent review into the above policy reform.

6.7 Discussion

The findings indicate that the energy efficiency of the Indian mining industry varies widely. Certain subsectors and companies are leading in terms of efficiency: coal- and petroleum-mining firms. In other cases, the efficiency is clearly below the industry average. For the industry sector as a whole, there exists important energy efficiency potential. As per our results, special attention should be given to non-metallic- and metallic-mining firms, which provide interesting opportunities to improve energy efficiency.

Analysis of different determinants of energy efficiency reveals that the size, CUR, and LP influence energy efficiency positively and significantly, making them the most important determinants of inter-firm heterogeneity in efficiency. In contrast, a firm's age and the Energy Conservation Act seem to have a neutral effect. Interestingly, the type of ownership has a significant positive effect on three subsectors (coal, metallic, and non-metallic), the exception being the petroleum subsector.

The energy efficiency of the mining industry assumes importance in the context of rapidly growing industrial production as this industry is the basic resource provider to other industries, especially manufacturing. The International Energy Agency (IEA) projection shows that India's GDP will increase from 3.7 trillion to 12.6 trillion US dollars by 2030, which represents a 240% rise (IEA, 2006). On the other hand, Tata Energy Research Institute (TERI) projections show that the GDP growth would be 400–900% over the same period (TERI, 2006). These high growth projections have important implications for industrial production. Such a high growth implies enormous material needs for the future and thereby greater industrial production. This increased demand for industrial output will ultimately put pressure on basic industries such as mining for its resource needs, thereby urging the mining industry to operate at its maximum. The maximum use ultimately necessitates high energy consumption. Thus, with the rapid increase in industrial production, both energy use and CO_2 emission will rise, which is a matter of concern. In such a case, energy efficiency gain plays a vital role in helping produce the output with low energy consumption and fewer emissions. Thus, the policy implication here is, given the rapid expansion in industrial production, it is of key importance that new investments should be based on energy-efficient mining equipment, keeping in mind the cost-effectiveness.

Due to the modest share of mining (approximately 2.7%) in total industrial energy use and the efficiency potential, it is evident that a substantial reduction of GHG emissions compared with today's level cannot be achieved by focusing on energy efficiency in the mining industry alone. A nationwide effort is required, and energy efficiency must be combined with other strategies, such as fuel switching and CO_2 capture and storage, to achieve a meaningful emissions reduction countrywide.

The energy efficiency estimation of the mining industry has immense implications for policymakers. One of the important implications is that energy efficiency gain in any subsector indicates an equal resource gain, which is key for climate change policymaking. The energy efficiency dimension provides insights into how the industrial operation affects energy consumption, and thereby CO_2 emissions. Subsectoral comparison brings into the limelight the subsectors that are poor performers in terms of energy performance and thereby provides the direction to policymakers on where to shift the focus of investment for efficiency enhancement.

In times of ever-increasing domestic energy prices, growing international geopolitical instability, and concerns over climate change risks, the case for energy efficiency improvement from all industrial segments, including mining, is becoming stronger. Mining companies' sincere efforts to boost energy efficiency—the level of output produced from energy consumed—could have spectacular results. There exists a substantial opportunity to enhance energy efficiency. For instance, by investing in energy-efficient equipment and adopting readily available technology to improve energy productivity in mining, mining companies could cut the energy demand growth by a substantial proportion, thereby helping to bring down the sector's energy demand. Now the typical question is what restricts the mining companies from taking advantage of these opportunities. Most likely, the answer could be the existing energy market imperfection, which discourages mining firms from investing in energy-efficient equipment. Mining firms may also tend to consider this type of investment in energy efficiency too risky and expensive. So here, the role of policymakers in bringing energy policy reforms that are beneficial for the mining industry in particular and businesses of all types in general becomes important.

One such policy initiative could be to make energy efficiency tradeable. This could be implemented in the same way as carbon emissions trading. In the context of mining companies, a system that makes energy efficiency tradeable would enable the mining firms to sell credits when they exceeded new standards. This would reduce the TPE consumption, putting a check on carbon emissions. When this sort of market mechanism is added to trade efficiency improvements, many firms may come forward to accept the energy efficiency standards that they may have resisted in the past. The policymakers should also impose stringent energy standards on the least energy-efficient subsector, the biggest energy consumer in the industry.

The need of the hour is that the policymakers, instead of focusing more on an uninterrupted energy supply, should focus on reducing energy consumption by bringing an improvement in energy efficiency. In the absence of such a course of action, the mining industry may fail to achieve fully achievable energy efficiency and continue to operate sub-optimally by becoming an energy consumer and producer of carbon emissions.

6.8 Conclusion

This chapter attempts to estimate the energy-use efficiency of mining firms at the subsectoral level of the mining industry in India in a production theoretic framework. For the same, the SFA is used on CMIE Prowess data for a period of seventeen years, covering 2000–2017. Drawing upon Schmidt and Lovell (1979) and further described in, for example, Kumbhakar and Lovell (2000) and following Filippini and Hunt (2010), the energy-demand frontier for power (fuel and electricity) has been constructed for the four subsectors of the mining industry to estimate energy efficiency. These energy-demand frontiers depict the minimum amount of energy consumed to produce a certain amount of output, all other things remaining constant. The empirical findings reveal that there is scope for energy-saving potential by improving energy-use efficiency in all the subsectors. The highest energy-saving potential seems to exist in the non-metallic-mining subsector. Further, this chapter attempts to analyse the factors that contribute to interfirm heterogeneity in energy efficiency. This is done by applying a second-stage panel regression. The results of this regression show that the larger the size of the firm, the greater the energy-use efficiency. On the other hand, age has a neutral effect on the energy efficiency of the firm. The quality of labour also has a significant positive impact on energy efficiency performance. The coefficient of the regulation dummy is insignificant in all the four subsectors, implying that the implementation of the Energy Conservation Act (2001) does not have much impact on energy efficiency. The results also reveal interesting outcomes concerning ownership, which show a significant positive effect on three subsectors—coal, metallic, and non-metallic; the petroleum subsector shows the opposite result. Finally, this chapter discusses certain policy measures to improve energy-use efficiency. In the wake of expanding industrial production from all industrial quarters, it is advocated that new investments should be based on energy-efficient mining equipment, keeping in mind the cost-effectiveness.

It is also suggested that as the mining industry is not a large consumer of industrial energy use, unlike the manufacturing industry, for substantial GHG emission, a countrywide effort is necessitated and alternative strategies for energy reduction (such as fuel switching, CO_2 capture, and storage) should be attempted for meaningful GHG reduction. It is also advocated that the focus of investment should be directed towards those sectors that are constantly poor energy performers to improve the energy efficiency of the whole industry. Finally, it is suggested that improvement in energy efficiency can be achieved by adopting policies such as energy efficiency trading.

This chapter is not free from limitations. One of the important limitations is the unavailability of carbon emissions data. When energy is used by any industry, carbon emissions take place as a by-product. So, along with the desirable output, an undesirable output is released by energy consumption. The carbon emissions intensity, which can be measured as carbon emissions per unit of output, can be an important determinant of energy-use efficiency. The relationship between carbon intensity and energy efficiency is usually assumed to be negative; higher carbon intensity may lead to less energy-use efficiency and vice versa. In the absence of carbon emissions data, we are not able to include this in our analysis.

Another limitation is related to the composition of energy expenditure. We have considered the total value of spending on power and fuel as total energy consumption. However, energy use can emanate from various sources, such as coal, electricity, liquefied petroleum gas (LPG), or diesel. As per the India Energy Statistics Report (CSO, 2019), in the mining industry mostly LPG and diesel are used for production. Thus, energy efficiency can be estimated with respect to different types of energy as they can influence the efficiency aspect. However, as the data set does not distinguish between different types of energy and considers the energy consumed as the TPE consumption, we are not able to disentangle the energy efficiency for different types due to data limitations.

7

Mining

Social and Environmental Performance

7.1 Introduction

Chapters 4–6 analysed the mining industry from the economic dimension (productivity and efficiency). The mining industry is expected to have a significant impact on the country's environmental and social fabric and analysis of this industry would be incomplete without examining these two aspects of mining. This chapter aims to fill this gap by examining the environmental and social performance of the mining industry from the perspective of their compliance. The necessity to comply with environmental and social norms arises from the negative impacts that the mining industry imposes due to its operation.

Mining companies acquire land either from government or private individuals to commence their operation activities. In return for the acquired land, they provide compensation to the households and make other provisions for the settlement of the displaced population. Obtaining a social licence necessitates compliance with certain social parameters. In the absence of this social compliance, there may be public protests, conflicts, and chaos, leading to the closure of the mining operation. The Pohang Steel Company (POSCO), Tata, and Vedanta projects in Odisha and Tata's project at Singur in West Bengal stand witness to this fact (Bhattacharya, 2007; Chandra, 2008; Fernandes, 2007; Sarkar, 2007). Das (2013) observed that these protests may lead to two types of problems. First, they can accentuate the distributional problem and augment chaos; second, if these protests are ill motivated, then they may generate a sense of disinterest among the investors and demotivate them to

The Indian Mining Industry. Meenakshi Parida and S. Madheswaran, Oxford University Press.
 DOI: 10.1093/9780198954392.003.0007

invest in the sector, thereby reducing the output. Given these facts, the issue of social compliance assumes some importance in the context of mining firms.

Mining activities also generate enormous environmental hazards in the form of air pollution, water pollution, noise pollution, and so on, thereby making it difficult to achieve other sustainable development goals, such as climate action, good health, and clean water. The adverse impact that this industry creates has made environmental scientists worry about environmental sustainability. Therefore, there is upward pressure on this industry to minimize the negative environmental hazards through responsible environmental performance by adhering to pre-set environmental standards and parameters. Hence, environmental compliance by this sector is envisaged to be key to establishing a green economy that is sustainable.

There are several questions to ponder here. Which social and environmental parameters or norms should they comply with? How should mining companies compensate for the social and environmental damage they create due to their acquisition of land and operational activities? Are the affected households satisfied with the compliance measures? Given these questions, the present chapter seeks to examine the environmental and social compliance of mining firms in the context of the Odisha mining industry from the perspective of project-affected households.

Based on a survey of eighty households, which have been affected by the mining projects in one of the mineral-rich districts of Odisha, the chapter examines the social and environmental compliance of mining firms from the perspective of affected households. The rest of the chapter is organized as follows: sections 7.2 and 7.3 describe the concept of social and environmental compliance, respectively. Section 7.4 discusses the review of literature on the social and environmental performance of the mining industry. Section 7.5 outlines the methodology and data, and section 7.6 presents the results, which are once again presented in two parts: the first part shows the findings concerning social compliance and the second part depicts the results for environmental compliance. Finally, section 7.7 provides the concluding remarks of the chapter.

7.2 The Concept of Social and Environmental Compliance

Hardly any literature is found on the topic of 'social compliance' in economics. So, it is imperative to define the concept of 'social compliance' before we delve deep into the subject matter. We define 'social compliance' as the direct and indirect benefits provided to the individual or community for the direct and indirect economic, environmental, and social losses made due to the transfer of land, displacement, and damage to natural resources. As such, the term 'social compliance' seems synonymous with the terms 'social performance' and 'corporate social responsibility'. At the outset, it has to be made clear that though both the concepts of corporate social responsibility and social compliance are visibly similar, they are not the same. Social compliance is a broader concept when compared with corporate social responsibility.

7.2.1 Social Compliance versus Corporate Social Responsibility

In today's world, companies are increasingly facing greater scrutiny regarding their environmental and social impact. Two important concepts guiding responsible business practices are social compliance and corporate social responsibility (CSR). While seemingly interrelated, they are two diverse approaches.

Social compliance, in general, refers to adhering to rules and regulations established to protect the environment, workers, and the communities. These laws usually address issues related to labour standards, environmental regulations, and occupational safety and health. Under labour standards, social compliance means compliance concerning minimum wages, child labour, working hours, forced labour, and discrimination. Environmental compliance concerns pollution control, waste management, and resource utilization. Compliance for occupational safety and health focuses on safe working conditions, accident prevention, and exposure to hazardous materials.

Compliance is the foundation upon which a responsible business is developed, and it ensures that companies operate within a defined ethical framework without harming the social fabric.

CSR is a broader concept than social compliance and delves deeper than just merely meeting the minimum legal standards. It is a strategic business approach that considers the company's impact on the environment and the society. CSR goes beyond social compliance in many respects, such as concerning proactive initiatives, stakeholder engagement, transparency, and accountability. CSR necessitates that companies engage in activities that positively contribute to society and the environment. CSR recognizes the interests of all the stakeholders: shareholders, employees, communities, and the environment. Companies, by reporting on their CSR activities and holding themselves accountable for their social and environmental performance, become transparent in their operations and social impact.

Social compliance forms the baseline of CSR. A company cannot be considered truly socially responsible without complying with the basic minimum legal standards. On the other hand, CSR pushes companies to go beyond compliance, encouraging positive contributions and long-term sustainability. As such, social compliance and CSR are complementary approaches to responsible business practices.

CSR is defined differently by different organizations. The World Business Council for Sustainable Development (1998) defines it as 'the continuing commitment by a business to behave ethically and contribute to economic development while improving the quality of life of workforce and their families as well as local community and society at large'.

According to the European Commission, CSR is a concept whereby companies integrate social and environmental concerns in their business operations and in their interaction with their stakeholders on a voluntary basis. The Federation of Indian Mineral Industries (FIMI, 2009) defines CSR as an investment that provides social licence to continue to operate a business, which is increasingly becoming very challenging. It points out that CSR results in 'a win-win situation for companies as well as for all its stakeholders, which ensures sustainability in the long-term' (FIMI, 2009).

By social compliance, we mean here all the promises made to the affected households and how far these promises have been kept. Before acquiring the land for mining operations, the mining companies undertake negotiations with the mining surface rights owners in relation to the offerings in the form of benefits, both direct and indirect. Under direct benefits, they sometimes offer direct cash payments or employment offers, while under indirect benefits, the companies consider contributing financially to the local area development activities, improving the livelihood of project-displaced people, contributing to infrastructure development activities, and much more. This is referred to as the social performance of the mining companies, which they undertake for the sustainable operation of their activities. However, it is essential to examine whether or not the promises made by them are kept; in other words, to what extent the companies have complied with their own promises.

Social compliance includes all aspects of CSR and the compensation made to the individual or community in return for the acquired land. Social compliance is statutory, whereas CSR is voluntary. In case of social compliance, compensation in cash or an alternative house or land is provided before the beginning of the mining operation. Alternatively, employment in the project or expenses in local area development activities, restoring the environment, infrastructure, and so on is done after the project starts. The second group basically comprises all CSR activities. Hence, social compliance is a broader concept than that of CSR, though having some resemblance to it.

7.3 The Concept of Environmental Compliance

Environmental compliance can be defined differently based on the perspective of the different stakeholders—government, mining companies, and financial companies sponsoring the funds; communities directly affected by the mining operations; and the broader community, loosely defined as the non-government organizations. All these stakeholders seem to have a legitimate interest in the environmental performance of the mining industry (Jones, 2008). To the majority of people, environmental compliance is meeting with the legislated environmental standards set by the government. In the context of India, important legislations that relate to environmental matters are the Air (Prevention and Control of Pollution)

Act (1981), the Water (Prevention and Control of Pollution) Act (1974), and the Forest Conservation Act (1980). All these Acts specifically mention environmental regulation, and the term 'environment compliance' has not been exclusively defined anywhere. However, all these Acts provide for various norms and standards for industries to comply with the environmental parameters. Now the question arises whether or not meeting these environmental standards is enough to correct the damage created by the mining operations. In a world where everything is changing at a fast pace, the environmental aspects of mining, community aspirations, industry attitude, guidelines, and legal and legislative regulations have significantly changed over the years and will continue to do so. This poses a significant risk to those companies who simply choose to meet the prescribed current standards. Having the current benchmark in the form of prescriptive legislation results in environmental risk, as it encourages the lowest-common-denominator approach rather than an optimal solution for a specific site (Jones, 2008). Further, whether environmental compliance has been achieved or not cannot be determined in the present time frame. Sustainable ecology cannot be created in a day, a month, or a year. It takes years to cover up the damage created by the mining firms. Hence, considering these aspects, it cannot be said with certainty that environmental compliance has been attained. However, these prescribed limits can provide direction towards the achievement of sustainable ecology and the best chance of creating an acceptable long-term environmental outcome. Thus, notwithstanding these complex issues that revolve around the definition of environmental compliance, in this chapter, we accept the same definition of environmental compliance (EC) as is accepted by the majority of stakeholders. However, we attempt to assess the EC from the project-affected people's perspective. Specifically, we examine the people's opinions on the EC performance of mining firms.

7.4 Studies on Social and Environmental Performance

7.4.1 Theoretical Literature

Mineral extraction, due to the nature of its operation, has a colossal impact on society and the environment as well. Thus, the mining firms must follow socially and environmentally responsible behaviour to remain in business. As mining involves several stakeholders and can negatively impact the environmental diaspora, there is huge scope for the mining industry to operate sustainably. To operate sustainably, the mining industry has to perform well on key social and environmental performance parameters. Thus, sustainable development theory explains a great deal of why the mining industry has to undertake social and environmental performance.

In the context of social performance, many dimensions can be brought into the picture. One of the key dimensions that could explain the mining industry's social performance concerns the compensation packages provided to the mining-affected people. The other dimensions could be social performance in health, education, infrastructure, and so on. Now the question arises why mining-affected people should be compensated and what the mechanisms to pay compensation are in exchange for the land provided for mining. Does the type of firm have any impact on compensation? Answers to a few of the above questions can be found in the property rights theory literature. However, property rights theory varies from country to country, and a uniform application of this theory for all countries is unsuitable.

In India, minerals fall under national property and the central government is entrusted with the power to formulate required laws and control the production, development, and conservation of key minerals, which are defined in Schedule A of the Mines and Minerals (Regulation and Development) Act (1957), whereas the respective state governments are empowered to regulate, develop, and conserve minor minerals specified in Schedule B. Since land is enlisted in the state list, the responsibility for issuing surface rights lies with the state governments. Thus, mining firms are required to obtain two different rights in India before they commence their operation. One is related to the extraction right of a mineral and the other is the surface right, which gives the mining companies the right to the surface land under which the mineral exists. Extraction rights are sanctioned by either the state or central government, while surface rights are sanctioned by the state governments only. Mining firms can obtain surface rights either from the government (where the government is the landholder) or from private individuals (where private individuals are landowners).

Now, the question arises as to why a surface rights holder should agree to transfer their land to mining firms. Definitely, the answer is in exchange for something—maybe in terms of financial or non-financial benefits. These benefits can be transferred to the affected people through social and environmental performance. Again, a surface right holder would be willing to transfer his or her land only when the firm pays as much as he or she expects. In other words, when the reservation price of the surface right holder matches with the willingness to pay of the firm, the transaction would be materialized. However, this smooth exchange seldom happens in reality, and consequently, the government has to intervene to take possession of the land. This opens several questions related to the social performance of the mining companies. For instance, how should the landowners be compensated for the transfer of their land? Should they be provided with some special compensatory measures for their loss? Does the surface right holder deserve a part of the mineral revenue?

In his study, Long (1995) stresses the fact that a surface right holder has no claim to the earnings from mineral extraction and processing. However, they have every right to exploit the opportunity of the geographical specificity of mining sites. Surface right holders demand higher payments than they would obtain from the alternative uses of their land, which is referred to as their reservation price. However, they will attempt to negotiate for the best possible deal that is above the reservation price. In the land transfer process, both the parties (landowners and mining firms) negotiate for their share of the best possible differential rents. Differential rents are the profits over what is required to make mineral investments (Long, 1995). By this definition, the mines that require low investment in terms of exploration, development, extraction, and processing will generate the highest differential rent and vice versa. Thus, the surface right owners will obtain the highest price for their land when the differential rent is high. Alternatively, they may get a lower price for their land, and in cases where it is equally expensive to extract, the surface right owners will get only the reservation price. Thus, the question of whether or not the landowners should be paid based on the value of the minerals extracted seems untenable. In this context, Long (1995, p. 78) mentions, 'Surface right owners are paid what is necessary to induce them to forego all other alternative land uses plus the differential rents they can bargain for.' However, in India, there is no such definite mechanism to decide on the compensation packages.

Apart from providing financial compensation to the landowners, the social performance of mining firms also constitutes compensating them non-financially in a variety of ways, such as making provision for education, improved health facilities, quality infrastructure in their area, and local area development activities. This non-financial performance can be related to the CSR literature. The overall social performance takes into account both the financial and non-financial compensation made by the mining firms to make good for the loss that arises due to their operation activities.

Further, there may be differences in the social performance based on the type of ownership of mining firms. The literature points towards many theoretical factors that contribute to this difference in social performance between public-sector and private-sector mining firms. One of the key factors responsible for this difference is the objective of firms. As the primary goal of public-sector firms is to maximize social welfare, contrary to the objective of profit maximization by private firms, this provides them with the incentive to perform better socially compared with private firms. However, as against this, private-sector firms cannot use coercive power to acquire private land, which the public-sector firms can do. This leaves the private-sector firms with one option (i.e. incentives) to soothe the land acquisition process. Thus, in this case, the private sector's social performance, in terms of providing better compensation, would be more than that of its counterpart. Another important factor that can cause the performance differential is the budget limitation faced by the mining firms. Private-sector mining firms, contrary to public-sector firms, may face financial constraints in providing both cash and employment opportunities to the affected people, thereby resulting in poor performance in comparison to the public-sector firms. The bargaining strength of mining firms, to a large extent, also influences the performance differences. The public-sector firms can exercise more bargaining power with the regulating authorities compared with private firms. However, private firms, through their rent-seeking activities, can influence the regulatory authorities and can change the game. However, public-sector firms have no such scope to bribe the authorities and move the decision in their favour. Besides, the above factors, the differences in social performance could also be explained by the principal–agent and public choice theory. In the public sector, managers are least bothered about the firm and its profit. Their fixed salaries and tenure do not provide any incentive to work for the interest of the organization by showing impressive social performance. On the other hand, in the case of private firms, managers are keen to have the utmost interest in the reputation and image of their organization. So, they could work in the better interest of the business by planning to provide for a good compensation deal. However, the private-sector firms could also influence the regulatory agencies and political leaders through bribing and thereby provide low compensation.

The above discussion on theoretical factors causing differences in social performances does not bring any definite conclusion with regard to who performs better socially—the state-owned firm or the privately owned firm. This inconclusive theoretical argument makes this issue an empirical one, necessitating further investigation.

In the context of the environmental performance dimension, the need for environmentally sustainable behaviour is pronounced because of the environmental costs generated by the mining firms due to their operation. Theoretically, it is argued that as the mining firms generate negative externalities in the form of varied types of pollution, it is customary for them to follow some environmentally responsible practices to minimize the damage they cause to the society. The CSR literature speaks at length about this issue.

On a similar line of argument, there may exist differences in the environmental performances of different types of firms. This difference may be due to several factors. One of the key factors is related to the objective of the firm. The ultimate objective of each firm is to minimize its total cost, given a certain level of output. Generally, a firm faces three types of costs—production costs, which include expenses on pollution abatement; fines paid to the regulatory agencies; and the social cost resulting from pollution. However, the private firms do not usually take into account the third type of cost, that is, the social costs. The overall performance of a firm takes into account all these three types of costs.

One key contributing factor to the differences in environmental performance could be production inefficiencies. If a firm is technically efficient, it will show better ecological performance by generating less pollution. Thus, based on extraction efficiency, the public- and private-sector firms may exhibit different ecological performance.

Another factor that can result in a difference in performance is related to the internalization of the environmental cost the firms are inflicting on society. Public firms, having the objective of social welfare, do not have the chance to neglect this cost. However, private-sector firms do not always internalize the damaging effect of the pollution externality and often pay least attention to the environmental cost. Baumol et al. (1988) observe that private-sector firms may exhibit high resource utilization efficiency, but they may fail to internalize environmental costs. So, they would continue using inputs that are pollution-creating, ignoring their social responsibility. They may compromise the environment to circumvent the potential expenditures on environmental restoration. In this case, the public-sector firm's environmental performance would be better than that of the private firm.

The differential environmental performance may result from regulatory differences. The public-sector firms may have a greater influential power, and thereby strong bargaining power with the environmental regulatory authorities. This may result in lower environmental performance. On the other hand, private-sector firms may alter the situation through their rent-seeking activities. However, public-sector firms have no scope to bribe the regulatory agencies to refrain from stringent punishments. On the contrary, private firms could adopt bribery to avoid punitive actions. In such a situation, public firms would be less polluting than private firms. Wang and Jin (2002), in their study, mention that private and public firms will have different environmental bargaining power with the pollution control authorities, as a result of which their environmental performance would vary. In addition, different types of firm are guided by various levels of informal regulatory norms, and community pressure, which may also cause performance differences.

Besides the above factors, economic and technological constraints may result in differences in environmental performance (Hilson, 2000). For instance, though highly efficient pollution-minimizing technologies are available, fund constraints may inhibit investment in these cleaner technologies by mining firms. In certain instances, structural barriers may also constitute obstacles in the implementation of these technologies. In addition, switching to this advanced technology requires adept and skilled personnel, necessitating imparting training to existing employees. However, investment in these training programmes may add to the cost of the firms already facing budget constraints. Another important barrier that prevents the adoption of newer and improved technology is the absence of a proper system.

7.4.2 Empirical Literature

As discussed earlier, hardly any studies exist that examine the social performance of mining firms in the literature. All the literature points to the concept of CSR, when social performance is the focal point of discussion. Hence, assuming CSR and social compliance are somewhat similar, we intend to draw insights from the CSR literature.

A study of two mining communities in Ghana made by Siawor-Robertson and Churchill (2015) reveals that CSR has a visible impact mostly on the infrastructure development of mining communities; the CSR activities lag in empowering the people and improving their livelihood. Studying the world's largest mining multinational company, the Rio Tinto Group (Kapelus, 2002), one finds that although the firms undertake measures to appear socially responsible, in reality, they fail to implement their idealistic principles and guidelines. Literature on CSR points to several indicators—such as size, ownership, age, and profitability—that have a significant impact on social performance. A study on the relationship between CSR and the profitability of the firm by Aupperle, Carrol, and Hatfield (1985) establishes no direct link.

Szablowski (2002), studying a mining company, Compania Minera Antamina (CMA), in Peru, revealed that the company was accused of inappropriate social impact assessment, low compensation to project-affected persons, and breach of trust. He pointed out that the CMA violated the norms by not engaging the local people and social experts in the social impact assessment procedure.

In the context of India, Herbert and Lahiri Dutt (2004) mentioned the failure of Coal India Limited (CIL), the state-owned coal company, which is one of the largest coal producers in the world, to provide satisfactory compensation to the project-affected people in Parej East in

Jharkhand. The promises made by CIL authorities, in terms of job assurance and substitute land, have never been met. Bhengara (1996) pointed out that the baseline survey on which the rehabilitation was based was flawed. It did not value the assets like trees, wells, or other non-movable assets, which were entitled to compensation under the Coal Bearing Areas (Acquisition and Development) Act (1957) and the Land Acquisition Act (LAA). Similarly, the people were not paid for the land and other common property resources over which the community had only the sole rights but no legal records.

Many studies have attempted to analyse the environmental performance of the mining industry.

In a study of artisanal, small and medium firms in Bolivia, Chile, and Peru, McMahon (1999) pointed out that, on average, although the artisanal and small mine subsector (ASM) is significantly dirtier per unit of output than other types of mining, this is not always the case. In contrast to the common belief that the ASM would be unviable if they included environmental costs into their production costs, these firms have proved themselves to be economically viable even when they internalize these environmental costs. The findings of the study showed that there was no significant difference in the environmental performance of medium and large-scale mines as well as new and old mines. The study also pointed out that ownership does not make any significant difference in environmental performance. This was evident from the case study of Chile. In Chile, although the state-owned company, Empresa Nacional de Mineria (ENAMI), is entrusted with smelting all of the output of small and medium producers, its smelters are heavy polluters, and there have been several lawsuits against them.

McMahon et al. (2000), in another study in the context of mining in Indonesia, revealed that medium-scale mines showed poor to very poor environmental performance and that ASM firms had very little consideration towards the environment. Contrarily, the environmental performance of large-scale mines showed improvement due to the use of state-of-the-art technologies and practices.

Chakravorty (2001), in his study, observed that small-scale mines in India did not pay any heed to environmental damage. They inadvertently destroyed the vegetation and the trees (at times deliberately for extra income), particularly at and near the area of mining operation, and they also did not take any steps to compensate for the environmental loss they caused.

Ghose (2003) pointed out that Indian mining was dominated by small-scale mining. Approximately 90% of India's mines operate on a small-scale basis. These mines use conventional techniques in their exploration activities. However, a few of them use semi-mechanized techniques. Conventional exploration techniques, lack of planning, and low-to-intermediate technology result in the poor recovery of mineable deposits. These mines hardly take any steps towards better environmental performance.

The above review of literature points towards a lack of serious research on the issues of mining displacement, rehabilitation, and community development. Development economics still has to respond to these aspects concerning the social cost of development. Similarly, the literature lacks serious studies on the environmental performance of mining companies. Our study makes a swift attempt to tide over this deficiency through our examination of the social and environmental performance of mining companies in the context of Odisha's mining industry.

7.5 Data and Methodology

7.5.1 The Case Study Area and Data Collection

To examine the environmental and social performance of mining firms in terms of their compliance regarding the environmental and social cost created by them due to their operation, the study considers the state of Odisha, one of the mineral-rich states situated in the east of India, as the study area. Particularly, we chose one district of Odisha (namely Jajpur) for conducting a household survey. We chose the Sukinda block of the Jajpur district as our survey area as 97% of the proven chromite reserves (chromite ores) in the country are in this valley, extending over an area of approximately 200 square kilometres (CSE, 2008). The selection of the district was purely based on the concentration of the mining companies in the said area and the volume of chromite ore production. This region produces the highest volume of chromite ores in the country (GoI, 2019). In addition, as our objective is to assess EC, the selection of this survey area, which is the sole chromite-producing region in India, can add value as chromite mining is considered to generate a huge volume of hazardous pollutants, hexavalent chromium, and other toxic metals that pollute air and water. So, selecting this area for survey purposes is justified to examine the extent to which these mining companies are environmentally complying from the household perspective.

Again, in this block, we zeroed in on two villages from one *panchayat* to obtain the number of households affected by the mining projects. The selection of these villages was done based on a maximum number of households who had given their land for mining purposes. As most of the households in these two villages in one *panchayat* have given their land for mining, we decided to conduct our survey here. The lists of affected households were collected from the district collectorate and the Department of Mines, Government of Odisha. Of the eighty households surveyed, fifty-nine provided their land for mining operations through different modes. Out of the fifty-nine households, a majority, thirty-nine, have surrendered their land to public-sector mining companies, and twenty to the private sector. These fifty-nine households are involved in a total of sixty-nine land transfer cases. The detailed information on the sample has been provided in Table 7.1

To conduct the survey, we designed a questionnaire that was initially framed in the English language and later translated into Odia. With this questionnaire, we conducted a pilot survey of a few households, and accordingly, necessary changes were made in the questionnaire. After this, the full phased actual survey was conducted with this pre-tested questionnaire during the period January–March 2021 and information was collected on the direct and indirect benefits that these mining firms created for the local community. The variables on which data were

Table 7.1 Data on surveyed villages

District	Jajpur
Block	Sukinda
Panchayat	Kaliapani
Villages	Ostapal and Saruabil

Source: Authors.

collected were mode of land transfer, nature of compensation, satisfaction of households with respect to compensation received and capacity-building exercise undertaken, environmental upgradation activities, and any other development activities performed. The questionnaire used for this purpose is provided in Appendix A7. This survey primarily aimed to study the environmental and social compliance activities from the perspective of local communities.

7.5.2 Methodology

We use the primary survey method to examine the social and EC of mining firms situated at Jajpur district of the state of Odisha. The data collected are analysed with the help of frequencies, percentages, and means and cross tabulation for the analysis. To compare the environmental performance between public- and private-sector firms, we use the proportion test.

7.6 Empirical Findings

7.6.1 Findings on Social Compliance

The main objective of this piece of work is to examine the degree of compliance made by the mining firms for the social and environmental damages they inflict. We attempted to assess compliance with respect to the compensation packages, infrastructure facilities, and education and health facilities provided through our primary survey.

The villages in which we conducted our survey were mostly remotely located. Most of the areas were hilly areas, having a shortage of rainfall, which had made them dry. The majority of the households surveyed consisted of the Adivasi population. At the time of the survey, each of the villages had *kuchha* roads. All of them had one primary school each. None of them have any upper primary or high school facilities. Most of the households did not have any interest in sending their children for higher education. However, a few of them, who wanted their children to get more education, sent them to the nearby upper primary and high schools, far off from their place of residence. Most of the households believed that higher education would not help them in any way to earn a better income and gain a better standard of living. Rather, they felt that if they spent their time learning other ancillary activities, such as animal rearing, agriculture, and other vocational work, this could fetch them a decent living. The older population of the villages felt that higher education would mean they drifted away from their own culture and heritage. They wanted to live their life in the beauty of nature by upholding their tradition and culture. Thus, education was not at all a priority for most of the households; barely a few children were high school certified, and no modern education has touched the villages. Table 7.2 presents the socio-economic characteristics of the surveyed households.

Mining companies acquired land from households in three ways—by means of direct purchase, on lease, and by means of paying compensation to them. Our results reveal that out of eighty households surveyed, fifty-nine households transferred land to the mining companies. In total,

Table 7.2 Socio-economic characteristics of the surveyed households

Variables	Frequencies	% of population
Gender		
Female	241	42.8
Male	321	57.2
Age category (years)		
<18	122	21.7
18–35	159	28.2
36–53	225	40
54>	56	10
Education		
Illiterate	153	27.3
0–8	293	52.1
9–10	96	17
10–12	20	3.6
Total population: 562 (n)	**562**	**100**
Occupation		
Agriculture	175	31.2
Mining	43	7.6
Small business	10	1.7
Livestock rearing	12	2.2
Construction	7	1.3

Source: Primary survey.

sixty-nine land transfer cases were identified where a few households were involved in more than one land transfer. Out of the total sixty-nine land transfers, two were by direct purchase, twenty-five by paying compensation, and the remaining forty-two were based on lease. Out of sixty-nine land transfers, forty-six transfers were made to public-sector firms and the remaining twenty-three to private-sector firms. Leaving aside the case of direct purchase, in all other cases, many of the households received jobs as compensation. Compared with the households that transferred land on lease; those households that had given their land after receiving compensation got more job opportunities in the mining companies (Table 7.3). The results show that out of the twenty-five households that transferred their land after receiving compensation, 92% obtained employment in the mining firms. But of the forty-two households that had given their land on lease, only 31% got jobs in the mining companies.

According to 65% of the households, mining companies have taken steps to increase the provision of education, health, and supplies of drinking water in the locality. However, a majority of them opined that education facilities are restricted only to the primary level. No efforts have been made to improve the employability of local youths through imparting vocational and technical skills. No higher education facilities have been created. As regards the provision of health facilities, a majority have admitted that health facilities have improved after the mining companies began their operations. The majority of households surveyed said that they have access to the free medical treatment provided by the doctor of the mining company and his or her staff when they visit their village.

Table 7.3 Job compensation on the basis of mode of land transfer

Mode of land transfer	No. of households	% of households
Compensation	23 (25)	92
Lease	13 (42)	31

Note: (1) In the case of direct purchase as a mode of land transfer, no job compensation was paid. Only one-off financial compensation was provided. (2) The figures in parentheses show the total number of households that transferred their land according to the corresponding mode of transfer.

Source: Primary survey.

This has led to a reasonable reduction in the medical expenses incurred by the households before the opening up of mining projects. Now they are able to receive health services provided by the mining companies on their doorstep, and referral to a government or private hospital for any disease has been tremendously reduced, resulting in a reduction in travel expenses. Most of the households also expressed satisfaction towards the 'Health awareness camps' organized by the mining firms at regular intervals, which help them to take preventative measures against health risks. However, despite these benefits, many households surveyed also expressed dissatisfaction with some of the facilities and the quality of services provided. For instance, they complained about the frequency of visits of doctors and staff. Respondents pointed out that doctors visited the villages once in a week. 'However, the disease comes without giving any prior notice,' mentioned one of the respondents. Respondents mentioned that major facilities were only meant for those who surrendered their land to the mining companies.

In our survey, we attempted to examine what kind of compliance measures have been undertaken by the mining firms for compensating the livelihood and common property loss resulting from the mining operations. Surprisingly, eight out of ten households were of the view that the companies have not taken any appropriate measures to make up for their loss. The majority of the households (87%) said that their livelihoods have been adversely affected by the mines. Households said that prior to the opening up of mines, they relied heavily on agriculture, livestock rearing, and collection of non-timber food products (NTFPs) for their livelihood. But now, after having lost their lands to mining firms, they are deprived of the benefits that they used to get from the land. This has led to food problems, reduced cash savings, and in some cases has brought down their additional income. Respondents said that due to the surrender of land, they are now unable to access the natural resources, such as fruit, fuelwood, and medicinal plants, referred to as provisioning services or NTFPs. They lamented that these NTFPs were commonly used for subsistence as well as commercial use, and as such they used to provide them with a means of income. They also said that these resources used to serve as a safety net or fall-back option for them during tough times, often in response to socio-economic and ecological shocks.

It was found from our survey that losses of land and associated livelihood for the affected households and local community were inadequately compensated. After the land acquisition, the mining companies did not pay proper attention to compensating the various losses. Respondents said that despite people's clamour against the compensation packages, the deals were sealed and agreed upon. Our findings reveal that as compliance for the land and livelihood loss, the firm's only made provision for one-time cash compensation, in some cases job and both job and cash compensation. No efforts had been taken to compensate for the livelihood loss by means of creating alternative livelihoods.

About 62% of the people were of the view that they had experienced no perceivable improvement in their standard of living in terms of asset holding, and 20% of households opined that this had actually deteriorated after mining begun. In terms of livestock ownership, 52% households observed a decline, whereas 45% reported no change. The respondents viewed that mining companies have not taken any steps towards making provisions for subsidies or providing common grazing land for livestock rearing. In the absence of alternative livelihood generation, the cash and job compensations to the households that surrendered their land was not enough to bring them out of poverty and provide them with a sustainable living. Lack of provisions with respect to alternative livelihood generation has more than offset the benefits of available employment opportunities. The jobs which most of the households got were either casual or low grade in nature. Mining firms cited the low level of skills as the reason behind such job offerings, according to the respondents. However, the mining firms have taken no efforts to improve the skills of the people by imparting capacity-building exercises. The majority of households believe that the mining jobs have not compensated for the land loss, as well as common pool resources loss. This might be the reason why the households said that there are no perceivable improvements in their economic condition and standard of living.

More than 90% of households were of the view that the mining firms did not adhere to the compliance measures that were promised by them before taking the lands. They said that besides providing job and cash compensation, the firms promised to devote funds towards the purchase of private land nearby to be used by the community to compensate for the loss of natural resources and common pool land. Also, promises were made to set aside a larger chunk of funds towards the development of land for agricultural production, and word was given that a part of the funding would be made for community development purposes. However, unfortunately, these were blank promises made to the households to persuade them to surrender their land. There was no written contract/agreement as regards these compliance measures, which provided the mining firms enough room not to deliver on their promises.

As regards compliance concerning compensation packages, 85% of the households expressed unhappiness and said that they had approached the concerned legal authority to get a better deal. In an attempt to obtain the point of view of the other party on this aspect, we tried to contact the mining officials, but our efforts were in vain as neither the public- nor the private-sector mining firms were ready to disclose any information. Thus, in the absence of the other party's perspective, we present here the social and economic compliance of the mining firms solely from the household perspective, which undeniably constitutes a major limitation of this chapter. Thus, we assess the compliance aspect concerning the promises made about compensation packages, economic and social infrastructure generation, and environmental upgrade efforts.

Our findings reveal that the rate of cash compensation was the same for each household, which was estimated on the amount and category of land transferred. As the cash part of the compensation was determined by the statutory authority, here the government itself, the rate of cash was fixed for different categories of land, and our household survey made it clear that all the mining companies abided by the rates prescribed by the agency. The only difference observed concerned job compensation, where the mining firms got the opportunity to bargain. To learn which type of firms complied better concerning promises made for compensation packages, we asked the question about which firms had kept their promises in relation to compensation packages (job).

As jobs were not provided as compensation in the case of direct purchase, we dropped the land transfers through direct purchase from our analysis to learn which type of company provided better job compensation. After dropping two cases of land transfer made by direct purchase, we had sixty-seven land transfer cases made based on either lease or by paying compensation. Around 82% (thirty-two out of thirty-nine) of households who had given their land to public-sector mining firms expressed dissatisfaction over compensation. Similarly, around 94% (nineteen out of twenty) of households that transferred their land to private mining firms revealed dissatisfaction over the compensation (Table 7.4).

The results show that thirty-eight households who were involved in sixty-seven land transfer cases (lease and compensation) got jobs in the concerned mining firms as compensation. Households involved in twenty-six (around 58%) of the forty-four land transfers (either compensation or lease) to public-sector mining companies got jobs. Households involved in twelve (around 53%) of the twenty-three land transfers (either by compensation or lease) to private-sector firms also received jobs as part of their compensation.

Thus, it can be said from Table 7.5 that the public-sector firms provided more jobs than the private-sector firms.

Besides assessing the difference in job compensation, we attempted to examine the opinion of households on the overall compliance measures adopted (both direct and indirect) by both types of firms. Given

Table 7.4 Percentage of households dissatisfied with compensation (job)

Type of firms	% of households dissatisfied	No of households	Total no. of households
Public	82	32	39
Private	94	19	20

Source: Primary survey.

Table 7.5 Percentage of households that received a job as compensation

Type of firm	Total no. of land transfers made (dropping two direct-purchase cases)	No. of households involved in the land transfers	% of households that received a job as compensation
Public	44	26	58
Private	23	12	53
Total	67	38	57

Source: Primary survey.

this, households were asked which type of firm had better compliance in terms of providing better compensation. We received four types of response: 'public', 'private', 'no difference', and 'cannot say'. As many as 44% (out of thirty-nine) of the households that transferred land to public-sector mining firms, opined that public-sector firms provided better compensation as compared with private firms. However, 28% of the households believed that private firms were better compared with private firms. Of the remaining, 21% of households believed that there was no difference and 7% chose to remain silent. Likewise, out of twenty households that transferred their land to private-sector mining firms, around 39% of households said that public-sector firms provided better compensation. Overall, 42% of households said that public firms performed better in providing compensation as against the private firms, 28% believed that private firms provided better compensation, 16% did not see any difference between the performance of both types of mining firms and 14% did not say anything (Fig. 7.1).

From the responses of households, we did not find any conclusive answer to who provided better compensation. It is evident from Fig. 7.1 that overall, 42% opined that public-sector firms gave better compensation, but 30% (16% indifferent and 14% with no response) did not say the same. Also, 28% of households believed private firms were better than public firms in providing compensation. Thus, we are unable to derive

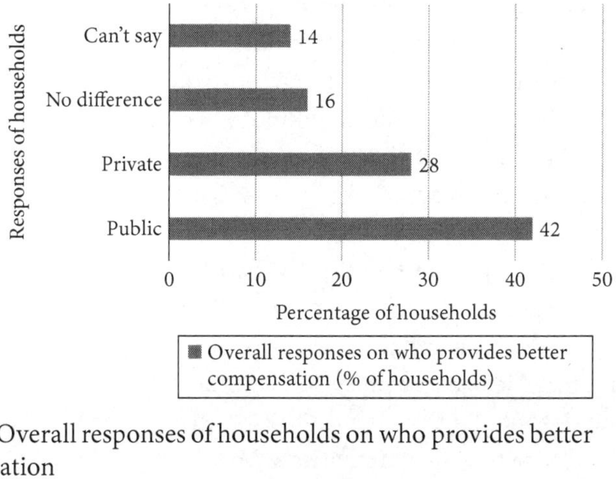

Fig. 7.1 Overall responses of households on who provides better compensation

Source: Primary survey conducted by the author (2020).

any definite conclusion based on the above results. This inconclusiveness is in line with our finding showing that the majority of households were dissatisfied with the compensation packages, irrespective of who had provided it.

7.6.2 Findings on EC

Along with examining the social compliance of mining firms from the perspective of affected households, our survey also assessed the EC aspect. Mining firms are required to adhere to certain environmental regulations prescribed by the State Pollution Control Board (SPCB) (in this case, Odisha State Pollution Control Board) to get the environmental clearance certificate. The SPCB specifies maximum limits for various environmental parameters, such as air quality, water quality, noise level, tree plantation, and overburden management. So, as per these standard norms, the mining firms have to keep their operations below these limits. If they do so, then they are referred to as environmentally compliant firms. However, though on paper these firms adhere to the prescribed limits, the ground reality is significantly different. This is evident from our results on the EC measures adopted by the mining companies from the perspective of one of the key stakeholders—the local community. We present our results in this section.

Respondents claim to understand the effect of mining activities on the environment, and they are aware of the need to improve the environmental condition. They are of the view that if companies want to do business, then they have to do it without harming them. A majority of the respondents reported that the environmental climate has undergone tremendous change since the mining firms started their operations. According to one of the respondents, companies are only interested in extraction, and they pay little attention to restoring the environment, which has been damaged due to their activities: 'Since the commencement of the mining project, we are not getting clean air to breathe.' Another respondent said, 'The firms are insensitive towards the effects of their activities and do not adopt adequate measures to restore the initial conditions. They have no idea how their activities are badly impacting our lives.'

It is clear that 95% of surveyed respondents said that there was a significant deterioration of environmental quality in the locality after mining operations began. The air is full of dust causing breathing problems and suffocation. Water contamination is evident from the quality of the water, which is full of dust particles.

To assess whether or not the mining companies are undertaking any activities to improve the environmental condition of the area to comply with the prescribed EC norms, we gathered responses for whether or not mining companies have undertaken any practices to improve the environment concerning air and groundwater quality, noise level, treatment of mine drainage water, and tree plantation. Using a three-point Likert scale, we gathered responses from the affected households on the EC of mining firms (Fig. 7.2).

As can be seen in Fig. 7.2, a significant proportion of the households expressed strong disagreement regarding the EC exercises undertaken by the mining firms. For instance, 93% of respondents believed that no significant steps have been undertaken by the mining firms to improve the air quality of the area. The only respite was the provision of drinking

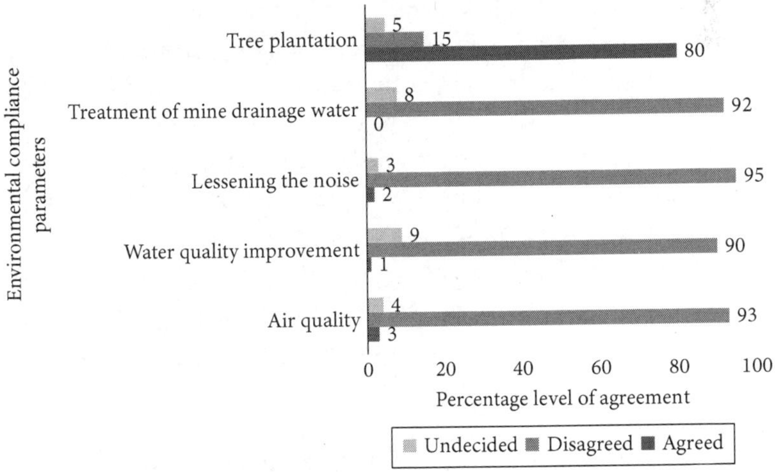

Fig. 7.2 Perceived responses of households for environmental compliance of mining firms

Source: Primary survey conducted by the author (2020).

water supplied by the mining firms through tankers. However, some respondents observed irregularities in the supply of drinking water. A few respondents complained that the drinking water facilities were provided only for those households who gave their land for mining.

One of the respondents lamented, 'Although we have not given our land, we stay in the same locality and suffer all the harmful effects of their operation. How can you differentiate in providing drinking water?'

Every eight out of ten households responded that the quality of groundwater had deteriorated since the beginning of the mining operation. The water is contaminated with toxic dust particles, the impact of which is felt in the form of waterborne diseases among the local population. Although the mining companies conduct health camps from time to time and have made provision for health-care facilities, 90% of the respondents were of the opinion that they have not undertaken any action to improve the water quality in the locality.

As regards the question related to noise creation and the measures taken to ease the effect, 95% responded that no significant effort has been made to mitigate the noise and vibrations resulting from blasting in the mine sites.

Regarding the treatment of mine drainage water, a majority of them responded (around 92%) that the firms release their toxic water into nearby water bodies, causing contamination. This has brought down the number of freshwater animals, such as fish. The flora and fauna of the locality have been greatly affected by the release of this untreated water. On the same point, they also revealed that no specific steps have been taken to improve the condition of freshwater resources and restore the flora and fauna in the locality.

However, 80% of respondents opined that mining firms have taken up tree plantation activities as a part of green area development in surrounding areas. However, that is not adequate to mitigate the pollution created by the firms, as one respondent asserted.

7.6.2.1 Comparison of environmental performance between public- and private-sector firms

Having discussed the EC of mining firms concerning several parameters, such as air quality, water quality, noise level, and tree plantation, we also attempted to look into the difference between the environmental performance of private- and public-sector mining firms. To achieve this, we gathered responses from households on the overall environmental performance (related to improving air quality, water quality, noise management, tree plantation, etc.) of the private and public mining firms. In this regard, we asked our respondents which type of company, public or private, is more environmentally non-compliant. We received responses of four types: 'public', 'private', 'both', and 'do not know'. Of the thirty-nine households that provided their land to public-sector mining firms, twenty-four (62%) households opined that both were equally non-compliant. On the other hand, of the twenty households that transferred their land to private-sector firms, eleven (55%) believed that both types of firms were equally non-compliant. It can be inferred from this that both private- and public-sector firms are equally non-compliant when it comes to environmental performance. However, to ascertain the statistical significance of the difference between public- and private-sector mining firms in adhering to EC, we undertook a proportion test.

We present the result of the proportion test to determine whether or not ownership of a firm makes any difference to the EC of mining firms in Table 7.6.

Samples 1 and 2 consist of the responses of the households that provided their land to public-sector and private-sector mining firms respectively. P1, P2, and P are the proportions of responses corresponding to the households that transferred their land to the public sector and private sector, respectively. While n1 and n2, are the size of households that provided their land to the public sector, the private

Table 7.6 Results of two-proportion Z-test

Column 1	Proportion (P1)	Size n1, n2, N
Sample 1	0.62	39
Sample 2	0.55	20
Pooled sample	0.593220339	59
Z	0.295310192	–
P value	0.767756931	–

Source: Author's estimation.

sector (N) is the pooled sample size. Our null hypothesis here is that both private- and public-sector firms are equally non-compliant in respect of their EC performance. It can be seen that the *p*-value of the Z statistic is greater than 0.05, indicating that we do not have sufficient evidence to reject the null hypothesis. Thus, we accept the null hypothesis and conclude that there are no significant differences between public- and private-sector firms in their EC performance, and they are equally non-compliant.

From all the above field responses, we can infer that mining companies care least about the environment. This is evident from the overall dissatisfaction of the respondents concerning the compliance measures adopted. This is in stark contrast to the results that the mining companies declare in their EC reports to the SPCB, wherein they show their environmental performance with regard to various parameters well below the permissible limits (Table 7.7). This indicates that mining performances on the ground are significantly different to how they present on reports, which is a matter of concern.

In Table-7.7, we show the environmental performance of four mining firms to whom our surveyed households have transferred their land. Among these, one is a public-sector firm and the remaining three are private-sector mining firms.

Tables 7.7 and 7.8 show the performance of the concerned mining firms on six indicators—air pollution, fugitive emissions, noise pollution, quality of groundwater, quality of mine drainage water, and overburden

Table 7.7 Environmental performance of mining firms situated at Odisha

Firms	Type	AAQ	FE	ANL	GWQ	MDQ	OBR
1	Public	47	272	47	0.037	0.024	1
2	Private	45.1	312	52	0.041	0.22	2
3	Private	52.3	315	55	0.022	1.025	2
4	private	43.2	285	61	0.035	0.69	3
Permissible limits		100	1,200	85	0.05	0.1	1

Source: Odisha State Pollution Control Board, Bhubaneswar, and EC reports of the concerned mining firms, 2019.

Table 7.8 Environmental compliance parameters with standard permissible limits

Parameters	Permissible limits
AAQ (PM10 (µg/m3))	100
Fugitive emissions (µg/m3)	1200 (µg/m3)
Ambient noise level	85 dB(A) during daytime
Groundwater quality, hexavalent chromium (mg/l)	0.05
Quality of mine discharge water (mg/l) Cr (VI)	0.1, 2.0
OBR (overburden removal)	Satisfactory, partial, poor (1, 2, 3)

Source: Odisha State Pollution Control Board, 2019.

management.[1] It can be seen that most of the firms comply with the prescribed standards (Table 7.8) on most of the indicators. A few firms deviate on parameters such as quality of mine drainage water and overburden removal. This result is in stark contrast to what we found on the ground. This is evident from the responses of the majority of households, who feel that no significant steps have been taken by the mining companies to improve the environmental condition of the area. Thus, our study indicates a wide discrepancy in the performance of mining firms on compliance measures—ground reality is different from what is shown on paper.

7.7 Discussion

It is of paramount importance to draw inferences from the results of our analysis against the basic premises we made in the beginning of

[1] Mineral extraction usually involves the removal of the topsoil in the case of underground mining and, in the case of open-cast mining, removal of other unwanted soil from the pit. This unwanted soil contains hazardous material, which can have a detrimental impact on the environment. Run-off of this soil in water may contaminate the surrounding water bodies and thereby hurt agricultural productivity. Thus, before the mining operation begins, mining firms are required to submit a plan to the Indian Bureau of Mines regarding the management of this unwanted soil and minimize environmental damage. Mining firms usually achieve this by stabilizing dumps with plants, mat fixing, or constructing retention walls.

our chapter. The study does not attempt to examine the performance of mining firms against any prescribed standard social and environmental norms. Rather, we aim to assess the social and EC performance of mining firms from the perspective of mining-affected households. A few inferences can be drawn from our study that may help improve the condition. Our results reveal that land acquisition has led to land-based livelihood losses to a large extent, indicating no significant effort by mining firms in the generation of alternative livelihood options. Again, the dissatisfaction of the majority of households with inadequate generation of livelihood options points towards the failure on the part of the mining firms in keeping their promises given before the land acquisition. Most dissatisfaction was observed with regard to compensation packages, which could be seen as part of non-compliance. The probable reasons for this non-compliance could be attributed to policy and regulatory lapses. The mining companies took into account only the direct economic losses that resulted from land transfer, ignoring the indirect losses, such as loss of common land resources and forest degradation, and therefore these affected households have not been compensated for this. Thus, our results indicate that the time has come to take more than a cursory look at the existing compensation policy of the mining firms and bring in necessary changes to provide maximum benefits to mining-affected households.

Mining causes serious damage to the environment, which in turn poses a problem in obtaining a social licence to operate. Our survey reveals that despite well-established environmental regulations by the government; compliance varies significantly on the ground. This weak implementation may be the result of various factors, such as a lack of local government focus, an unhealthy nexus between local government and mining firms, and firms' resistance to compliance based on cost-cutting. In such a situation, if firms can be convinced about the compliance benefits for the business, there would be greater EC as adhering to environmental norms can single out a firm in a crowd and thereby create favourable conditions for them to gain social acceptance by improving their image in the eyes of the local community.

In achieving a higher degree of EC, the role of government (both local and state) cannot be negated. The degree of EC is a joint outcome of government regulation and firm initiative (Wang and Wheeler, 2005). The cost of checking pollution and the resultant government fines increases with the rise in output. This implies that the relative cost of EC falls, with an increase in output implying that better environmental performance leads to better financial performance.

As, during the past two decades, people and society have become more aware of environmental and social issues, they are now pressing for a cleaner and greener environment. The affected households have now started to raise their voices for more practical environmental and social compliance measures requiring more than simple publication of environmental reports. In this respect, the time has come for the mining firms to formulate their business plans around some practically sustainable environmental and social practices.

Compliance measures (social and environmental) have a market mechanism associated with them that secretly carves out a path for mining firms for their long-term existence and operation and paves the way for obtaining a social licence to operate. Affected households and the local community care about their income, livelihood options, standard of living, development of their local area, a better future for their children, and a healthy environment free from pollution. The mining firms that provide them with all these benefits send a signal to the community about their competence. It cannot be denied that these compliance measures are expensive, but they are highly correlated with the firm's competence. Only those firms that can bear the costs will eventually gain local community acceptance for their operation, which can make a strong business case for their profitability.

Thus, through this chapter, we suggest to the mining firms that there is significant benefit in being compliant. By adhering to better social and environmental compliance, firms can increase the possibility of obtaining society's approval for their business operations and thereby their profitability opportunities.

Finally, it is worth mentioning that social and environmental compliance has important practical implications for business and the government. Our results indicate that implementing EC measures will have a long-term positive impact on the sustainability of business. For local and state governments, our findings seem to be an eye-opener indicating that there is a greater need for more stringent environmental monitoring and swift actions to compel the mining firms to adhere to environmentally sustainable practices.

7.8 Conclusion

In this chapter, we examined the environmental and social compliance of mining firms in the context of the Jajpur district of Odisha. Specifically, we defined social compliance as the direct and indirect benefits provided to the individual or community for the direct and indirect economic, environmental, and social losses made due to the transfer of land, displacement, and damage to natural resources. To explore whether or not the mining firms are socially and environmentally compliant and whether or not there is a possibility of difference between public- and private-sector firms in this regard, a survey of eighty households was conducted, out of which fifty-nine surrendered their land to mining companies in one of the minerals-rich districts of Odisha.

Our findings about social compliance reveal that land acquisition has led to land-based livelihood losses to a large extent, indicating no significant effort by mining firms in the generation of alternative livelihood options. The highest dissatisfaction was observed concerning compensation packages, which could be seen as part of the non-compliance. The results also show that in terms of providing job compensation, public-sector firms outperform private-sector firms. However, when it comes to overall compliance performance (both financial and non-financial compensation), our results do not find any difference between the two types of firm.

Our findings concerning EC highlight the least compliance and commitment to the environment. Though mining companies inflict serious environmental damage, they do not exhibit responsible behaviour to mitigate those environmental risks. Our findings point out the failure of mining firms on several environmental parameters, such as maintaining air and water quality, lessening noise pollution, and taking care of biodiversity loss—from the affected household perspective. This is in stark contrast to the results that they mention in their environmental reporting, which indicates that in respect of EC, the reality on the ground is significantly different. This difference in results may be due to a lack of local government focus, an unhealthy nexus between local government and mining firms, and firms' resistance to compliance based on cost-cutting.

The findings also reveal that public and private firms are equally non-compliant about adopting EC measures.

While the literature provides evidence that the social and environmental performance of mining firms is improving (Hodge, 2014), our results stand diametrically opposed to this. This may be because our study assesses the performance of mining companies from the perspective of the people affected by the project and is not based on the social and environmental reports of companies, which many of the studies are. Thus, our study presents the actual reality with respect to the social and environmental performance of mining companies. The fact that emerges from our study is that the local community is increasingly becoming aware of the impacts of mining operations and has started to expect adequate compliance measures to mitigate the loss they suffer. This awareness may be the result of an improved world communication system, which has empowered communities to have a larger say in their own future. If the mining companies are unable to make provisions of the required measures, conflict would be the natural outcome. Thus, social and environmental compliance can be viewed as a key success factor for the sustenance of any mining operation.

In this chapter we suggest that environmental and social compliance brings benefit to businesses by helping them obtain a social licence to operate. Thus, the time has come for mining firms to formulate their business plans around some practically sustainable environmental and social practices.

Appendix A7

Environmental Impacts of Chromite Mining

Chromite mining consists of a process to extract chromium ore. This process can have significant negative consequences for the environment. The key areas of impact are water contamination, land degradation, and air pollution. A detailed breakdown of key areas of impact is presented below.

Water Contamination

- **Chromium leaching**: chromite contains chromium, which can exist in various forms, such as trivalent (Cr (III)) and hexavalent (Cr (VI)) forms. Hexavalent Cr (VI) is highly soluble and harmful. During mining, hexavalent Cr (VI) can leach from waste rock and overburden piles, thereby contaminating ground and surface water sources.
- **Mine drainage**: large volumes of water run-off are generated in the case of opencast mining. This might prove harmful if not treated properly as this chromium-laden water coming from opencast mining can heavily pollute nearby water bodies.
- **Tailing disposal**: tailings are produced while processing chromite ores. Tailings are waste products that can also contain chromium and other heavy metals. Improper storage of tailings can lead to contamination of water bodies.

Land Degradation

- **Habitat loss**: chromite deposits are often largely found in forested areas. Chromite mining results in deforestation, destroying wildlife habitats and thereby impacting the biodiversity system.
- **Soil erosion**: mining activities disrupt the soil, making it vulnerable to erosion by wind and water. Ultimately, this can result in the loss of fertile topsoil and sedimentation in waterways.
- **Overburden dumps**: large amounts of waste rock (overburden) are generated to access the ore body. Ineffective and improper disposal of overburden pollutes surrounding areas if not managed effectively.

Air Pollution

- **Dust generation**: different stages of mining activities (such as drilling, blasting, and transportation of ore) generate a large volume of dust containing chromium and other particles. This dust generation can be one of the key reasons for respiratory problems in nearby communities.

Exposure to chromium through contaminated water, soil, and air can have serious health impacts, including respiratory problems, skin irritation, and even cancer. Overall, extracting chromium through the process of chromite mining can have significant negative environmental consequences. Thus, it necessitates due consideration in terms of mitigating the environmental challenges created by mining before the chromite mining process takes place. Mitigating these impacts requires robust laws, responsible mining practices, and adequate and effective pollution control measures.

8

Summary and Conclusion

8.1 Introduction

Minerals are considered vital natural resource endowments that have enormous value for any nation. The finiteness and non-renewable nature of minerals makes them most valuable in the commodity basket. Almost every aspect of modern life depends on minerals and mineral products such as base metals, precious metals, coal, iron, sand, limestone, and industrial minerals.

Everything that people use—household appliances, computers, farm equipment, mobile phones, fertilizers, medicines, transport vehicles, beauty products—relies heavily on minerals and mineral products for their production and distribution. As such, minerals constitute key raw materials for many basic industries and are therefore considered as a major source of development (GoI, 2010). India is a nation blessed with many key mineral resources. The availability of key mineral resources makes India a resource-rich nation among the global key players. In India, the mining industry provides basic raw materials to many key sectors of the economy, such as manufacturing and power. It is envisaged that as a primary resource supplier to many key sectors, this industry has the potential to affect the growth, employment, and income of the economy through its direct and indirect impact. Thus, low production and productivity of this industry may bring a halt to the production and productivity in related manufacturing industry and curtail overall economic growth. Improving the productivity efficiency and competitive performance of this industry can be seen as a strategy to accelerate the growth of the nation. Along with having the potential to influence the growth of the nation via output, income, and employment, this industry has its negative side too in the form of generating negative externalities. These negative externalities can be broadly divided into two

The Indian Mining Industry. Meenakshi Parida and S. Madheswaran, Oxford University Press.
 DOI: 10.1093/9780198954392.003.0008

dimensions—environmental and social. Mineral extraction causes serious environmental damage in terms of changes in land use patterns and environmental pollution. The mining industry is considered to be one of the most polluting industries. Mineral extraction also causes displacement and marginalization of local communities by having a large impact on their livelihoods. The environmental and social dimension of mining makes it a problem for firms to obtain the social and economic licences needed to operate. Obtaining a social licence to operate necessitates both environmental and social compliance on the part of the mining firms.

Against this backdrop, the aim of this book was to evaluate the performance of the mining industry, a primary resource supplier industry in India, from three dimensions: productivity, social, and environmental. The book also offered policy suggestions in case of the existence of further scope for performance improvement. To accomplish these objectives, the book was divided into eight chapters.

8.1.1 Economic Impact of the Mining Industry in India

Chapter 2 dealt with the evaluation of the economic impact of the mining industry on some important macroeconomic variables—output, income, and employment. We used the latest input–output table of 2013–2014 to examine this objective. The findings showed that the mining industry had a noticeable impact on these macroeconomic variables, though not significantly so. The effect of mining on output showed that one additional output production in mining leads to an increase in the total output of the economy by approximately two units. This total effect consists of both direct and indirect effects. Our results reveal that out of the total effect, the total indirect effect of mining output expansion is 0.88 (industrial support effects + production-induced effects), which signifies the interconnectedness that this industry has with others. This high interconnectedness with the suppliers of the inputs industry and the industries that consume its product as their intermediate product is expected to bring positive results in both directions, such as productivity generation throughout the economy, as well as supporting the productive activity of others. Our results also find the income multiplier for this industry to be high (i.e. 0.98), indicating the prevalence of a relatively higher wage rate in this industry. Our findings also establish that the contribution of this industry to the country's output and income will be more via intersectoral linkages if the demand requirements of this industry (both domestic and export) increase. This book suggests that domestic and export demand boost needs key policy intervention from the Government of India.

The results also show a considerable impact of the mining industry on employment generation, which is visible from a high employment multiplier of 0.72 in this sector. This high employment creation potential is all the more important from the viewpoint of a labour-abundant country like India. The large workforce and increased capital–labour ratio in the organized sector for a labour-abundant country like India is truly a grave concern, which has been well highlighted by the Government of India (GOI, 2013). If India has to meet the demographic dividend challenge anyway, it has no choice but to target industries where the employment multiplier is higher. In this context, the mining industry assumes importance due for its high employment-generating potential. A study by Chakraborty (2013), pointed out that roughly 10 million people would need a job every year for the next fifteen years. Finding productive jobs for such a huge number is a big challenge, and the answer lies in stepping up the employment intensity of growth. Further, these additional jobs would have to be created keeping in mind the fact the overall structural changes that the Indian labour market has been going through, particularly in terms of movement of people away from agriculture. Thus, the non-farming sector has to gear up to shoulder the burden of agriculture. Amongst the non-farming sector, while the services sector has already led India's growth and employment story for some time, now it is high time for the mining industry to play an important role in creating jobs in the coming years, as employment in manufacturing has also reached a stagnant position.

Similarly, our findings point to a reasonable high-income multiplier by showing that one unit increase in the output of this industry would result in 0.98 units of income generation for the entire economy. This figure would be more were the employee's expenditures to be included in the estimation procedure. The high-income creating potential of this industry may be due to the higher wage and salary payment of this sector due to the nature of risk involved in the mining activity, which is then translated into increased demand for goods and services of other industries, which in turn employs more workers to satisfy the increased demand, thereby leading to more income generation.

The results also reveal that within the mining industry, the output expansionary impact is high for the metallic subsector, which is followed by coal, non-metallic, and petroleum. Again, within the metallic subsector, manganese ore has the highest output expansionary impact. For non-metallic and petroleum, the output multipliers are the highest for mica and crude petroleum, respectively. The income expansionary impact is more or less the same for all the subsectors, implying that across the subsectors, the wage rate is same. However, the average employment multiplier values are the highest for the non-metallic subsector, followed by metallic, coal, and petroleum.

This chapter concludes by saying that although mining in India has a moderate impact on the economy compared with other sectors, government policies should not neglect the mining ecosystem and the associated businesses across the value chain. Rather, the Government of India should promote mineral development, giving priority to environmental and social concerns. In this context, it is suggested that key investment areas of mining operations should be identified, focusing on their respective strengths and weaknesses.

8.1.2 Challenges of the Indian Mining Industry

This chapter attempts to identify the key challenges faced by the Indian mining industry by using an extensive literature survey and referring to expert opinions. The findings indicate that despite India being abundant in some mineral deposits, its contribution to the national economy is rather meagre. This poor contribution can be attributed to many challenges faced by the industry. The chapter identifies factors such as low reserves-to-production ratio, lack of investment in exploration activities, inadequate infrastructure facilities, procedural and permit delays in mining operations, land acquisition issues, shortage of skilled human capital, corruption, sustainability, and the country's complex mining policy environment as the key challenges that the mining industry faces currently. Along with identifying the problems, this chapter also attempts to put forward some possible pathways to overcome these challenges. The chapter concludes by mentioning that several critical success factors, enablers, and building blocks in the form of supportive government policy, adequate infrastructure facilities, raw material security, and supply-chain optimization techniques, as well as sustainability and environment reforms, can help overcome the challenges.

8.1.3 Total Factor Productivity, Trends, and Effect of Ownership

Chapter 4 seeks to estimate the total factor productivity (TFP) of the whole mining industry and its coal, petroleum, metallic, and non-metallic subsectors. This chapter uses the Levinsohn and Petrin method to estimate the TFP levels. The results show that over the entire period of analysis, the TFP growth for the whole industry shows a declining trend. The decline in TFP growth is more visible during the period 2006–2011, considered the mining boom phase. The possible reason for this decline in TFP could be higher commodity prices due to the mining boom experienced during this period.

The results also reveal the existence of a productivity gap between public and private mining firms over the studied period. The results also show that private firms are more productive than public firms in three subsectors of the mining industry—metallic, non-metallic and coal, with the exception of the petroleum subsector. The non-metallic-mining subsector exhibited the highest productivity differential, where private firms were approximately two times more productive than their public counterparts. The metallic and coal subsectors followed suit, where private firms registered more productivity than public firms. Our results confirm the findings of Das (2012). However, our study differs from Das's assessment in several respects, such as study period, sample, and the variables construction. Again, the same methodological approach as used by Das was followed in this book, which helped us conclude that the old model is fully compatible with the new set of updated, latest, and larger data. The findings point towards a consistent productivity gap between public and private mining firms, raising concerns for policymakers. The continuing productivity differential defies the purpose of opening up the mining industry to private-sector participation as it fails to create a healthy competitive environment to give a boost to the public sector.

This chapter also highlights the probable reasons for the low productivity of public-sector firms. These reasons can be found in the public choice and property rights theory. According to the public choice theory, public-sector firms perform inefficiently due to the agency problem, which states that there is a difference in ownership (principals) and management (agents) in the case of a public-sector enterprise. As managers have more and better information than owners, there is every chance that they will take undue advantage of this information asymmetry and undertake wasteful projects in their own self-interest. In the absence of proper monitoring by owners, managers misuse their status for personal gain at the expense of the investor's interest (Li and Xia, 2008). Inefficient performance can also result from a lack of incentives at the organizational and individual level. At the organizational level, unlike private firms, the managers of public firms are seldom concerned about organizational improvements. The losses of these firms are very often adjusted through budgetary support, giving the public firm managers the least incentive to perform efficiently. Often, to accomplish their political career objectives, public-sector managers emphasize employment generation at the cost of efficiency. On the individual front, fixed tenure and pay scale do not provide much incentive to public-sector managers to perform efficiently. As their salaries are not linked to profit and they have an assurance of a fixed tenure, they do not put in much effort towards organizational improvement. Besides incentives and agency problems; the low productivity of public-sector firms can stem from property rights. As ownership, in the case of public firms, is diffused among all members of society, and no member has the right to sell his or her property, there is little incentive for owners to monitor the behaviour of managers. On the contrary, the ownership of private firms is concentrated among fewer individuals, and each individual has the right to sell his or her property shares. This gives the owners the incentive to keep an eye on the management to ensure better productivity. Apart from these issues, several other problems, such as inadequate and unskilled manpower, absence of upgraded technology, and inadequate infrastructural facilities, could be attributable to the low productivity of public-sector mining firms.

The reasons may vary from firm to firm and sector to sector. Since our findings point to the large productivity difference between public and private firms, as the previous study did (Das, 2012), it implies that the findings of the previous research have not been effectively implemented to bridge the gap between the two types of firm. Thus, all these pertinent causes provide us with enough impetus to call for the attention of policymakers to take the necessary steps to provide incentives to the public firms, improve infrastructural facilities, upgrade manpower by providing training and learning opportunities, facilitate better and improved technologies so that they can improve productivity levels, and thereby stand up to the private firms in the competitive field.

8.1.4 Technical Efficiency of Mining Firms

Chapter 5 estimated the technical efficiency of the coal-mining industry using the stochastic frontier analysis (SFA). The results reveal that coal-mining companies are operating at as high as 75% of their potential output; however, no company is able to follow the best practice technique and achieve 100% efficiency. The unavailability of advanced machinery and equipment, poor infrastructure, limited research and development facilities, a lack of adequate technology support services, and a shortage of skilled personnel may be some of the reasons for not achieving 100% efficiency. The findings also reveal that the coal-mining subsector is dominated by the presence of a considerable proportion of medium-efficient firms, implying that there exists the scope for improving technical efficiency (TE).

8.1.5 Energy Use Efficiency and Its Determinants

Chapter 6 focuses on the estimation of energy-use efficiency of the Indian mining industry at four subsectoral levels—coal, metallic, non-metallic, and petroleum. The chapter attempts to estimate the energy-use efficiency of the mining firms at subsectoral levels in a production theoretic framework. To accomplish the objective, the stochastic frontier approach is used. The data for this was extracted from the Centre for Monitoring Indian Economy (CMIE) Prowess database for a period of seventeen years, from 2000 to 2017. Drawing upon Schmidt and Lovell (1979) and further described in, for example, Kumbhakar and Lovell (2000) and following Filippini and Hunt (2010), the energy-demand frontier for power (fuel and electricity) was constructed for the four subsectors of the mining industry to estimate the energy efficiency. The energy-demand frontier showed the minimum amount of energy consumed to produce a given level of output, taking into account the production technology, input prices, and non-energy inputs, etc. The energy efficiency estimated in this way embeds both technical and allocative efficiencies (Filippini and Hunt, 2015).

The findings indicate the existence of energy inefficiency among the subsectors. The results show that the average energy efficiency of the firms under study during the sample period are 0.8536, 0.7924, 0.5116, and 0.8215 for coal, metallic, non-metallic, and petroleum, respectively. These efficiency scores imply that there exists scope for improving energy efficiency by reducing energy consumption. For instance, in the case of coal-mining, it would be possible to reduce the energy consumption by 14.64% and still produce the same amount of output without using any extra inputs. The results point towards the existence of the highest amount of energy saving potential (48.84%) with the non-metallic-mining subsector as it operates with the least energy efficiency.

A second-stage regression analysis, for identifying drivers of energy efficiency, reveals that size is an important determinant of energy efficiency, being positive and significant. On the other hand, age has a neutral effect on the energy efficiency of the firm. The quality of labour also has significant positive impact on the energy efficiency performance for all the subsectors, implying that the higher the quality of labour, the greater will be the energy-use efficiency. The coefficient of the capital–energy (KE) ratio is positive and significant for all the sectors, implying that improving energy efficiency requires more capital. The coefficient of regulation dummy is insignificant in all the four subsectors, implying that the implementation of the Energy Conservation Act (2001) has not had much impact on energy efficiency. The results also reveal interesting outcomes concerning ownership, showing a significant positive effect on three subsectors—coal, metallic, and non-metallic. The petroleum subsector shows the opposite result.

Finally, this chapter discusses certain policy measures to improve energy-use efficiency. In the wake of expanding industrial production from all industrial quarters, it is advocated that new investments should be based on energy-efficient mining equipment, keeping in mind the cost-effectiveness. It is also suggested that as the mining industry is not a big consumer of industrial energy, unlike the manufacturing industry, for substantial greenhouse gas emission, a countrywide effort would be necessary and alternative strategies for energy reduction, such as fuel switching and CO_2 capture and storage, should be attempted for meaningful greenhouse gas reduction. It is also advocated that the focus of investment should be directed towards those sectors that are constantly poor energy performers to improve the energy efficiency of the whole industry. Finally, it is suggested that improvement in energy efficiency can be achieved by adopting policies such as energy efficiency trading.

Chapter 7 examines the social and environmental compliance of mining firms in the context of the Jajpur district of Odisha. Specifically, social performance is defined as the direct and indirect benefits provided to the individuals or community for the direct and indirect economic, environmental, and social losses incurred due to the transfer of land, displacement, and damage to natural resources. To explore whether or not the mining firms were socially and environmentally compliant and whether or not there is any possibility of performance differences between public and private sector firms, this book surveyed eighty households, out of which fifty-nine surrendered their land to mining companies in one of the minerals-rich districts of Odisha state.

The major findings on social compliance reveal that land acquisition has led to land-based livelihood losses to a large extent, indicating no significant effort by mining firms in the generation of alternative livelihood options. In addition, the dissatisfaction of the majority of households with the inadequate generation of livelihood options points towards the failure on the part of the mining firms in keeping their promises given before the land acquisition. Most dissatisfaction was observed with respect to compensation packages, which could be seen as a part of the non-compliance. The results also show that in terms of providing job compensation, public-sector firms outperform private-sector firms. However, when it comes to overall compliance performance (both financial and non-financial compensation), our results do not find any conclusive evidence of difference between the two types of firm. The probable reasons for this non-compliance could be attributed to policy and regulatory lapses. Also, the mining companies took into account only the direct economic losses that resulted from land transfer, ignoring the indirect losses, such as loss of common land resources and forest degradation, and therefore these affected households have not been compensated for this. Thus, our results indicate that the time has come to take a detailed look at the existing compensation policy of the mining firms and bring in necessary changes to provide maximum benefits to the mining-affected households.

The findings on environmental compliance highlight least compliance and commitment to the environment. Mining companies, though inflicting serious environmental damage, do not follow responsible behaviour to mitigate those environmental risks. Our findings point to the failure of mining firms on several environmental parameters, such as maintaining air and water quality, lessening noise pollution, and taking care of biodiversity loss from the affected household perspective. This is in stark contrast to the results that the mining companies mention in their environmental reporting, indicating that the reality on the ground is significantly different. This difference in results may be due to a lack of local government focus, an unhealthy nexus between local government and mining firms, and the resistance of firms to compliance, based on cost-cutting. The findings also reveal that public and private firms are equally non-compliant with respect to adopting environmental compliance measures.

While the literature provides evidence of increasing social and environmental performance of mining firms (Hodge, 2014), our results stand diametrically opposed to it. This may be because this work assesses the performance of mining companies from the perspective of the project-affected people and is not based on the social and environmental reports of the companies, which many of the studies are. The fact that emerges from this piece of work is that the local community is increasingly becoming aware of the impacts of mining operations and has started to expect adequate compliance measures for the loss they suffer.

This awareness may be the result of an improved world communication system, which has empowered communities to have a greater say in their own future. If the mining companies are unable provide for the required measures, conflict would be the natural outcome. Thus, social and environmental compliance can be viewed as a key success factor for sustaining any mining operation. Finally, it is suggested in this chapter that since environmental and social compliance brings benefit to the business by helping it obtain a social licence to operate, mining firms should formulate their business plan around some practically sustainable environmental and social practices.

8.2 Policy Implications

In this book we attempted to analyse the Indian mining industry from three perspectives—economic, social, and environmental. Particularly, we examined the veracity of several questions: (i) What impact does the mining industry have on macroeconomic variables such as output, income, and employment, and what are the roadblocks in this industry? (ii) How is the mining industry performing in terms of productivity? (iii) Does private sector participation in the industry increase productivity level? (iv) How does the mining industry perform in terms of energy efficiency? and (v) How do mining firms perform in terms of social and environmental compliance? In the quest to answer these questions, we analysed the mining industry in the Indian context. Thus, our economic analysis provides us with some policy implications. However, all the policy implications drawn from our empirical analysis are indicative in nature due to the fact that it is not comprehensive. Thus, the primary aim of this book has been to develop and implement the most appropriate analytical and methodological framework to examine the above issues in the context of the performance of the mining industry in India.

The study demonstrates empirically that the mining industry has a noticeable impact on the Indian economy for the simple reason that it has considerable interconnectedness with other sectors as it is primarily a raw material supplier to other sectors. The study also establishes that the TFP growth of the whole mining industry shows a declining trend. The book brings to light the fact that in the majority of the sectors, private-sector firms are more productive than their public counterparts. With respect to energy saving, the study establishes the existence of energy-saving potential by enhancing energy-use efficiency. On social and environmental compliance measures, the study finds high overall dissatisfaction and no significant difference in the environmental compliance performance of public and private mining firms. However, we abstain from making any conclusion regarding the impact of the mining industry on social welfare as addressing this aspect needs more investigation of several questions about the industry's revenue generation and resource allocation process and the redistributive policy of the government.

As this industry has a noticeable economic impact, it tends to imply that the mining industry should be allowed to expand projects in all possible locations. However, this implication should be viewed cautiously, because the mining operation brings with it several associated problems pertaining to social and environmental concerns. However, presently it is difficult to imagine a modern society without this industry due to the invaluable contribution it makes in our day-to-day lives. The only way round the problem is to envisage a trade-off between how much to produce and social and environmental concerns.

Our results highlight the productivity gap between private and public mining firms. This raises questions about the stability of state ownership over time, because the superior performance of the private sector in terms of productivity may create the impression that only when a firm is privatized is its productivity enhanced, suggested by the public choice and property rights theory. In the long run, this would motivate policy-makers to further the privatization process by divesting the public-sector firms. Thus, the stability of the state ownership of mining firms is at stake as public-sector mining firms are experiencing low productivity growth, as indicated by our analysis. It cannot be denied that both public- and private-sector mining firms have their own challenges. While the public-sector mining firms are marred by rampant corruption, the private-sector firms indulge in large-scale illegal mining, which ultimately brings down the productivity of the whole mining industry. Nevertheless, notwithstanding these challenges in both sectors, if the best practices employed by both sectors are followed, then the Indian mining industry will experience a high growth rate. Thus, we call for the decision-makers involved in mining policymaking to follow the best practices of both public and private sectors to gain maximum leverage from this industry. However, as our results suggest that the public-sector mining firms are experiencing low productivity growth, this necessarily calls for policymakers to take appropriate and requisite steps to strengthen the public-sector firms by identifying the causes of their slow productivity.

The scope for improving energy-use efficiency to realize energy-saving potential advocates for new investments on energy-efficient mining equipment, keeping in mind cost-effectiveness. It is also suggested that as the mining industry is not a big consumer of industrial energy, unlike the manufacturing industry, a nationwide effort should be made to use alternative energy reduction strategies, such as fuel switching and CO_2 capture and storage to achieve substantial greenhouse gas reduction.

The non-compliance of mining firms with social and environmental commitment indicates the tangible failure of government regulatory and monitoring systems. Thus, in this context, it is suggested that there is a greater need for more stringent environmental monitoring and swift action to compel mining firms to adhere to environmentally sustainable practices. It is also advocated that mining firms would benefit from being compliant. By adhering to better environmental compliance, firms could increase the possibility of obtaining society's approval for their business operations and thereby their profitability opportunities.

8.3 Limitations

Despite making a considerable contribution towards the analysis of the Indian mining industry from three standpoints, this book suffers from a few limitations. However, the limitations of the present study are beyond the scope of uncomplicated remediation.

It is acknowledged that this work faced serious challenges concerning the systematic availability of data. A major problem related to data was identified with respect to the input–output data of this industry used for analysing the economic impact of the economy. As an industry can have an impact on output growth, employment, and income generation, the evaluation of such impact requires input–output transactions of the industry for each individual year. The impacts can be assessed more accurately if the available data is more recent. However, this book uses the input–output table for the year 2013–2014 as this is the latest available data. Another problem is the administered price of coal and petroleum subsectors. However, this does not undermine the significance of the study, as we abstain from making intersectoral comparisons between public and private firms. To avoid the data problem, we attempt an intra-sector comparison.

Within the productivity estimation, one of the key challenges faced is an estimation of capital and solving the endogeneity problem. These are two important problems that have become highly debatable (Griliches and Mairesse, 1998; OECD, 2001, 2009). We can only approach them by admitting that no methodology is free from criticisms and always gets embroiled in one problem or another.

In the estimation of energy efficiency, there are limitations related to the composition of energy expenditure. This book considers the total value of expenditure on power and fuel as total energy consumption. However, energy use can emanate from various sources, such as coal, electricity, liquefied petroleum gas (LPG), and diesel. As per the India Energy Statistics Report (CSO, 2019), in the mining industry mostly LPG and diesel are used for production. Thus, energy efficiency can be estimated concerning different types of energy as the type of energy does influence the efficiency aspect. However, as our data set does not distinguish between different types of energy and considers the energy consumed as the total primary energy used, we are unable to disentangle the energy efficiency for different types due to data limitations.

Another serious constraint in the energy efficiency estimation pertains to the unavailability of carbon emissions data. When energy is used by any industry, carbon emissions take place as a by-product. So, along with the desirable output, an undesirable output is released by energy consumption. The carbon emissions intensity, which can be measured as carbon emissions per unit of output, can be an important determinant of energy-use efficiency. The relationship between carbon intensity and energy efficiency is usually assumed to be negative; higher carbon intensity may lead to less energy-use efficiency and vice versa. However, this study faced serious constraints in the availability of carbon emissions data. In the absence of carbon emissions data, we are unable to include this in our analysis.

In the study of the social and environmental compliance performance of mining firms, this book faces limitations in two aspects. One is related to the availability of data and the other is about the subjectivity of the responses of the interviewed households. This study collected data for examining social and environmental compliance through primary surveys by conducting interviews with the project-affected households, who have transferred their land. As there was a large gap between the time of land acquisition, the compensation paid, and our survey, the responses may have been influenced by memory lapses. Thus, a certain amount of subjectivity could be expected from the responses of the households. However, to keep our work objective, the study attempted to gather as much data as possible from objective variables, such as cash compensation and job compensation.

As regards the problem associated with data collection, we considered only one district and two villages in our study. However, Odisha is one of the most mineral-rich states in the country, having mineral resources distributed across many districts. Apart from Jajpur district, Kendujhar is another mineral-rich region with a strong presence of mining companies. Thus, as the study relied on only two mining villages in one district, and conducted its analysis with the responses received from only eighty mining-affected households, there are problems associated with a small sample. Data on the social and environmental performance of a higher number of affected households would prove to have more merit than this small sample data.

8.4 Directions for Further Research

As this is a new area of study in the Indian context, there is ample scope to make further investigation in different areas. In this section, we make note of a few directions that further investigations could take.

First, our study examined the economic impact of this industry regarding macroeconomic variables such as income, employment, and output at broader and subsectoral levels. However, we only limited ourselves to direct and indirect impact assessment. However, it is acknowledged that any industry can influence the economy through induced impacts, which generate a series of subsequent impulses in the economy. Thus, further investigation could be made in this direction to arrive at the total multiplier impact, which is a combination of three types of effects, namely, direct, indirect, and induced effects.

Within the productivity and efficiency estimation, we studied the TFP of the whole industry and compared the four component subsectors. We also attempted to estimate the technical efficiency (TE) of coal-mining companies. Thus, there is scope to calculate the TE of other component sectors and compare them to ascertain which subsector is more technically efficient and what could be the possible contributing factors for this.

Within the social and environmental dimension, we examined the social and environmental compliance of mining firms from the perspective of project-affected households, taking Odisha as a case study. This could be extended to other mining states to arrive at a definitive conclusion regarding the performance of mining firms in this respect.

Finally, it is imperative to mention here that modern society would be unimaginable in the absence of this industry because of the invaluable contribution minerals make in our day-to-day lives. At the same time, the industry cannot be allowed to grow uncontrollably because of the enormous damage it causes to the environment and social fabric. Thus, it is essential to establish a trade-off between the quantity of minerals produced and the associated social and environmental concerns this will bring about. Figuring out this balance could constitute a scope for valuable further study.

Bibliography

Abramovitz, M. (1956). Resource and output trends in the United States since 1870. *American Economic Review, 46*(2), 5–23.

Ahammad, H., & Clements, K. W. (1999). What does minerals growth mean to Western Australia? *Resource Policy, 25*, 1–14.

Ahluwalia, I. (1991). *Productivity and growth in Indian manufacturing.* Oxford University Press.

Aigner, D., Lovell, C. K., & Schmidt, P. (1977). Formulation and estimation of stochastic frontier production function models. *Journal of Econometrics, 6*(1), 21–37.

Alchian, A. A. (1965). Some economics of property rights. *II Politico, 30*, 816–829.

Alchian, A. A., & Demsetz, H. (1972). Production, information costs and economic organizations. *American Economic Review, 62*(5), 777–795.

Ang, B., & Liu, F. (2001). A new energy decomposition method: Perfect in decomposition consistent in aggregation. *Energy, 26*(6), 537–548.

Ang, B. W., & Liu, N. (2007). Negative-value problems of the logarithmic mean divisia composition approach. *Energy Policy, 35*(1), 739–742.

Ang, B. W., Liu, F. L., & Chung, H.-S. (2004). A generalized Fisher index approach decomposition analysis. *Energy Economics, 26*(5), 757–763.

Arellano, M., & Bond, S. (1991). Some tests of specification for panel data: Monte Carlo evidence and an application to employment equations. *Review of Economic Studies. 58*(2), 277–297.

Asr, E. T., Kakaie, R., Ataei, M., & Mohammadi, M. R. T. (2019). A review of studies on sustainable development in the mining life cycle. *Journal of Cleaner Production, 229*, 213–231.

Aupperle, K. E., Carroll, A. B., & Hatfield, J. D. (1985). An empirical examination of the relationship between CSR and profitability. *Academy of Management Journal, 28*(2), 446–463.

Auty, R. (1993). *Sustaining development in mineral economies: The resource curse thesis.* Routledge.

Auty, R. (2001). *Resource abundance and economic development.* Oxford University Press.

Averch, H., & Johnson, L. L. (1962). Behaviour of the firm under regulatory constraint. *American Economic Review, 52*, 1052–1069.

Awuah-Offei, K., Osei, B., & Askari-Nasab, H. (2011). Modelling truck/shovel energy efficiency under uncertainty. *Transactions of the Society for Mining, Metallurgy, & Exploration, 330*, 573–584.

Balakrishnan, P. (2004). Measuring productivity in manufacturing sector. *Economic and Political Weekly*, 1465–1471.

Balakrishnan, P., & Pushpangadan, K. (1994). Total factor-productivity growth in manufacturing industry: A fresh look. *Economic and Political Weekly*, 2028–2035.

Balakrishnan, P., & Pushpangadan, K. (1998). What do we know about productivity growth in Indian industry? *Economic and Political Weekly*, 2241–2246.

Balakrishnan, P., Pushpangadan, K., & Babu, M. S. (2000). Trade liberalisation and productivity growth in manufacturing: Evidence from firm-level panel data. *Economic and Political Weekly*, 3679–3682.

Banker, R. D., Charnes, A., & Cooper, W. W. (1984). Some models for estimating technical and scale inefficiencies in data envelopment analysis. *Management Science*, *30*(9), 1078–1092.

Battese, G. E., & Coelli, T. J. (1992). Frontier production functions, technical efficiency and panel data: With application to paddy farmers in India. *Journal of Productivity Analysis*, *3*(1), 153–169.

Battese, G. E., & Coelli, T. J. (1995). A model for technical inefficiency effects in a stochastic frontier production function for panel data. *Empirical Economics*, *20*(2), 325–332.

Battese, G. E., Coelli, T. J., & Colby, T. C. (1989). Estimation of frontier production functions and the efficiencies of Indian farms using panel data from ICRISAT's village-level studies (No. 400-2016-24556). *Journal of Quantitative Economics*, *5*(2), 327–348.

Baumol, W. J., Baumol, W. J., Oates, W. E., Bawa, V. S., Bawa, W. S., Bradford, D. F., & Baumol, W. J. (1988). *The theory of environmental policy*. Cambridge University Press.

Berndt, E. R. (1990). Energy use, technical progress and productivity growth: A survey of economic issues. *Journal of Productivity Analysis*, *2*(1), 67–83.

Berndt, E. R., & Wood, D. O. (1975). Technology, prices, and the derived demand for energy. *Review of Economics and Statistics*, *57*, 259–268.

Bhattacharya, M. (2007). Nandigram and the question of development. *Economic and Political Weekly*, 1895–1899.

Bhengara, R. (1996). Coal mining displacement. *Economic and Political Weekly*, *31*(11), 647–649.

Blundell, R., & Bond, S. (1998). Initial conditions and moment restrictions in dynamic panel data models. *Journal of Econometrics*, *87*(1), 115–143.

Boardman, A. E., & Vining, A. R. (1989). Ownership and performance in competitive environments: A comparison of the performance of private, mixed, and state-owned enterprises. *Journal of Law and Economics*, *32*(1), 1–33.

Boyd, G. A. (2008). Estimating plant-level energy efficiency with a stochastic frontier. *Energy Journal*, *29*(2), 23–43.

Boyd, G. A., & Lee, J. M. (2019). Measuring plant level energy efficiency and technical change in the US metal-based durable manufacturing sector using stochastic frontier analysis. *Energy Economics*, *81*, 159–174.

Boyd, G. A., & McClelland, J. D. (1999). The impact of environmental constraints on productivity improvement in integrated paper plants. *Journal of Environmental Economics and Management*, *38*(2), 121–142.

Boyd, G. A., & Roop, J. M. (2004). A note on the Fisher ideal index decomposition for structural change in energy intensity. *Energy Journal*, *25*(1), 87–102.

Boyd, G. A., Hanson, D. A., & Sterner, T. (1988). Decomposition of changes in energy intensity: A comparison of the Divisia index and other methods. *Energy Economics*, *10*(4), 309–312.

Boyd, G. A., McDonald, J. F., Ross, M., & Hansont, D. A. (1987). Separating the changing composition of US manufacturing production from energy efficiency improvements: A Divisia index approach. *Energy Journal, 8*(2), 77–96.

Buchanan, J. M. (1978). *The economics of politics.* Institute of Economic Affairs.

Caves, D. W., & Christensen, L. R. (1980). The relative efficiency of public and private firms in a competitive environment: The case of Canadian railroads. *Journal of Political Economy, 88*(5), 958–976.

Caves, D. W., Christensen, L. R., & Diewert, W. E. (1982). The economic theory of index numbers and the measurement of input, output, and productivity. *Econometrica, 50*(6), 1393–1414.

Chakravarty K. C. (2013). Environmental & social sustainability: Key issues and concerns. Yes Bank–Deutsche gesellschaft für Internationale Zusammenarbeit (GIZ)–United Nations Environment Programme (UNEP) Sustainability series on environment and social risk management. GIZ.

Chakravorty, S. L. (2001). Artisanal and small-scale mining in India. No. 78. Mining, Minerals and Sustainable Development Project of the International Institute for Environment and Development.

Chamberlain, G. (1982). Multivariate regression models for panel data. *Journal of Econometrics, 18*(1), 5–46.

Chand, P., Thakkar, J. J., & Ghosh, K. K. (2020). Analysis of supply chain sustainability with supply chain complexity, inter-relationship study using Delphi and interpretive structural modelling for Indian mining and earthmoving machinery industry. *Resources Policy, 68*, 101726. https://doi.org/10.1016/j.resourpol.2020.101726

Chandra, N. K. (2008). Tata Motors in Singur: A step towards industrialisation or pauperisation? *Economic and Political Weekly, 43*(50), 36–51.

Charnes, A., Cooper, W. W., & Rhodes, E. (1978). Measuring the efficiency of decision-making units. *European Journal of Operational Research, 2*(6), 429–444.

Chatterjee, A., Zhang, L., & Xia, X. (2015). Optimization of mine ventilation fan speeds according to ventilation on demand and time of use tariff. *Applied Energy, 146*, 65–73.

Chen, T. Y., & Chen, L. H. (2007). DEA performance evaluation based on BSC indicators incorporated: The case of semiconductor industry. *International Journal of Productivity and Performance Management, 56*, 335–357.

Christensen, L. R. (1975). Concepts and measurement of agricultural productivity. *American Journal of Agricultural Economics, 57*(5), 910–915.

Clements, K. W., Ahammad, H., & Qiang, Y. (1996). New mining and mineral-processing projects in Western Australia: Effects of employment and the macro-economy. *Resources Policy, 22*(4), 293–346.

CMIE (Centre for Monitoring Indian Economy). (n.d.). Prowess Data Base.

CSE (Centre for Science and Environment). (2008). *Rich lands, poor people: Is 'sustainable' mining possible?* New Delhi Centre for Science and Environment.

CSO (Central Statistics Office). (n.d.). *National accounts statistics (NAS)* (various issues).

CSO. (2015). *National accounts statistics—sources & methods.*

CSO. (2019). Energy statistics. Issue 26. Government of India Ministry of Statistics and Programme Implementation. https://www.mospi.gov.in

Das, A. (2012). Who extracts minerals more efficiently—public or private firms? A study of the Indian mining industry. *Journal of Policy Modelling, 34*(5), 755–766.

Das, A. (2013). *Performance of public and private mining firms in India: In productivity, environmental and social dimensions.* Cambridge Scholars Publishing.

Das, D. K., Erumban, A. A., Aggarwal, S., & Wadhwa, D. (2010). Total factor productivity growth in India in the reform period: A disaggregated sectoral analysis. World KLEMS Conference, Harvard University.

Das, D. V., Azeez, A. E., Aggarwal, S., & Das, P. C. (2015). *INDIA KLEMS database manual.*

Davis, G. A. (1995). Learning to love the Dutch disease: Evidence from the mineral economies. *World Development, 23*(10), 1765–1779.

Davis, G. A., & Tilton, J. E. (2005). The resource curses. *Natural Resources Forum, 29*, 233–242.

Debreu, G. (1951). The coefficient of resource utilization. *Econometrica: Journal of the Econometric Society, 19*(3), 273–292.

Deloitte. (2014). The top 10 issues mining companies will face in the coming year. 2014. https://www2.deloitte. com /content/ dam /Deloitte/global/Documents/ Energy-and-Resources/dttl-er-Tracking-the-trends-2014_EN_final.pdf

Denison, E. F. (1962). *The sources of economic growth in the United States and the alternatives before us.* Committee for Economic Development.

Denison, E. F. (1985). *Trends in economic growth, 1929-1982. Brookings.*

Dewenter, K. L., & Malatesta, P. H. (2001). State-owned and privately owned firms: An empirical analysis of profitability, leverage, and labour intensity. *American Economic Review, 91*(1), 320–334.

Diewert, W. E. (1980). Capital and the theory of productivity measurement. *American Economic Review, 70*(2), 260–267.

DIPP (Department for the Promotion of Industry and Internal Trade). (2016). Mining sector achievement reports. Government of India Ministry of Mines.

Dorian James P. (1994). Economic impacts of mining: A changing role in the transitional economies. *Natural Resources Forum, 18*(1), 17–29.

Downing, T. E. (2002). *Avoiding new poverty: Mining-induced displacement and resettlement* (Vol. 52). International Institute for Environment and Development.

Downs, A. (1976). Inside bureaucracy: Little, Brown & Co. *Economics and Management, 38*(2), 121–142.

Ernst & Young/ASSOCHAM. (2011). Mining India: Sustainably for growth—a report by Ernst & Young and ASSOCHAM.

Edwards, A. (1985). South Africa's potential for mineral based added value products. Mintek, Randburg.

Ehrlich, I., Gallais-Hamonno, G., Liu, Z., & Lutter, R. (1994). Productivity growth and firm ownership: An analytical and empirical investigation. *Journal of Political Economy, 102*(5), 1006–1038.

Ellerman, D., Stoker, T. M., & Berndt, E. R. (2001). *New developments in productivity analysis.* University of Chicago Press. https://www.nber.org/books/hult01-1

Evans, J., Filippini, M., & Hunt, L. C. (2013). The contribution of energy efficiency towards meeting CO_2 targets. In R. Fouquet (Ed.), *Handbook of energy and climate change* (pp. 175–223). Edward Elgar Publishing.

EY. (2014). Productivity in mining: A case for broad transformation. https://www.ey.com/Publication/vwLUAssets/EY-Productivity-in-mining/$FILE/EY-Productivity-in-mining.pdf

Fama, E. F. (1980). Agency problems and the theory of the firm. *Journal of Political Economy, 88*(2), 288–307.

Fang, H., Wu, J., & Zeng, C. (2009). Comparative study on efficiency performance of listed coal mining companies in China and the US. *Energy Policy, 37*(12), 5140–5148.

Faraia, R. C. D., Moreira, T. B. S., & Souza, G. S. (2005). Public versus private water utilities: Empirical evidence for Brazilian companies. *Economics Bulletin, 8*(2), 1–7.

Farrell, M. J. (1957). The measurement of productive efficiency. *Journal of the Royal Statistical Society: Series A (General), 120*(3), 253–281.

Farsi, M., & Filippini, M. (1999). Sectors. In J. Evans & L. C. Hunt (Eds.), *International handbook on the economics of energy* (pp. 598–623). Edward Elgar Publishing.

Farsi, M., & Filippini, M. (2009). Efficiency measurement in the electricity and gas distribution sectors. In J. Evans & L. C. Hunt (Eds.), *International handbook on the economics of energy* (pp. 598–623). Edward Elgar Publishing.

Farsi, M., Filippini, M., & Greene, W. (2005). Efficiency measurement in network industries: Application to the Swiss railway companies. *Journal of Regulatory Economics, 28*(1), 69–90.

FIMI (Federation of Indian Mineral Industries). (2009). Corporate Social Responsibility. http://www.fedmin.com/fedmin/nmp08.pdf

Fernandes, A. M. (2007). Trade policy, trade volumes and plant-level productivity in Colombian manufacturing industries. *Journal of International Economics, 71*(1), 52–71.

Fernandes, W., & Paranjape, V. (1997). Hundred years of displacement in India: Is the rehabilitation policy an adequate response? In W. Fernandes & V. Paranjape (Eds.), *Rehabilitation policy and law in India: A right to livelihood* (pp. 1–34). New Delhi: Indian Social Institute.

FICCI (Federation of Indian Chambers of Commerce & Industry), Mines and Metals Division. (2013). Development of the Indian mining industry—the way forward.

Filippini, M., & Greene, W. (2016). Persistent and transient productive inefficiency: A maximum simulated likelihood approach. *Journal of Productivity Analysis, 45*(2), 187–196.

Filippini, M., & Hunt, L. C. (2010). *Energy demand and energy efficiency in the OECD countries: A stochastic demand frontier approach.* Surrey Energy Economics Centre (SEEC).

Filippini, M., & Hunt, L. C. (2011). Energy demand and energy efficiency in the OECD countries: A stochastic demand frontier approach. *Energy Journal, 32*(2), 59–80.

Filipini, M, & Hunt, L. (2012). US residential energy demand and energy efficiency: A stochastic demand frontier approach. *Energy Economics, 34*, 1484–1491.

Filippini, M., & Hunt, L. C. (2015). Measurement of energy efficiency based on economic foundations. *Energy Economics, 52*, S5–S16.

Filippini, M., Hunt, L. C., & Zorić, J. (2014). Impact of energy policy instruments on the estimated level of underlying energy efficiency in the EU residential sector. *Energy Policy, 69*, 73–81.

Fleming, D. A., & Measham, T. G. (2014). Local job multipliers of mining. *Resource Policy, 41*, 9–15.

Frederiksen, T. (2018). Corporate social responsibility, risk and development in the mining industry. *Resources Policy, 59*, 495–505.

Gelb, A. H. (1988). Growth and Efficiency: Policy Planning and Research. Policy Research Working Paper Series No. 202. World Bank.

Ghose, M. K. (2003). Promoting cleaner production in the Indian small-scale mining industry. *Journal of Cleaner Production, 11*(2), 167–174.

Gielen, D., & Taylor, P. (2009). Indicators for industrial energy efficiency in India. *Energy, 34*(8), 962–969.

Giri, V. V. (1958). *Labour problems in Indian industry.* Asia Publishing House.

GoI (Government of India). (1957). *The Mines and Minerals Development and Regulation Act.* Ministry of Law and Justice.

GoI. (1974). *The Water (Prevention and Pollution) Act.* Ministry of Environment, Forest and Climate Change.

GoI. (1980). *The Forest (Conservation) Act.* Ministry of Environment, Forest and Climate Change.

GoI. (1981). *The Air (Prevention and Pollution) Act*, No. 14 of 1981. Central Pollution and Control Board.

GoI. (2001). *Energy Conservation Act.* Bureau of Energy Efficiency, Ministry of Power.

GoI. (2005). *The Expert Committee on Road Map for Coal Sector Reforms.* Ministry of Coal.

GoI. (2006). *Minerals and Mining Act.* Ministry of Mines.

GoI. (2008). *National mineral policy: Report of the High-Level Committee.* Planning Commission.

GoI. (2010). *National mineral scenario.* Department of Mines.

GoI. (2011). *Unlocking the potential of the Indian mineral sector.* Government of India.

GoI. (2013a). *Economic survey.* Ministry of Finance.

GoI. (2013b, 2014a, 2015a, 2016a, 2018a, 2019a, 2020). *Indian mineral year book.* Ministry of Mines, Indian Bureau of Mines.

GoI. (2013c, 2014b, 2015b, 2016b, 2017, 2018b). *Statistics of mines in India.* Directorate General of Mines Safety; Ministry of Labour & Employment.

GoI. (2013d, 2014c, 2015c, 2016c, 2017b, 2018c, 2019b). *Indian mineral industry—at a glance* (various issues). Ministry of Mines, Indian Bureau of Mines.

GoI. (2015c). *The Mines and Minerals Development and Regulation Act.* Ministry of Law and Justice.

GoI. (2018). *Indian mineral years book.* Ministry of Mines, Indian Bureau of Mines.

GoI. (2019). *Indian mineral years book.* Ministry of Mines, Indian Bureau of Mines.

GoI and the United Nations (2018–2022). *Sustainable development framework.* United Nations Development Programme (UNDP).

Govindan, K., Kannan, D., & Shankar, K. M. (2014). Evaluating the drivers of corporate social responsibility in the mining industry with multi-criteria approach: A multi-stakeholder perspective. *Journal of Cleaner Production, 84*, 214–232.

Green, W. H. (1997). Frontier production function. In H. Pesaran & P. Schmidt (Eds.), *Handbook of applied econometrics, Vol. 2: Microeconomics* (pp. 81–166). Blackwell.

Greene, W. H. (2004). Distinguishing between heterogeneity and inefficiency: Stochastic frontier analysis of the World Health Organization's panel data on national health care systems. *Health Economics, 13*(10), 959–980.

Greene, W. H. (2005a). Reconsidering heterogeneity in panel data estimators of the stochastic frontier model. *Journal of Econometrics, 126*(2), 269–303.

Greene, W. H. (2005b). Fixed and random effects in stochastic frontier models. *Journal of Productivity Analysis, 23*(1), 7–32.

Greene, W. H. (2008). The econometric approach to efficiency analysis. *Measurement of Productive Efficiency and Productivity Growth, 1*(1), 92–250.

Greening, L. A., Davis, W. B., Schipper, L., & Khrushch, M. (1997). Comparison of six decomposition methods: Application to aggregate energy intensity for manufacturing in 10 OECD countries. *Energy Economics, 19*(3), 375–390.

Griliches, Z., & Mairesse, J. (1999). Production functions: The search for identification. In: S. Strøm (Ed.), *Econometrics and economic theory in the 20th century: The Ragnar Frisch Centennial Symposium* (pp. 169–223). Econometric Society Monographs. Cambridge University Press.

Gruenhagen, J. H., & Parker, R. (2020). Factors driving or impeding the diffusion and adoption of innovation in mining: A systematic review of the literature. *Resources Policy, 65*, 101540. http://10.1016/j.resourpol.2019.101540

Habakkuk, H. J. (1962). *American and British technology in the nineteenth century*. Cambridge University Press.

Hajkowicz, S. A., Heyenga, S., & Moffat, K. (2011). The relationship between mining and socio-economic wellbeing in Australia's regions. *Resources Policy, 36*, 30–38.

Haque, N., & Norgate, T. (2014). The greenhouse gas footprint of in-situ leaching of uranium, gold and copper in Australia. *Journal of Cleaner Production, 84*, 382–390.

Harris, P., McManus, P., Sainsbury, P., Viliani, F., & Riley, E. (2021). The institutional dynamics behind limited human health considerations in environmental assessments of coal mining projects in New South Wales, Australia. *Environment Impact Assessment Review, 86*, 106473. http://doi.org/10.1016/j.eiar.2020.106473

Hausman, J. A. (1978). Specification tests in econometrics. *Econometrica: Journal of the Econometric Society*, 1251–1271.

Henriksson, E., Söderholm, P., & Wårell, L. (2014). Industrial electricity demand and energy efficiency policy: The case of the Swedish mining industry. *Energy Efficiency, 7*(3), 477–491.

Herbert, T., & Lahiri-Dutt, K. (2004). Coal sector loans and displacement of indigenous populations: Lessons from Jharkhand. *Economic and Political Weekly, 39*(23), 2403–2409.

Herrera-León, S., Lucay, F. A., Cisternas, L. A., & Kraslawski, A. (2019). Applying a multi-objective optimization approach in designing water supply systems for mining industries. The case of Chile. *Journal of Cleaner Production, 210*, 994–1004.

Hilson, G. (2000). Pollution prevention and cleaner production in the mining industry: an analysis of current issues. *Journal of Cleaner Production, 8*(2), 119–126.

Hilson, G. (2002a). Small-scale mining and its socio-economic impact in developing countries. *Natural Resources Forum, 26*(1), 3–13.

Hilson, G. (2002b). An overview of land use conflicts in mining communities. *Land Use Policy, 19*(1), 65–73.

Hobbs, M. J. (2020). Conflict ecology: Examining the strategies and rationales of lobbyists in the mining and energy industries in Australia. *Public Relations Review, 46*(2), 101868. http://doi.org/10.1016/j.pubrev.2019.101868

Hodge, R. A. (2014). Mining company performance and community conflict: Moving beyond a seeming paradox. *Journal of Cleaner Production, 84,* 27–33.

Hu, H., & Kavan, P. (2014). Energy consumption and carbon dioxide emissions of China's non-metallic mineral products industry: Present state, prospects and policy analysis. *Sustainability, 6*(11), 8012–8028.

IBEF (India Brand Equity Foundation). (2020). Metals and the mining industry in India. https://www.ibef.org/industry/metals- and- mining.aspx

ICMM (International Council on Mining and Metals). (2014). *Role of mining in national economies: Mining's contribution to sustainable development* (2nd ed.). ICMM.

IEA (International Energy Agency). (2006). *World energy outlook.* IEA/Organisation for Economic Co-operation and Development (OECD).

Jensen, M. C., & Meckling, W. H. (1976). Theory of the firm: Managerial behaviour, agency costs and ownership structure. *Journal of Financial Economics, 3*(4), 305–360.

Jiskani, I. M., Cai, Q., Zhou, W., & Lu, X. (2020). Assessment of risks impeding sustainable mining in Pakistan using fuzzy synthetic evaluation. *Resources Policy, 69,* 101820. http://doi.org/10.1016.j.resourpol.2020.101820

Jondrow, J., Lovell, C. K., Materov, I. S., & Schmidt, P. (1982). On the estimation of technical inefficiency in the stochastic frontier production function model. *Journal of Econometrics, 19*(2–3), 233–238.

Jones, H. (2008). Environmental compliance. Maney on behalf of the University of Western Australia and the Australia International Monetary Market. https://doi.org/10.1179/037178411X12942393517651

Jorgenson, D. W., & Griliches, Z. (1972). Issues in growth accounting: A reply to Edward F. Denison. *Survey of Current Business 52*(5), 65–94.

Kalirajan, K. P. (1981). An econometric analysis of yield variability in paddy production. *Canadian Journal of Agricultural Economics, 29*(3), 283–294.

Kalirajan, K. P., & Shand, R. T. (1999). Frontier production functions and technical efficiency measures. *Journal of Economic Surveys, 13*(2), 149–172.

Kapelus, P. (2002). Mining, corporate social responsibility and the "community": The case of Rio Tinto, Richards Bay Minerals and the Mbonambi. *Journal of Business Ethics, 39*(3), 275–296.

Kasap, Y., Konuk, A., Gasimov, R. N., & Kiliç, A. M. (2007). The effects of non-controllable factors in efficiency evaluation of Turkish coal enterprises. *Energy Exploration & Exploitation, 25*(6), 429–450.

Kendrick, J. W. (1957). Productivity trends, capital and Labour. *Review of Economics and Statistics, 39*(3), 248–257.

Kinnunen, P. H. M., & Kaksonen, A. H. (2019). Towards circular economy in mining: Opportunities and bottlenecks for tailings valorization. *Journal of Cleaner Production, 228,* 153–160.

Kitula, A. G. N. (2006). The environmental and socio-economic impacts of mining on local livelihoods in Tanzania: A case study of Geita District. *Journal of Cleaner Production, 14*(3–4), 405–414.

Kohler, M. (2014). Differential electricity pricing and energy efficiency in South Africa. *Energy, 64,* 524–532.

Koopmans, T. C. (1951). An analysis of production as an efficient combination of activities. In T. C. Koopmans (Ed.), *Activity analysis of production and allocation.*

Cowles Commission for Research in Economics Monograph No. 13 (pp. 33–99). Wiley.

Kopp, R. J. (1981). The measurement of productive efficiency: A reconsideration. *Quarterly Journal of Economics*, *96*(3), 477–503.

Krugman, P. (1994) *Defining and measuring productivity*. The Age of Diminishing Expectations.

Kulshreshtha, M., & Parikh, J. K. (2001). A study of productivity in the Indian coal sector. *Energy Policy*, *29*(9), 701–713.

Kulshreshtha, M., & Parikh, J. K. (2002). Study of efficiency and productivity growth in opencast and underground coal mining in India: A DEA analysis. *Energy Economics*, *24*(5), 439–453.

Kumbhakar, S. C., & Lovell, C. A. K. (2000). *Stochastic frontier analysis*. Cambridge University Press. http://dx.doi.org/10.1017/cbo9781139174411

Laffont, Jean-Jacques, & Jean Tirole. (1993). *A theory of incentives in procurement and regulation*. Massachusetts Institute of Technology Press.

Lane, P., & Tornell, A. (1995). Power concentration and growth. Harvard Institute of Economic Research, Discussion Paper No. 1720. Harvard University Press.

Lei, Y., Cui, N., & Pan, D. (2013). Economic and social effects analysis of mineral development in China and policy implications. *Resource Policy, 38*, 448–457.

Leibenstein, H., (1976). *Beyond economic man*. Harvard University Press.

Leontief, W. W., & Inchausti, Á. A. (1984). *Análisis económico input-output*. Orbis.

Leontief, W. W. (1936). Quantitative input–output relations in the economic system of the United States. *Review of Economics and Statistics, 18*, 105–125.

Leontief, W. W. (1941). *The structure of the American economy 1919–1939: An empirical application of equilibrium analysis*. Oxford University Press.

Leontief, W. W. (1966). *Input–output economics*. Oxford University Press.

Levesque, M., Millar, D., & Paraszczak, J. (2014). Energy and mining: The home truths. *Journal of Cleaner Production*, *84*, 233–255.

Levinsohn, J., & Petrin, A. (2003). Estimating production functions using inputs to control for unobservables. *Review of Economic Studies*, *70*(2), 317–341.

Li, S., & Xia, J. (2008). The roles and performance of state firms and non-state firms in China's economic transition. *World Development*, *36*(1), 39–54.

Li, Z., Sun, L., Geng, Y., Dong, H., Ren, J., Liu, Z., & Higano, Y. (2017). Examining industrial structure changes and corresponding carbon emission reduction effect by combining input–output analysis and social network analysis: A comparison study of China and Japan. *Journal of Cleaner Production*, *162*, 61–70.

Liu, X. Q., Ang, B. W., & Ong, H. L. (1992). The application of the Divisia index to the decomposition of changes in industrial energy consumption. *Energy Journal*, *13*(4), 161–177.

Long, K. R. (1995). Economics of mining law. *Non-Renewable Resources*, *4*(1), 74–83.

Lovell C. A. K, & Lovell J. E. (2013). Productivity decline in Australian coal mining. *Journal of Productivity Analysis*, *40*(3), 443–455.

Lööw, J., Abrahamsson, L., & Johansson, J. (2019). Mining 4.0—the impact of new technology from a work place perspective. *Mining, Metallurgy & Exploration*, *36*(4), 701–707.

Lundgren, T., & Marklund, P. O. (2015). Climate policy, environmental performance, and profits. *Journal of Productivity Analysis*, *44*(3), 225–235.

Lundgren, T., Marklund, P. O., Samakovlis, E., & Zhou, W. (2015). Carbon prices and incentives for technological development. *Journal of Environmental Management, 150*, 393–403.

Lundgren, T., Marklund, P. O., & Zhang, S. (2016). Industrial energy demand and energy efficiency—evidence from Sweden. *Resource and Energy Economics, 43*, 130–152.Lutz, B. J., Massier, P., Sommerfeld, K., & Löschel, A. (2017). Drivers of energy efficiency in German manufacturing: A firm-level stochastic frontier analysis. ZEW—Centre for European Economic Research Discussion Paper.

Majumdar, S. K. (1998). Assessing comparative efficiency of the state-owned mixed and private sectors in Indian industry. *Public Choice, 96*(1), 1–24.

Mandal, S. K., & Madheswaran, S. (2011). Energy use efficiency of Indian cement companies: a data envelopment analysis. *Energy Efficiency, 4*(1), 57–73.

Marimuthu, R., Sankaranarayanan, B., Ali, S. M., de Sousa Jabbour, A. B. L., & Karuppiah, K. (2021). Assessment of key socio-economic and environmental challenges in the mining industry: Implications for resource policies in emerging economies. *Sustainable Production and Consumption, 27*, 814–830.

Marschak, J., & Andrews, W. H. (1944). Random simultaneous equations and the theory of production. *Econometrica, Journal of the Econometric Society, 12*(3/4), 143–205.

Marshall, A., (1920). *Principle of economics* (8th ed.). MacMillan.

Martin, S., & Parker, D. (1995). Privatization and economic performance throughout the UK business cycle. *Managerial and Decision Economics, 16*(3), 225–237.

McKinsey & Company. (2014). Putting India on the growth path: Unlocking the mining potential. Presented at CII Global Mining Summit.

McMahon, G. (Ed.). (1999). *An environmental study of artisanal, small, and medium mining in Bolivia, Chile, and Peru* (Vol. 23). World Bank Publications.

McMahon, G., Subdibjo, E. R., Aden, J., Bouzaher, A., Dore, G., & Kunanayagam, R. (2000). *Mining and the environment in Indonesia: Long-term trends and repercussions of the Asian economic crisis.* East Asia Environment and Social Development Unit, World Bank.

Meeusen, W., & van Den Broeck, J. (1977). Efficiency estimation from Cobb–Douglas production functions with composed error. *International Economic Review, 18*(2), 435–444.

Megginson, W. L., & Netter, J. M. (2001). From state to market: A survey of empirical studies on privatization. *Journal of Economic Literature, 39*(2), 321.

Mehta, P. S. (2002). The Indian mining sector: Effects on the environment and FDI inflows. *Conference on Foreign Direct Investment and the Environment*, 7–8.

Miller, R. E., & Blair, P. D. (2009). *Input–output analysis: Foundations and extensions.* Cambridge University Press.

Ministry of Coal. (1957). *The Coal Bearing Areas (Acquisition and Development Act).* Act No. 20, Act ID: 195720. Government of India.

Ministry of Law and Justice. (1984). *The Land Acquisition Act.* Government of India.

MoM (Ministry of Mines). (2011). Unlocking the potential of Indian mineral sector. Government of India.

MoM. (2015, 2016, 2017, 2018, 2019). *Annual Report.* Government of India.

Mishra, D. P., Sugla, M., & Singha, P. (2013). Productivity improvement in underground coal mines—a case study. *Journal of Sustainable Mining, 12*(3), 48–53.

Motlogelwa, O. G., & Minnitt, R. C. A. (2013). Optimization of diesel usage at Uitvlugt Mine. *Journal of the Southern African Institute of Mining and Metallurgy, 113*(4), 345–349.

Mukherjee, K. (2008). Energy use efficiency in the Indian manufacturing sector: An interstate analysis. *Energy Policy, 36*(2), 662–672.

Nadolski, S., Klein, B., Kumar, A., & Davaanyam, Z. (2014). An energy benchmarking model for mineral comminution. *Minerals Engineering, 65*, 178–186.

Napier-Munn, T. (2015). Is progress in energy-efficient commination doomed? *Minerals Engineering, 73*, 1–6.

Nasih, M., Harymawan, I., Paramitasari, Y. I., & Handayani, A. (2019). Carbon emissions, firm size, and corporate governance structure: evidence from the mining and agricultural industries in Indonesia. *Sustainability, 11*(9), 2483. http://dx.doi.org/10.3390/su11092483

Neingo, P. N., & Tholana, T. (2016). Trends in productivity in the South African gold mining industry. *Journal of the Southern African Institute of Mining and Metallurgy, 116*(3), 283–290.

Nikulin, A., Ikonnikov, D., & Dolzhikov, I. (2019). Smart personal protective equipment in the coal mining industry. *International Journal of Civil Engineering and Technology, 10*(4), 852–863.

Nimana, B., Canter, C., & Kumar, A. (2015). Energy consumption and greenhouse gas emissions in the recovery and extraction of crude bitumen from Canada's oil sands. *Applied Energy, 143*, 189–199.

Nishimizu, M., & Page Jr, J. M. (1986). Productivity change and dynamic comparative advantage. *Review of Economics and Statistics*, 241–247.

Niskanen, W. A. Jr. (1971). *Bureaucracy and representative government*. Aldine.

Norgate, T., & Haque, N. (2010). Energy and greenhouse gas impacts of mining and mineral processing operations. *Journal of Cleaner Production, 18*(3), 266–274.

NSSO (National Sample Survey Office). (2016). 68th round unit-level data on employment and unemployment. Government of India, Ministry of Statistics and Programme Implementation.

O'Connor, R., & Henry, E. W. (1975). *Input–output analysis and its applications*. MacMillan Publishing.

Odhams, A. M. C., Roebuck, R. L., Lee, Y. J., Hunt, S. W., & Cebon, D. (2010). Factors influencing the energy consumption of road freight transport. *Proceedings of the Institution of Mechanical Engineers, Part C: Journal of Mechanical Engineering Science, 224*(9), 1995–2010.

Oladiran, M. T., & Meyer, J. P. (2007). Energy and exergy analyses of energy consumptions in the industrial sector in South Africa. *Applied Energy, 84*(10), 1056–1067.

Olley, G. S., & A. Pakes. (1996). The dynamics of productivity in the telecommunication equipment industry. *Econometrica, 64* (6), 1263–1297.

Olson, M. (1965). *The logic of collective actions: Public Goods and the theory of groups*. Harvard University Press.

Pactwa, K., Woźniak, J., & Dudek, M. (2020). Coal mining waste in Poland in reference to circular economy principles. *Fuel, 270*, 117493.

Palaniandy, S., Powell, M., Hilden, M., Allen, J., Kermanshahi, K., Oats, B., & Lollback, M. (2015). VertiMill®—preparing the feed within floatable regime at lower specific energy. *Minerals Engineering, 73*, 44–52.

Panda, G. (2014). Mining sector and its impact on Odisha economy: Poor utilization of limited resources using forecasting techniques. *Journal of Business and Management Sciences, 2*, 41–45.

Pandey, A., Ashta, A., Spiegelman, E., & Sutan, A. (2020). Exploration of financial stress indicators in a developing economy. *Strategic Change, 29*(3), 285–292.

Parida M., & S. Madheswaran. (2018). The Indian mining industry: Present status, challenges and the way forward. Working Paper No. 430. Institute for Social and Economic Change.

Parida, M., & Madheswaran, S. (2021). Effect of firm ownership on productivity: Empirical evidence from the Indian mining industry. *Mineral Economics, 34*, 87–103.

Parry, I. W. (1997). Productivity trends in the natural resource industries. RFF Working Paper Series dp-97-39. Resources for the Future.

Penrose, E. T. (1959). *The theory of the growth of the firm*. Basil Blackwell.

Peter. F. D. (1991). The new productivity challenge. *Harvard Business Review*, November–December.

Petrick, S., Rehdanz, K., & Wagner, U. J. (2011). Energy use patterns in German industry: Evidence from plant-level data. *Jahrbücher für Nationalökonomie und Statistik, 3*(231), 379–414.

Pitt, M. M., & Lee, L. F. (1981). The measurement and sources of technical inefficiency in the Indonesian weaving industry. *Journal of Development Economics, 9*(1), 43–64.

Planning Commission of India. (2006). Integrated Energy Policy: Report of the Expert Committee. Government of India.

Pollitt, M. G. (1995). *Ownership and performance in electric utilities: The international evidence on privatization and efficiency*. Oxford University Press.

Pothina, R., Kecojevic, V., Klima, M. S., & Komljenovic, D. (2007). Gyratory crusher model and impact parameters related to energy consumption. *Mining, Metallurgy & Exploration, 24*(3), 170–180.

Prescott, E. C., & Visscher, M. (1980). Organization capital. *Journal of Political Economy, 88*(3), 446–461.

Productivity Commission. Measurement and interpretation. Staff Working Paper. Productivity Commission, Commonwealth of Australia.

PwC (PricewaterhouseCoopers). (2012). *Opportunities in the India mining sector*. Asia School of Mines.

Rábago, K. R., Lovins, A. B., & Feiler, T. E. (2016). Energy and sustainable development in the mining and minerals industries. Mining, Minerals and Sustainable Development Working Paper No. 41.

Lovins, A. B., Feiler, T. E., Rábago, K. R., et al. (2021). Assessment of key socioeconomic and environmental challenges in the mining industry: Implications for resource policies in emerging economies. *Journal of Sustainable Production and Consumption, 27*, 814–830.

Ray, S. C. (2004). *Data envelopment analysis: Theory and techniques for economics and operations research*. Cambridge University Press.

RBI (Reserve Bank of India). (2014a). *Estimates of productivity growth for Indian economy*. RBI.

RBI. (2012, 2013, 2014b, 2015, 2016, 2017, 2018). *Handbook of statistics on Indian economy*. RBI.

Roldán, J. J., Crespo, E., Martín-Barrio, A., Peña-Tapia, E., & Barrientos, A. (2019). A training system for Industry 4.0 operators in complex assemblies based on virtual reality and process mining. *Robotics and Computer-Integrated Manufacturing, 59*, 305–316.

Rose, A., & Miernyk, W. (1989). Input–output analysis: The first fifty years. *Economic Systems Research, 1*(2), 229–272.

Sachs, J. D., & Warner, A. M. (1995). Natural resource abundance and economic growth. National Bureau of Economic Research (NBER) Working Paper No. 5398. http://www.nber.org/papers/w5398

Sachs, J. D., & Warner, A.M. (1997). Fundamental sources of long-run growth. *American Economic Review, 87*, 184–188.

Sachs, J. D., & Warner, A. M. (1999). Natural resource intensity and economic growth. In: J. Mayer, B. Chambers, & F. Ayisha (Eds.), *Development policies in natural resource economics* (pp. 184–188). Edward Elgar Publishing.

Sachs, J. D., & Warner, A. M. (2001). The curse of natural resources. *European Economic Review, 45*, 827–838.

Sahoo. L. K. *Energy efficiency in the mining sector*. Central Institute of Mining and Fuel Research (CIMFR)/Council of Scientific and Industrial Research (CSIR).

Sahoo, L. K., Bandyopadhyay, S., & Banerjee, R. (2014a). Benchmarking energy consumption for dump trucks in mines. *Applied Energy, 113*, 1382–1396.

Sahoo, A. K., Sahoo, D., & Sahu, N. C. (2014b). Mining export, industrial production and economic growth: A co-integration and causality analysis for India. *Resources Policy, 42*, 27–34.

Sahoo, L. K., Bandyopadhyay, S., & Banerjee, R. (2014c). Water and energy assessment for dewatering in opencast mines. *Journal of Cleaner Production, 84*, 736–745.

San Cristobal, J. R., & Biezma, M.V. (2006). The mining industry in the European Union: analysis of inter-industry linkages using input–output analysis. *Resource. Policy, 31*, 1–6.

Sandberg, J., Holmström, J., & Lyytinen, K. (2020). Digitization and phase transitions in platform organizing logics: Evidence from the process automation industry. *Management of Information System, 44*(1), 129–153.

Sarkar, A. (2007). Development and displacement: Land acquisition in West Bengal. *Economic and Political Weekly, 42*(16), 1435–1442.

Schmidt, P., & Lovell, C. K. (1979). Estimating technical and allocative inefficiency relative to stochastic production and cost frontiers. *Journal of Econometrics, 9*(3), 343–366.

Shannon, H. A., & Parker, A. W. (2020). Evaluation of a health literacy instrument designed for the mining industry. *Health Literacy Research and Practice, 4*(2), e84–e93.

Shepherd, W. G. (1986). On the core concepts of industrial economics. In H. W. Jong & W. G. Shepherd (Eds.), *Mainstreams in industrial organization* (pp. 23–67). Springer.

Sheshinski, E., & López-Calva, L. F. (2003). Privatization and its benefits: Theory and Evidence. *CESifo Economic Studies, 49*(3), 429–459.

Shrivastava, P., & Vidhi, R. (2020). Pathway to sustainability in the mining industry: A case study of Alcoa and Rio Tinto. *Resources, 9*(6), 70.

Siawor-Robertson, D., & Awaworyi Churchill, S. (2015). The mining industry and corporate social responsibility: Evidence from two mining communities in Ghana. ZBW Liebniz Information Centre for Economics.

Singh, K., & Kalirajan, K. (2003). A decade of economic reforms in India: The mining sector. *Resources Policy, 29*(3–4), 139–151.

Singh, K., & Saluja, M. R. (2017). India input–output table for 2013–14. National Council of Applied Economic Research (NCAER) Working Paper No. 111. http://www.ncaer.org/papers/w111

Singh, R. K., Kumar, A., Garza-Reyes, J. A., & de Sá, M. M. (2020). Managing operations for circular economy in the mining sector: An analysis of barriers intensity. *Resources Policy, 69*, 101752. https://doi.org/10.1016/j.resourpol.2020.101752

Solow, R. M. (1957). Technical change and the aggregate production function. *Review of Economics and Statistics, 39*(3), 312–320.

Srivastava, V. (1996). *Liberalisation, productivity and competition: A panel study of Indian manufacturing.* Oxford University Press.

Stigler, G. J. (1971). The theory of economic regulation. *Bell Journal of Economics and Management Science, 2*, 3–21.

Stiglitz, J. E. (1988). *Economics of the public sector.* W. W. Norton.

Stilwell, L. C., Minnitt, R. C. A., Monson, T. D., & Kuhn, G. (2000). An input–output analysis of the impact of mining on the South African economy. *Resource Policy, 26*, 17–30.

Stinchombe, A. L. (1965). Social structure and organizations. In J. G. March (Ed.), *Handbook of organizations* (pp. 142–193). Rand McNally.

Stoker, T. M., Berndt, E. R., Ellerman, A. D., & Schennach, S. M. (2005). Panel data analysis of US coal productivity. *Journal of Econometrics, 127*(2), 131–164.

Sutomo, S. (2020). The determinants of capital structure in the coal mining industry on the Indonesia Stock Exchange. Investment management. *Financial Innovation, 17*(1), 165.

Szablowski, D. (2002). Mining, displacement and the World Bank: A case analysis of compania minera antamina's operations in Peru. *Journal of Business Ethics, 39*(3), 247–273.

TERI (Tata Energy Research Institute). (2001). Overview of the mining and mineral industry in India. TERI Project Report (2001EE42).

TERI. (2006). National energy map for India. Technology vision 2030. PSA/2006/3.

Tinbergen, J. (1942). On the theory of long-term economic development. *World Economic Archives*, 511–549. Indian Development Update, March 2018. https://openknowledge.worldbank.org/entities/publication/25b7f4a3-0367-5559-bba4-f52d053fe8ee

Topp, V., Soames, L., Parham, D., & Bloch, H. (2008). Productivity in the mining industry. Australian Productivity Commission.

Transparency International. (2014). Corruption Perception Index, 2014. https//www.transparency.org/cp 2013/results

Tsolas, I. E. (2011). Performance assessment of mining operations using nonparametric production analysis: A bootstrapping approach in DEA. *Resources Policy, 36*(2), 159–167.

US DoE (US Department of Energy). (2007). Mining industry energy bandwidth study.

US DoE. (2007). Mining industry energy bandwidth study. http://www.energy.gov/sites/prod/files/2013/11/f4/mining_bandwidth.pdf

US DOE. (2009). Industrial technologies program: Summary of program results for CY 2009. http://www1.eere.energy.gov/manufacturing/about/pdfs/impacts2009_full_report.pdf

Van Biesebroeck, J. (2007). Robustness of productivity estimates. *Journal of Industrial Economics, 55*(3), 529–569.

Van Greunen, D., Schutte, A. J., & Kleingeld, M. (2014). Energy efficiency through variable speed drive control on a cascading mine cooling system. In *2014 International Conference on the Eleventh Industrial and Commercial Use of Energy* (pp. 1–6). Institute of Electrical and Electronics Engineers (IEEE).

Vickers, J., & Yarrow, G. K. (1988). *Privatization: An economic analysis* (Vol. 18). MIT Press.

Victor, N. M. (2007). On measuring the performance of national oil companies. Program on Energy and Sustainable Development. Stanford University.

Virmani, A. (2004). Sources of India's economic growth: Trends in total factor productivity. Working Paper No. 131. Indian Council for Research on International Economic Relations.

Wagner, J. E., & Deller, S. C. (1998). Measuring the effects of economic diversity on growth and stability. *Land Economics. 74*(4), 541–556.

Walton, A. L. (1981). Variations in the substitutability of energy and non-energy inputs: The case of the Middle Atlantic region. *Journal of Regional Science, 21*(3), 411–420.

Wang, H., & Wheeler, D. (2005). Financial incentives and endogenous enforcement in China's pollution levy system. *Journal of Environmental Economics and Management, 49*(1), 174–196.

Wang, H., & Yanhong Jin. (2002). Industrial ownership and environmental performance: Evidence from China. World Bank Policy Research Working Paper No. 2936.

Wang, L. W., Tran, T. T., & Nguyen, N. T. (2015). An empirical study of hybrid DEA and grey system theory on analyzing performance: A case from the Indian mining industry. *Journal of Applied Mathematics, 1*, 395360. http://doi.org/10.1155/2015/395360

Warhurst, A., & Bridge, G. (1996). Improving environmental performance through innovation: Recent trends in the mining industry. *Minerals Engineering, 9*(9), 907–921.

WBCSD report on CSR. (1998). *Meeting Changing Expectations.* WBCSD's first report on corporate social responsibility. https://growthorientedsustainableentrepreneurship.wordpress.com/wp-content/uploads/2016/07/csr-wbcsd-csr-primer.pdf

Wei, Y. M., Liao, H., & Fan, Y. (2007). An empirical analysis of energy efficiency in China's iron and steel sector. *Energy, 32*(12), 2262–2270.

Williamson, O. E. (1964). *The economics of discretionary behaviour: Managerial objectives in a theory of the firm.* Prentice-Hall.

Windmeijer, F. (2005). A finite sample correction for the variance of linear efficient two-step GMM estimators. *Journal of Econometrics, 126*(1), 25–51.

Wolf, C. (2009). Does ownership matter? The performance and efficiency of State Oil vs. Private Oil (1987–2006). *Energy Policy, 37*(7), 2642–2652.

World Bank. (2018). India development update: India's growth story, March. https://documents1.worldbank.org/curated/en/814101517840592525/pdf/India-development-update-Indias-growth-story.pdf

World Economic Forum. (2009). *The global competitiveness report: 2008–2009*. World Economic Forum.

Xue, X., Shen, Q., Wang, Y., & Lu, J. (2008). Measuring the productivity of the construction industry in China by using DEA-based Malmquist productivity indices. *Journal of Construction Engineering and Management*, *134*(1), 64–71.

Zhang, H. (2017). Head-mounted display-based intuitive virtual reality training system for the mining industry. *International Journal of Mining Science and Technology*, *27*(4), 717–722.

Zhang, J., Fu, J., Hao, H., Fu, G., Nie, F., & Zhang, W. (2020). Root causes of coal mine accidents: Characteristics of safety culture deficiencies based on accident statistics. *Process Safety and Environmental Protection*, *136*, 78–91.

Zhou, P., Ang, B. W., & Poh, K. L. (2008a). A survey of data envelopment analysis in energy and environmental studies. *European Journal of Operational Research*, *189*(1), 1–18.

Zhou, P., Ang, B. W., & Poh, K. L. (2008b). Measuring environmental performance under different environmental DEA technologies. *Energy Economics*, *30*(1), 1–14.

Zhou, P., Ang, B. W., & Zhou, D. Q. (2012). Measuring economy-wide energy efficiency performance: A parametric frontier approach. *Applied Energy*, *90*(1), 196–200.

Index

For the benefit of digital users, indexed terms that span two pages (e.g., 52–53) may, on occasion, appear on only one of those pages.

Tables and figures are indicated by an italic *t* and *f* following the page number.